Unspeakable Cults

An Essay in Christology

Paul J. DeHart

BAYLOR UNIVERSITY PRESS

Waco, Texas 76798

Cover and book design by Kasey McBeath

The Library of Congress has cataloged this book under ISBN 978-1-4813-1555-5.
Library of Congress Control Number: 2021014882

Printed in the United States of America on acid-free paper with a minimum of thirty percent recycled content.

For Jonathan Z. Smith

Truth is necessarily stranger than history.
Morton Smith | *The Secret Gospel*

The disintegration of culture began with culture itself.
Jonathan Z. Smith | *Violent Origins*

There is thus no phenomenality reducing the sign or the representer so that the thing signified may be allowed to glow finally in the luminosity of its presence.
Jacques Derrida | *Of Grammatology*

I have yet many things to say to you, but you cannot bear them now.
John 16:12 (RSV)

Contents

III Cult of the Unspeakable
From Aretalogy to Teratology

Introduction

Lagging Epiphany

In this shrine are placed the statues, one of which is Hera,
the other Zeus, though they call him by another name. . . .
Between the two there stands another image of gold, no part
of it resembling the others: this possesses no special form of its
own. . . . The Syrians speak of it as "sign" [*semeion*] but they have
assigned to it no definite name.
Lucian | *On the Syrian Goddess*

Thanks be to God for his unspeakable gift!
2 Corinthians 9:15

I.

This book is an "essay" in two senses. First, it is a brief and schematic treatment of an enormously complicated and interlocking set of problems in Christology. This means that it covers a lot of ground rapidly; it intends only to lay out suggestive lines of thought which would require further explication and development elsewhere. Second, it is an essay in the sense of an experiment or trial run. A theology of incarnation is not simply articulated here but also confronted with some potentially disruptive historical considerations in order to test its viability. However, the experimental character of the proposals should not be interpreted as radical novelty. Although some Christological points are being pushed further and emphasized more vigorously than is typically the case, the overall position defended intends to be quite orthodox (defined, for purposes of this essay, as fidelity to the definitions of Nicaea and Chalcedon). No great claim to originality is being made; those for whom the ancient creeds have only the validity of bygone opinions, or who yearn for fundamental revisions to Christological doctrine, will be disappointed.

The essay is driven by a basic problem, and shaped around a basic hypothesis. The problem is that an orthodox or catholic theology of the incarnation or hypostatic union (granting absolute significance to a discrete event or set of events centering on Jesus of Nazareth) appears to clash with modern historical consciousness (for which all temporal events are essentially finite and relative). The hypothesis is that semiosis is a promising master-image or model for understanding the metaphysics of the incarnation, and that such a model helps address the problem described. Thinking of the incarnation along communicative and linguistic lines goes back to the New Testament, and theologians have handled the theme in many different ways. Karl Barth, for example, proposed to speak of Jesus as God's "self-interpretation."[1] But the hypothesis here focuses on *human* interpretive activity as a fundamental component of the total event of God's disclosure in Jesus. This in turn suggests an essential role for the reception of the Word uttered in him; the believing communities and their Spirit-directed labor of understanding are not just a secondary result of the incarnation, but the vehicle of its expression and actualization in history.

The various influences that have shaped my view of this problem and guided me toward this hypothesis are not evident from my previous publications, so here at the beginning I am bound to call attention to my sources of inspiration.[2] This duty is also a pleasure, as it will enable me to acknowledge intellectual debts which I keenly feel, but which would not otherwise be obvious to the reader. Starting with the basic problem, what needs clarification is not the obvious tension between modern historical thinking and incarnational faith, but rather the conviction suffusing this entire essay that historical consciousness is a precious gift of the modern

1 See, for a perceptive discussion of the phrase, Eberhard Jüngel, *God's Being Is in Becoming: The Trinitarian Being of God in the Theology of Karl Barth*, trans. John Webster (Edinburgh: T&T Clark, 2001), 27ff.

2 And to the source of my title, which is borrowed from F. W. von Juntzt's now hard-to-obtain *Unaussprechlichen Kulten* (1839).

age whose delicate critical mechanics are easily and routinely thrown out of balance by Christian apologetic bias, whether unconscious or open.

This happens in two ways. The systematic evaluation of sources and evidence and the tentative narrative reconstruction of possible scenarios of the past requires a skeptical reserve, a rigorous attention to canons of probability, and an openness to inconvenient conclusions that are all routinely endangered by the need of the Christian historian to mold the past into agreement with claims of the faith. Alongside this often-unwitting source of bias is a second, more self-conscious theological attitude to the past that suppresses the historian's fundamental sense of the continuity across all times and places of individual and social possibilities and dynamics. Sometimes, for example, the apologist argues directly for the discontinuity between all other history and the founding and sustaining events of Christianity, appealing to the interventions of omnipotence to account for this exceptional status. Or, as has sometimes happened in recent decades, theology borrows from critical genealogies of modern thought and post-foundationalist epistemologies to relativize and subvert the historian's sense of the veridical. Against these moves, I remain deeply convinced of the irreplaceable heuristic value of critical and historicist assumptions in authentically apprehending the past. The invocation of miracle and the temptations of what might be called "apologetic postmodernism" are dangerous expedients. Christians must know what they are about in jettisoning, for reasons of theological convenience, the canons of modern historical judgment, for the cost will be high; such an inevitably self-serving and arbitrarily selective maneuver can never really be principled, and thus corrupts all historical judgment and in time subverts intellectual honesty.

If I may speak autobiographically for a moment, this pressing concern with both the value and the fragility of forthright historical judgment stems in large part from former teachers whom I am happy to honor here. As an undergraduate I was initiated into the mysteries of sifting evidence and reasoning about the past by two marvelous historians, one a specialist in Renaissance Italy (Eric Cochrane), the other a student of ancient Greek culture (Arthur W. H. Adkins). They modeled a tough-minded pursuit of objectivity (though never forgetting the scholar's subjective limitations) that has stuck with me ever since. When, many years later, I read an exchange in the *Journal of Biblical Literature* between representatives of more traditionalist ("Neo-Albrightian") and more skeptical historiography of ancient Israel, I instantly sympathized on historical grounds with the so-called "minimalists" even though my theological instincts were (and are) quite different than theirs.[3] To this day I find something compelling in the reconstructions of Jewish history and the interpretations of the Old Testament furnished by scholars of a more radically critical temper (Lemche, Thompson, Davies, Liverani, Ahlström, Garbini) despite the massive divergence from the biblical storyline. For me, their work forcefully instantiates the necessary discursive discrimination between history and myth.

To be clear, my inclination to these authors springs from an approval of their overall stance toward historical investigation of the Bible, not from a global acceptance of their historical judgments on particular issues (which in any case differ among them). So while in general I find their bold reconstructions of ancient Israelite history often persuasive or at least worthy of serious consideration, and some of their postulated dating of biblical traditions plausible and fruitful, I freely admit no expertise, and I am aware that these positions have been sharply contested by reputable historians and biblical scholars. More important for my assessment of these thinkers is rather the framework of assumptions with which they approach the historical evidence within and beyond the Bible. Briefly, I think they have accurately identified and justifiably resisted a syndrome that afflicts reconstructions specifically of the biblical past, namely a tendency to begin from a broad acceptance of the basic veracity of the Old Testament narrative of Israelite history, entertaining corrections on any number of details but preserving as much of the Bible's narrative world as possible.

All the scholars I have named rightly, I believe, point out the ways such an approach diverges from the canons guiding the historical investigation of other ancient societies, where a far more skeptical attitude reigns toward a given culture's cherished narratives of its own origins, past glories, religious orientation, etc. Whereas historians of ancient Greece and

3 Iain W. Provan, "Ideologies, Literary and Critical: Reflections on Recent Writing on the History of Israel," *Journal of Biblical Literature* 114 (1995): 585–606. Responses by Thomas L. Thompson, "A Neo-Albrightian School in History and Biblical Scholarship?" *Journal of Biblical Literature* 114 (1995): 683–98; and Philip R. Davies, "Method and Madness: Some Remarks on Doing History with the Bible," *Journal of Biblical Literature* 114 (1995): 699–705.

Rome learned more than two centuries ago that the *Iliad* or the early books of Livy could not provide a baseline for grasping the actual shape of the periods they claim to treat, in biblical scholarship there still seems to be a faith in the general factuality of the Books of Kings, or of Judges, or even of Exodus, that is unwarranted on purely historical grounds. That this faith might in many cases be connected with the religious commitments of Christian and Jewish scholars, and even on occasion to the perceived imperatives of Middle Eastern politics, is surely further ground for the historian's suspicion.

Turning specifically to the New Testament, the reluctance among even "radical" Christian critics of the Old Testament to apply the same standards of judgment and draw the same challenging conclusions when it comes to the second part of the biblical canon, especially the Gospels, was noted long ago by David Friedrich Strauss.[4] Here, too, however, some under whom I studied inspired me to strenuous critical openness even on this (for Christian believers) most sensitive historical terrain. Early in my theological training the ground was prepared, surprisingly, by teachers suspicious of radical critique. Yet Richard Hays, for example, rightly warned us students against the temptation, in face of historical skepticism, to devise in response a Christology that renders questions of factuality simply irrelevant. False attempts to insulate Jesus' "existential impact" from his real human history forget that Christian faith in him really does depend upon certain things actually having happened. Like Hans Frei (whom I knew only from his publications), Hays showed us that for a theological reading of the New Testament, the skills of the literary critic are equally important to those of the historical critic, but that the historical questions must continue to serve as a crucial check on the plausibility of specific theological interpretations.

I never forgot these lessons, which kept me alert to the risks of faith's special pleading even when the disturbing historical problem of Christian origins was brought sharply home to me by later professors—not only historians like Arthur Droge and especially Jonathan Z. Smith (of

4 David Friedrich Strauss, *Das Leben Jesu, kritisch bearbeitet*, vol. 1 (Tübingen: C. F. Osiander, 1835–1836), 54ff.; English translation of the 4th edition: trans. anon. [George Eliot] as *The Life of Jesus Critically Examined*, 3 vols. (London: Chapman Bros., 1846), ed. Peter Hodgson (Philadelphia: Fortress, 1972). Unless noted otherwise, all page citations will be to the 4th German edition, followed by the corresponding pages of the Eliot translation available in the single volume edited by Peter Hodgson, in this case 65ff.

whom much more below), but also Brian Gerrish, a formidable mentor whose elegantly written essays modeled a principled refusal to evade the challenge of modern historicism. He also introduced me to the seminal work of Van Harvey, whose concerns with the distinct demands of historical and theological reasoning have remained alive for me ever since.[5] The result has been a determination on my part to entertain theologically even drastic departures from the received narrative of Christian origins, if the evidence and arguments adduced seemed to warrant it: from Bultmann to Betz and Koester and on to Burton Mack and the fascinating conversations springing from the SBL's Consultation on Ancient Myths and Modern Theories of Christian Origins.[6] In short, the sensibility I bring to the historical problem of the present essay is, to a great degree, a product of influences from these esteemed teachers and texts.

So much for the basic problem which has prompted this essay—what about the basic hypothesis that it develops in response? It will be more fully described below, but the already-stated main theme is the constitutive incarnational role of the human use and interpretation of signs, of pneumatically illuminated ecclesial reception. Some paragraphs should be devoted to the figures guiding my thinking along this path, for (as with my historical inclinations) certain theological influences on the basic approach are not easily gauged from the essay itself or its documentation. There are, first, figures whose fleeting appearance in the essay belies their actual importance for the Christological thesis itself: Rowan Williams and Michel de Certeau. It would be difficult for me to state all that I owe to the writings of the first of these in particular.[7] Next, Søren Kierkegaard

5 Van A. Harvey, *The Historian and the Believer: The Morality of Historical Knowledge and Christian Belief* (New York: Macmillan, 1966).

6 For the last mentioned see Ron Cameron and Merrill P. Miller, eds., *Redescribing Christian Origins* (Leiden: Brill, 2004), and *Redescribing Paul and the Corinthians* (Leiden: Brill, 2011).

7 Although this essay was written before I had seen Williams' *Christ the Heart of Creation* (London: Bloomsbury Continuum, 2018), I was privileged to hear, and benefit from, the Bonhoeffer material as initially aired in the DuBose lectures at the University of the South (2016). But his many earlier published articles and chapters had already influenced my thinking for some time, and at more than one level. However, an anonymous reader of this essay in manuscript has helpfully identified a central strategy connecting Williams' book with my own: appropriating creation *ex nihilo* in order to account conceptually for God's ability to fashion his own humanity in Jesus, such that divinity neither opposes nor interferes with Jesus' creaturehood, but is rather expressed by it. This reader went on to identify Ian McFarland's *The Word Made Flesh: A Theology of the Incarnation* (Louisville:

and Dietrich Bonhoeffer, though granted slightly more prominent roles, have influenced my thinking about the meaning of Christ in modernity at a much deeper level than the glancing discussions below might suggest. But ultimately, in terms not so much of its argumentative details as of its broader orientation, this project goes forward under the sign of two thinkers who never appear in it: the German church historian Erik Peterson (1890–1960) and the French theologian Yves Congar OP (1904–1995).

In spite of any number of disagreements, I regard Peterson as something of a kindred spirit, both biographically and, on crucial points, theologically. A deep resonance between my own course of thinking and Peterson's intellectual journey and orientation has shaped the approach of this essay. First there is his path, the earnest evangelicalism of his youth and young adulthood revealing itself to be a gradual preparation for reception into the Catholic Church in middle age.[8] The intellectual dimension of this complex religious transformation reveals three theological determinants, each of which bears fruit in the hypothesis of this essay. First, Peterson's experience and research convinced him that Protestantism's late medieval/early modern systematic centralization of a saving but quasi-extraneous transaction between God and the individual soul (*sola fide*, imputation) is unwarranted by the collective witness of the New Testament, and tends toward a serious impoverishment of the full meaning of salvation in Christ, diminishing or even abandoning its incorporative, communal, and eschatological dimensions. Second, this subject-oriented reduction is linked to the erosion of the ancient soteriological role (far beyond mere practical utility) of the church, not just as an idea or an affinity group but specifically as a divine yet public institution. It is

---

Westminster John Knox, 2019) as yet another recent Christology evincing the same orientation. I am grateful for that reader's perceptive insight into the role of creation in the present treatise. In fact, before it grew into a volume of its own, it had been envisioned as part of an essay collection thematically united around the infinity of God in light of a theology of *ex nihilo* creation, and the implications of that infinity for other Christian doctrines. By exploring what happens when the creator's infinity fully annexes the historical-cultural "body" of a human person, this essay maintains its original continuity with the approach of that volume. See Paul J. DeHart, *Creation and Transcendence: Theological Essays on the Divine Sublime* (forthcoming 2021 from T&T Clark).

8 Peterson's thorough, often quite critical but never finished engagement with Kierkegaard's thought is another mark of affinity. For an exhaustive and insightful treatment of Peterson's life and ideas, see Barbara Nichtweiss, *Erik Peterson: Neue Sicht auf Leben und Werk* (Freiburg: Herder, 1992). The points only touched on here are fleshed out at length by her extensive archival research.

a fundamentally liturgical society in which the ongoing incarnate life of God is made really visible and available in this world. Peterson rediscovered this church as an integral part of the Christian gospel, an undeniably juridical and political entity with its own modes of belonging and authority, announcing and instancing (however far from perfectly) the coming sovereignty of God among humanity.

Third, Peterson not only negotiated his transition to Catholicism without retreating into the then increasingly fashionable rightist, racist, or revanchist trends that proved so enticing to many Catholics in the interwar period (Fritz Stern's "politics of cultural despair").[9] More central to the concerns of this book, he managed to relocate himself in the world of Catholic scholarship without abandoning the historical consciousness and the high discipline of non-apologetic critical history which had shaped his mind as a Protestant. Peterson the scholar ultimately became something *sui generis*, an atypically adventurous and rather lonely figure among the Catholic church historians of his time. Shaped by Richard Reitzenstein amid the Göttingen milieu of the *religionsgeschichtliche Schule*, he somehow managed to retain, despite his later embrace of Catholic orthodoxy, a fundamentally critical and comparative orientation as a scholar of antiquity.[10] Alongside (and in subtle connection with) his theological reflections, his historical work partly inspires the determined insertion of early Christianity into Hellenistic religious culture employed below, just as his combination of hard-edged, non-apologetic interrogation of tradition with full Christian conviction forms a personal ideal.

Even more centrally for this essay, Peterson recovers the cosmic-political dimension of God's incarnation in Christ, as well as the essential continuation of the bodily, human presence of Christ in the public-cultic

9 Though, inevitably, his writings are marked in places by some of the particular blind spots and prejudices prevalent in his context.

10 Which is not to say that he feigned theological neutrality, for in fact he openly argued that only a proper theological orientation grants genuine historical insight into ancient Christianity. One need not accede to this doubtful claim (and I do not) to acknowledge Peterson's peculiar talents as an historian. On his achievement in this field, see Nichtweiss, *Erik Peterson*, 261–339. For a quirky but warm tribute to Peterson the historian, see the reflections of the prominent Dutch scholar of Gnosticism Gilles Quispel, "The Study of Encratism: A Historical Survey," in *Gnostica, Judaica, Catholica: Collected Essays of Gilles Quispel*, ed. Johannes van Oort (Leiden: Brill, 2008), 329–63, esp. 329–41. In 1959 Jean Daniélou called Peterson "one of the great pioneers in the renewal of the study of ancient Christianity" (Nichtweiss, 338).

act that is the church.[11] This intrinsically public character of the church (as itself only instrumental to, not identical with, the eschatological *polis* inaugurated by Jesus' resurrection) grants it a proper though always troubling presence within the open field constituted by political struggle. This must be kept in mind as necessarily complicating any too-simple approximation of Christianity to the mystery religions. As Peterson well knew, the Romans at least were not fooled: they slowly realized that in this new Oriental sect they were dealing with something much more, and much more threatening, than just another exotic cult.[12] But Peterson's ecclesial conception also requires critical supplementation, due to a problematic tendency to identify the church as a "political" institution straightforwardly with the clerical hierarchy. The necessary corrective for this lies in the pneumatological ecclesiology of Yves Congar, another lodestar for our theological hypothesis.[13] If Peterson was right to reemphasize the public-cultic and cosmic-eschatological aspects of the church (the final paragraphs of this essay clearly nod toward that last point), Congar was just as correct in rethinking the human transactions that make up the public ecclesial body in collective-interpretive rather than legal-executive terms, as apostolic-prophetic negotiations that cannot be reduced to an apostolicity construed one-sidedly as episcopal jurisdiction.

The incarnational model of pneumatic-ecclesial reception developed in the essay attempts to take up and extend Congar's critical supplement to Peterson's thematic. I read Congar's stress on the church as the people of God in light of the idea, intimated toward the end of my book *The Trial of the Witnesses*, of the Spirit as a force deploying or animating the dynamics of culture.[14] In the Eucharist the Spirit really unites the offering of the people with Jesus' own historical and bodily self-offering; this sign effects and encapsulates what is happening on a much larger scale, as the Spirit operates to retroactively constitute Jesus as God's historical body by

11 These crucial themes are superbly expounded, with valuable attention to Peterson's university lectures and correspondence and a special focus on his complex relation to the legal philosopher Carl Schmitt, in Nichtweiss, *Erik Peterson*, 722–830.

12 See Nichtweiss, *Erik Peterson*, 750.

13 A fine synthetic exposition of Congar from this point of view is Elizabeth Teresa Groppe, *Yves Congar's Theology of the Holy Spirit* (Oxford: Oxford University Press, 2004).

14 Paul J. DeHart, *The Trial of the Witnesses: The Rise and Decline of Postliberal Theology* (Oxford: Blackwell, 2006).

means of the semiotic body perpetuating and creatively realizing his identity. Thus Peterson's "public body," already "socialized" by Congar, comes to be "culturalized" here. Both these figures, it should be added, exemplify as well the same commitment to Catholic ecclesiology and faithfulness to classic creedal tradition that informs this entire project, whatever its success in its particular proposals.

Finally, the kind of thinking that informs this essay on both its historical and theological levels has been deeply if unexpectedly influenced by its dedicatee, Jonathan Z. Smith. This is partly a matter of style and example. Smith was for me the ideal scholar, a model in writing, speaking and teaching whose work displayed profound and creative erudition, exacting argumentation, and a sophisticated yet vibrant prose style. But his substantive insights, too, on the challenge and dignity of academic thinking in general, as well as in religion and religious studies in particular, continually stimulated my development. On both levels he was formative for me, starting with the momentous course I took with him as a doctoral student, leading to the reading (and eventual re-readings) of his marvelous essay collections, and ending in later years with my rapt attention at a number of his impressive presentations at the American Academy of Religion annual meetings.

Upon finishing the initial draft of this essay and deciding to dedicate it to him, I sent Smith a copy along with a brief letter reminding him of that long-ago class and letting him know of my intended dedication, offering to drop it if he had objections. I do not believe he ever saw the letter; four months after it was posted, I sadly read of his death. To some who admired and learned from this man as much and more than I, the use of his studiedly nontheological scholarship in service to an explicitly theological undertaking might appear impertinent, if not disrespectful. I am not unaware of the apparent incongruity, as the following excerpt from my letter shows.

> [Y]our ideas have been seminal for the thoughts developed herein. Please understand that it has not been my intention to pervert your own insights into a kind of unwitting religious apologetic. It is precisely your wariness of apologetics, and your commitment to the utter humanity of all religious history, that has challenged and informed my own quite different project. I have learned so much from reading you, and I wished to acknowledge that by dedicating

> this piece to you. I hope, if you get a chance to read it, you will not be offended at the contents. I also hope I have, to some degree at least, gotten you right.

That last hope remains. But what would he have made of the rash invoking of his name upon a Christological essay? And why the dedication, apart from the personal intellectual debts already noted?

My impression always was that Smith had a gentle, half-amused, and half-respectful tolerance for skilled theological thinking *in its own sphere*. However, though not necessarily intellectually or ethically suspect in itself, it needed to be mercilessly exposed and purged when it appeared within, or tacitly distorted the criteria of, the properly humanistic disciplines treating religion academically, that is, as an immanent exercise in cultural meaning-making strictly subject to exhaustive comparison and theoretical explanation. So though he would no doubt have had little use for the more theological and confessional dimensions of the piece, I like to think he would not have taken the dedication amiss. As for the specific intellectual connections between his thought and this essay, there is a complex relevance of Smith's way of thinking not just to the historical issues aired in the third chapter, but even (and especially) to the semiotic incarnational hypothesis that is the essay's main concern. With my roster of its hidden inspirations now complete, that hypothesis can now be more fully stated.

The human word, the intelligible utterance, must be received as a sign. That is to say, it does not "shine," emitting meaning like a beacon. Rather, first, it is effective only as inserted into a semantic network, linked with many other signs; second, it must be read, interpretively construed by its recipient via an act that is always to some degree imaginative or creative; and third, this act always takes place against the background of possible failure, of misunderstanding. Only under these conditions can a word actually be humanly heard. These semiotic conditions reign in all human cultural endeavors, including in that realm of collective meaning-making called religion. As will be clarified in the last part of the essay, characteristic of the work of J. Z. Smith was, first, the elaboration of these principles into a percipient theory of culture with a particular stress on the active and inventive character of all symbolic interchange and reception of tradition; and, second, the illuminating application of this theory to religious phenomena compared across multiple cultural settings.

The specifically theological hypothesis of this essay calls for the prolongation of these semiotic conditions for human meaning-making in the direction of the supreme act of meaning for Christian believers: when God, the infinite creator and goal of all things, utters herself into the world, into history, as the human being Jesus. But more is involved than just extending the conditions of human meaning to the temporal utterance of the eternal Word; further, the incarnation, it will be suggested, should be interpreted as involving a relation or synergy between human religious symbolization and the divine ontological mission. The divine Word is said to be uttered into history because that utterance constitutively incorporates the utterance of human words about the Word. Otherwise put, the divine self-expression does not happen alongside or instead of the human culture of worship; the latter is rather the vehicle of the former.

Jesus as the divine Word could not have assumed the semantic status of a human sign without both the entanglement of Jesus' own consciousness within the symbolic networks of his period and the interpretive work of the later cultic communities coming gradually to recognize him via their own symbolic performances. The Spirit is the divine agency in history unifying this process into the incarnation, such that ancient Hellenistic and Semitic religion becomes the "matter" that is "formed" by God into the advent of the divine person. This model is intended to point the way toward a rapprochement between the incarnation and historicist relativity. The divine person is present in time as a personal history in its interaction with other individual and communal histories, and this network of histories, unfolding according to the purely immanent logic of finite events, is itself taken up, "assumed" by the creative omnipotence that, far from interrupting or violating it, establishes and energizes its agency.

But the entry of the Word into the human "flesh" of history brings serious theological consequences in its train. The semiotic rule is: the sign does not shine, it must be read. In the context of this essay that means two things. First, even though the fullness of deity was present as the person Jesus, the phenomenon of deity, its appearance and reception as such, was inevitably stretched out into a temporal interpretive process through communal cultural activity. His epiphany, so to speak, had to "lag behind" his advent and departure.[15] The Gospels are the early fruit of this

15 "Lagging epiphany" is my translation of a phrase (*adventus longe extractus*) found in a curious passage of the seventeenth-century author John Selden. Part of an unpublished manuscript, it has been added as an appendix to this essay.

process; more than that, it will be argued below that the gospel genre itself symbolically inscribes the "lag" into a narrative convention whereby the hero's intensified transcendence results in repeated misrecognition and failures of definition. Second, this cultural imagining of transcendence is the immanent reflex of the ontological "unfinishedness" of the incarnation. The unbounded surplus of human meaning concentrated in Jesus can only find expression through the endless historical construction of a cultic community whose worship and collective activity is the interpretive "hearing" of the Word once given. The lag of epiphany, then, is not just cultural but eschatological; as long as the community of disciples fails to enact or catalyze perfect human community (i.e., as long as history lasts), for so long it cannot adequately name or fully utter God's truly human meaning. Though it rightly identifies Jesus as the Word, short of the eschaton the church remains a cult of the unspeakable.

II.

The argument has a number of moving parts; an overview of the whole will make its unity easier to grasp.

The first part of the essay sets the basic terms of the discussion: the apparent incompatibility between modern historical thinking and the religious affirmation of Jesus' divinity, and the historical and theological proposals that might reconcile them (without eliminating their mutual tension). *Chapter 1* begins with Ernst Troeltsch, who presented in exemplary form the quintessential liberal ("Neo-Protestant") response to the Christological challenge of modern historical consciousness: the saving principle of Christianity must be detached from effective dependence on the historical human being Jesus. Troeltsch tried to hold on to a merely functional centrality of Jesus by appealing to the social and psychological necessity of the community's cultic veneration of his personality, but Albert Schweitzer showed on historical grounds both that this cultic conception fails to establish the desired continuity with the premodern worship of Jesus, and that it is driven to historical judgments that illegitimately accommodate Jesus to modern sensibilities. The dialectical theologians Barth and Bultmann mounted a different, theological critique of Troeltsch's cult: faith in Jesus implies an absolute or transcendent status which Troeltsch's historicist metaphysics of spirit could not supply. The solution lies in a "strong pneumatology" which bestows eschatological significance on the historically given. These dual critiques, historical and theological, respectively, begin to indicate the path beyond the Neo-Protestant conception, but before that path can be taken, the relation of historical consciousness to Troeltsch's dichotomy of person and principle requires more detailed analysis than he provides.

Chapter 2 turns to D. F. Strauss, who best articulated the structure of the Neo-Protestant Christology. Adapting Hegel's dialectic to argue that the Christian message of divine-human reconciliation conceptually negates its appearance in a single individual (Jesus), Strauss set up a double opposition: (1) between the "factual" human Jesus and his transcendent "appearance" to later worshipers, and (2) between this apparent divinity and the metaphysical "truth" that all historical entities are merely relative. This clarifies the twofold response needed for the essay to overcome the opposition between high Christology and history: first, if it is historically conceivable that Jesus' own practice and self-conception were not negated but recognized and continued in his cult, the necessary opposition of fact and appearance would be undermined; second and more centrally, if a theology of God's relation to history were developed that conceptualized the bestowal of ultimate significance on historic entities without cancelling their causal relativity, the resulting "absolute fact" would collapse the opposition of appearance and truth. With the latter task deferred to part 2, the remainder of part 1 turns to the former task by starting with Strauss' conception of myth as the subjective back projection of the communal religious imagination upon Jesus, obliterating his objective human reality. The final section of the chapter outlines what kind of resources would enable an historical reconstruction of Jesus' "cultic recognition," thereby questioning the inevitability of that obliteration. Ideally, such reconstructive speculations would make sense of his later deification by means of the cultural terms also informing his own self-understanding; they would be free of any theological or apologetic agenda; and they would distance themselves from the confessional categories shaping the New Testament saga of Jesus and his church.

Chapter 3 experiments with some historical speculations that might fit the bill, deliberately utilizing the work of two historians of ancient religion quite outside the mainstream of "historical Jesus" scholarship. Morton Smith begins from the historical evidence of Jesus' attested healings and superhuman acts to propose the magician or wonder-worker as the key interpretive category for understanding him. Two motifs are thereby highlighted: salvation through participation in Jesus' quasi-divine agency, and the generative openness of his legacy to multiple overlapping and competing interpretations due to his syncretic and secretive cultural aura. The work of Jonathan Z. Smith, in turn, identifies large scale trends in the late Hellenistic religious imagination exemplified in both these motifs. The concentration and reconfiguration of archaic sacred symbols into the figure of the "holy man" and his community elevate the healer into a cult deity; the revolutionary new vision of salvation as nothing less than liberation from a cosmos become oppressive and carceral expands the local theophany to universal proportions, appropriating his categorical unspecifiability as the positive mark of an indefinable transcendence. The mere feasibility of motifs like these, not as sufficient in themselves to account for Jesus but as elements available for use in various imaginable reconstructions, undercuts the supposedly necessary opposition between the "objective" Jesus and his "subjective" cultic reception. They point toward a unification of Jesus and Jesus-worship within a single trajectory of shared meaning; their alienating distance from the official saga presented in the New Testament also makes them part of an "extreme" test case for the historical flexibility of the incarnational model that can now be developed.

Part 2 outlines the constructive hypothesis at the heart of the essay: a scheme in which the divine persons of Son and Spirit appropriate the historical complex of Jesus and his cultic tradition on the analogy of a formal integration of matter, granting the personal divine presence as historical fact without the rupture of finite causal relations. *Chapter 4* initiates the turn of the argument: from part 1's appeal to historical possibilities able to conciliate the opposition between Jesus' divine appearance and his human factuality to the fabrication of a noninterventionist theology of the Word's eternal incarnation. Such a theology will accommodate an historicist relativism of interwoven circumstance, thereby reconciling Jesus' appearance as a limited event with his absolute truth. The key to this incarnational theology will be a pneumatology of culture, the providential work of the Spirit informing and shaping human cultural transactions as the vehicle of the Word's advent. Avoiding a Barthian pneumatology suspended elusively above these transactions, and a Bultmannian one encapsulated within the structure of existential decision, the claim here will be that the Spirit operates within the imaginative and creative dimensions of culture, yet without appeal to epiphanic moments where divine meaning is directly given. The chapter works by building a causal model, beginning from the noncompetitive layering of physical and semantic efficacy in the event of speech, but then adding further mechanisms to account for the special complications of the Word's utterance in Jesus: posthumous propagation, constructive reception, and truth as self-disclosure rather than passive mirroring of reality. These interlocking components are modeled by the "allegory" of a musical event, the advent of a pop music genius via concert recording.

But can such an account really model the case of Jesus, where the figure embodies not just a musical epiphany but the presence of the infinite creator? Strauss denied the possibility of such an absolutization of a human individual in a classic critique of Friedrich Schleiermacher, who affirmed it. *Chapter 5* provides a scorecard of their bout, noting both the weaknesses exposed by Strauss but vindicating and preserving for critical development Schleiermacher's most promising insights. Besides exposing the critical liabilities of Schleiermacher's history of Jesus, Strauss rightly questioned the latter's attempt to cast the human redemptive connection with Jesus in terms of an immanent historical development, and to localize God's presence in him within an impossible, culturally quarantined psychological zone. But certain ingenious elements of Schleiermacher's incarnational scheme hold up well under Strauss' attack. His concept of the archetypal status of the Redeemer intriguingly points toward a formal identity of Jesus' redeemed subjectivity and that of those united to him in faith. Though weakened by its psychological scaffolding, his analysis of Jesus' human subjectivity rightly locates the decisive presence of God in him in terms of the primordial conditioning of his selfhood through the creator's formative proximity. Finally, Schleiermacher correctly saw that, if it is conceived as the enhanced reception of human intentionality, the "local" presence of the infinite creator within a delimited historical space need not involve a disruptive notion of miracle inimical to the world's causal continuity.

Chapter 6 argues that the best way to retrieve Schleiermacher's insights, and thereby secure an incarnational concept that accepts Jesus' real identity with God without interrupting the flow of historical relativity, is to critically resituate them within a Thomist framework. It begins by showing the superior utility of Thomas Aquinas' scheme of three ascending modes of God's presence in the world (in everything, in human souls, in Jesus) in comparison to the Spinozist scheme underlying Schleiermacher's Christology. Rather than the latter's simple gradation of intensity, Aquinas offers a differentiated scheme where the more profound modes of divine presence depend on prior, functionally distinct modes. Thus the union of Jesus' selfhood with the divine person rests on the intentional presence of God in created intellects and wills; and that intentional presence in turn rests on the providential omnipresence of the creative activity. This latter dependence ensures that the higher modes, though distinct, need not be conceived as disruptions in the continuity of physical or historical causality. With this framework in place, the essay can then exploit the Thomist theology of a twofold Trinitarian mission; such a conception allows a better use to be made of Schleiermacher's shrewd perceptions as to how Jesus' absoluteness in history works. The assumption of Jesus by the Son allows the total shaping of Jesus' human consciousness by God's special contiguity, but without any appeal to a mental zone of "inwardness" free of cultural conditioning. Likewise, the ecclesial community, animated by the ongoing descent of the Spirit that like Jesus bears the divine presence, continues and actively unfolds his divinized human form; it is freed from the one-sidedly passive incarnational role assigned to it by Schleiermacher (as recipient of a supposed historical influence of Jesus' redemptive power). Through the creative play of its interpretive practices, it co-constitutes the full expression of the Word in history. With this concluding chapter of part 2, the broad lines are now in place of an incarnational theology that might overturn the opposition between Jesus' divine appearance to faith and his metaphysical truth.

However, this comes at a price. Reconciling the incarnation with historical consciousness in this way means the compatibility in principle of creedally orthodox Christology with extreme historical departures from the Gospel story of Jesus. That is because the Word's assumption of an integral history means the necessary occlusion of any direct view of Jesus' divinity (i.e., unmediated by the interpretive venture of faith); though accommodated theologically, this has potentially disorienting consequences for how Jesus and the Gospels become available to the believer. The object of faith now presents threatening aspects; yet, as *chapter 7* attempts to explain, even the most troubling of these can actually be understood as springing from the radical acceptance of God's historical and cultural embodiment in the Christ-event. First, layered causality indeed means that Jesus' divinity could never be directly disclosed as the extraordinary, whether the historically "great" or the religiously numinous; however, the revelation of his true status through the cultural processes of the faithful imagination is inherent to the lowliness of his mission. Second, Jesus' non-transcendent consciousness, i.e., the total humanity of his psychological constitution and cultural horizon, is still compatible with a perfect, even blissful awareness of unity with God once certain unique characteristics of the subjective apprehension of God are taken into account. Third, the irreducibility of Jesus' transcendence to historical data, and the various mythic constructs necessarily employed to communicate it, does make it difficult to account for the truth of the canonical evangelical testimony to him. Yet the providential involvement of God in the communal processes leading to the composition and selection of the New Testament Gospels means that their direct factual inaccuracy on innumerable points cannot hinder a kind of partially fictional yet "hyperrealistic" veracity as renderings of his true identity.

The final two chapters continue to think through the consequences of Jesus' "lagging epiphany," i.e., the invisibility of his transcendence to inspection and its consequent extended and ongoing manifestation through interpretive reception. Unlike the previous chapter, though, the focus is not on the qualities of the faith-object but on the subjective challenge inherent within the faith-act itself, i.e., offense. *Chapter 8* deals with a first such scandal, the inability of faith either to definitively affirm or deny the superhuman character of the wondrous performances attributed to Jesus. It is argued that faith in Jesus' divinity can have no interest in assigning these acts to a defined category of divine efficacy, and that the model of layered causality employed in the essay suggests that their truth as signs for belief of Jesus' identity does not obviate their historical embodiment in him as human exercises consciously interpreted through traditional, culturally available paradigms. It is then suggested that this ontological ambiguity of the miraculous in fact extends and deepens older theological insights of Bonhoeffer and Kierkegaard as to how Jesus' divinity must inhabit his temporal humanity. The chapter concludes with a reminder that the testimony to the wondrous has always reflected the inevitable intertwining of the historical and the symbolic in the communication of Jesus' truth. Reading such testimony aright has in fact always presented a challenge to faith, but modernity pushes belief beyond its naïve habitation within the "magic realism" of the Gospels toward a self-aware discernment and differentiation of their literal and mythical discursive levels.

Chapter 9 concludes the essay with an interrogation of another stumbling block whose threat can never be removed from incarnational faith, what might be called the monstrosity of Jesus, meaning the strange and repellent visage he ever threatens to turn toward those attempting to grasp his divinity. For the incognito of the Word within the flesh of the world and of history has always been faith's trial. As it looks back into the past to find him, it can neither lay hands on nor imagine Jesus' single and ultimate identity, but can only perpetually construct a series of pictures that are all more or less "wrong." This wrongness is not, as with Hegel, rooted in a conceptual incongruity, the fantastic hybrid of deity and creature; it springs from the metamorphic character of Jesus' incarnate reality, the fact that his full human meaning is in process of disclosure, beginning from the definitive yet still rudimentary rendering of the New Testament and continually assimilating the multiplicity of redeemed life in its forms over time. The latter half of the chapter shows how this perennial challenge involves a vision not only of the past but of the future. For not just faith's object is in motion, but its own standpoint is shifting as well; every construction of the past Jesus also points toward an ideal future not yet attained, where the collective body of the faithful fully exemplifies Christ's infinite humanity in the breadth and harmony of full and undistorted communion. Just as surely, every failure of the church means that in interpreting who Jesus is it falsely projects its own disfigurement outside itself, onto his aspect. In sum, the believers in Jesus as God must have the courage to keep "reacquiring" Jesus interpretively, a task rendered all the more daunting in face of the modern critical exposure of Christianity's cultural and moral complicity with fallen history. They can never finally exorcise the distorted faces that Jesus will sometimes bear, partly from the multiplicity and metamorphosis of his unfinished meaning, partly because he must repeatedly judge the failure of the church to be the Kingdom. Short of the eschaton, the believers can only continually purify their love and thus their vision.

III.

Such, in brief, is the arrangement of the essay, an attempt to affirm both classic incarnational thinking and modern historical consciousness as necessarily in tension yet not finally incompatible. Though the discussion takes a rather gothic turn toward the end, the basic claims and warrants will hopefully be evident. However, additional clarification on a couple of points will prove beneficial.

First, readers of this essay should not misconstrue its intent.[16] One mistaken impulse would be to treat the "historical Jesus" discussion in the third chapter as itself part of, or even central to, the hypothesis of the essay. Had any kind of positive contribution to "historical Jesus" discussions been intended here, the scanty account given in that chapter, utilizing decades-old material from two scholars quite marginal to those discussions, would rightly be dismissed. However, the ideas broached in that chapter are not trying to present a true or even likely argument from historical evidence for who Jesus "really" was. The chapter is designed not to explain Jesus as an historical phenomenon, but to alert readers to certain possible interpretations of Jesus and the Jesus movement, deliberately drawn from nontheological authors outside mainstream New Testament scholarship, which will always be available for critical incorporation into the total historical picture. The relative historical merits of these specific motifs are not argued here; it is their theological utility that is important. First, if these or similar elements can be feasibly worked into the Jesus story, then historical reason itself is shown to possess the resources for connecting the culture of Jesus-worship that arose after his death with his own life history and self-awareness. In other words, the assumption of much modern revisionist Christology that the Jesus cult was an alien imposition on the "real" historical man from Nazareth is not axiomatic. Second and more importantly, the way Jesus and his cult are unified in that chapter touches off theologically fruitful considerations, pivoting the reader toward the actual incarnational hypothesis at the heart of the book. For the unified "Christ-event" as portrayed in the chapter both foreshadows the lines of the theological hypothesis of part 2, and serves as its "extreme" historical test case: since such an historically hostile picture of Jesus, totally contrary to the *Tendenz* of the Gospels, can never be fully ruled out by history, it is important to see that the form of Christological

16 I note here my sincere gratitude for the work of several anonymous readers of earlier versions of the essay in manuscript. In some cases, their misunderstandings alerted me to confusions and obscurities in the presentation of the argument. In other cases, their sharp interrogation of certain rhetorical gambits and infelicities of tone prompted valuable stylistic revisions. The work has been greatly improved thanks to their efforts; the remaining flaws rest with me.

orthodoxy commended by the essay could be sustained even in light of the most inhospitable historical possibilities. But the theological utility of the historical reconstructions delineated in the third chapter does not rest on a claim that this is how it "really" was.

Another misreading of this essay's intention would see it as replacing a (real) ontological understanding of the incarnation with a (merely) cultural one. But the whole point of the essay is that such an either/or view is unnecessary and impossible. The incarnational hypothesis pursued here is a matter of both/and: it is concerned with relating the ontological reality of God in Christ to the created, historical realities that must correspond to it if God really has taken on the flesh of this world. This simply extends the logic of Chalcedon: just as Jesus is not either uncreated (God) or a creature (a human being), but is rather a created human personality assumed by the person of the divine Word; so in this essay the complex of historical events going to make up the cultural psychology of Jesus and the mythic modes of religious veneration in which his divinity was apprehended by his followers are created temporal happenings assumed and formed by the omnipotent creator to project the presence of the divine persons (the Son/Word and Spirit) into the world. The council insisted that Jesus was truly and fully human as well as truly and fully divine; according to our hypothesis, this should be construed to mean that the entire "Christ-event" was truly and fully historical and cultural, precisely as the vehicle of the missions of Son and Spirit.

The challenge to be faced is how to bring together the relativity of history and the absolute character of the divine missions. For the quintessentially modern tradition of historical consciousness, any factual element of the past is appropriable only as utterly contextualized and relativized by the overall flow of causal contingency. On this view, which our incarnational hypothesis seeks to uphold, the human past qua human (like its present and future) is a seamless web of events in temporal flux, the identity of each defined by the mutual reciprocal influences reigning within its context of contiguous events, such that it could attain any more enduring significance only through being taken up into and causally mediated by further events of equally conditioned character. On the other hand, the hypothesis just as seriously adopts the classic posture of Christian religious veneration, absolutizing certain past events centered on Jesus of Nazareth as of universal human significance. To carry forward the latter tradition is to attempt to live one's life into, and out of, the conviction (with all its peculiar implications) that the hero of the four New Testament Gospels is alive, and is God. The discord is conspicuous.

The book seeks to arbitrate these apparently competing loyalties not by smoothing and cushioning their encounter (i.e., through massaging historical judgments into maximal agreement with dogmatic imperatives), but by arranging for them to crash into each other, so to speak. A model of "layered" agency is developed, whereby omnipotent quasi-formal causality assumes as its matter an immanently shaped yet unruptured tract of purely historical causality. This is designed to leave orthodox Christology open to direct contact with skeptical and antitheological historical conclusions concerning Jesus. On the understanding worked out here, the presently saving incarnation of the Word could have taken a far more "alien" human shape than the one depicted in the Gospels, because the Word's advent took place by way of the divine Spirit's activity, self-deployed within the human cultural transactions that produced the meanings-to-themselves of Jesus and his early worshipers. This implies, however, that the metaphysical reality of Jesus' divinity was not simply given, a brute fact to which his deification in the Christ-communities was merely the culturally conditioned response; the cultural dynamics at play in his self-understanding and in the exercise of his cult were themselves essential conditions of, and the ongoing vehicle for, his presence in history as God.

Referring to the rapid dissemination and persistent evolution of cultural traditions and communities revering Jesus as savior, Rowan Williams pregnantly remarked, "[T]he actual concrete meaning of logos in the world, the pattern decisively and transformingly embodied in Jesus, could only be seen and realized through the entire process of the history to which the event of Jesus gives rise, with all its fluidity and unpredictability."[17] The suggestion seems to be that this posthumous development flowing from him is inseparable from the constitution of God's incarnation in him. Perhaps his body *had* to disappear in order to release his meaning into history, just as each sound within a word must suffer instant displacement in order that the whole be heard. As a saving gift to humanity, God in (as) Jesus is an event of meaning, and the actualization of the

17 Rowan Williams, "Trinity and Pluralism," in *On Christian Theology* (London: Blackwell, 2000), 172.

Word's incarnation in him is a process that includes not just Jesus' human self-interpretation, but the interpretive acts of worship that actualize his divinity as a collective, cultural reality. This does not mean that the divine Word's act of self-bestowal on Jesus is partial or processual. But it does mean that the "taking into" human reality of this gift must unfold with the temporal course of human life, that of Jesus but also, with different but equal necessity, that of his extended living body in human history, the faithful collective (and even beyond the latter's visible bounds). The complete manifestation of his inexhaustible meaning for humanity, though fully implicit in his person, trails well behind the completion of his brief biological career. It is the "extended" effect within time of the eternal moment of hypostatic union.

The argument of the book is not concerned with defending any particular historical hypothesis as to what the historical Jesus looked like. It briefly elaborates the possibility of Jesus as a "magician" in order to test whether he could have been that and still be the incarnate Word of Christian belief. More than that, the choice of the "extreme" historical possibility is not random for, whatever its historical plausibility in itself, it brings to light the dynamic cultural elements (myth, thaumaturgy, cultic apotheosis) that, in some combination, were definitely at work in his story and that can on our premises now be seen as providing not a primitive alternative to but an essential component of the reality of incarnation. This constellation of interpretive practices provides the cultural machine, as it were, that then and still now negotiates the metaphysical meeting within history of infinite God and finite world.

Something like this dynamic was operative no matter how Jesus appeared among his contemporaries, magician or no. But the reflections below do not stop with this proposal. As the final part of the essay argues, if Jesus was indeed God, and continues to be so, by means of this progressive expansion into purely human cultural terrains, a deep though salutary insecurity is introduced into Christian belief (or rather we are reminded that it has always been there). Notwithstanding Jesus' assured familiarity, faith cannot grasp him once and for all, but must keep seeking and asking *who he is*.

The final part of the essay is dedicated to the exploration of what one might call this *traumatic* dimension of the "God in time" and its aggravation under modern conditions. That Jesus is God, or, better, that God is the creator of all things and is *also* Jesus, when pondered in its true range of significance for deity, for humanity, and for history, is an astonishing possibility. The meaning of this state of affairs (the "good news") is just what Christians are attempting, presumptively or really, well or badly, to embody in their individual and collective activity. But even to grasp this meaning, much less assimilate one's life to it, is neither straightforward nor easy. The concluding chapters are designed to show where the difficulty lies: the immensity of deity infused into Jesus' human history *necessarily* lends him an elusive and imponderable appearance to all temporally situated viewers.

To put it differently, there is a troubling and uncontrollable side of Jesus' presence within pious consciousness that is all too readily suppressed or evaded, but always at work nonetheless. Because the divine humanity of this man is still currently underway, it is hard to "see" it rightly, and to some degree is frightening when so seen; it takes a lifetime of thought and of labor upon oneself and the world at once to embrace and to get over this (never fully absent) fear, all the more so for modern persons. Yet this is not sheer misfortune; when the claim that Jesus is God shocks and offends, it is a sign that it is beginning to be more fully understood. This essay attempts to raise this frightful element of belief in Jesus, what Kierkegaard named "offense," to fuller consciousness. It hopes to suggest just where between Christian faith and modern minds the true point of tension, the scandal or stumbling block, does not lie, and where it does.

This invocation of Kierkegaard can fittingly conclude the introduction. The irremovable grounds for offense, which Kierkegaard located in faith's need to penetrate the "incognito" of the "God in time," can and should be reconceived to allow the destabilizing entry of modern historical consciousness into the Christian existential problematic. That is the surmise lying behind the entire project of this essay. Then, too, it follows a course already mapped out by Kierkegaard in insisting that modern faith in the Word's incarnation in Jesus must seek not to mitigate the historicity of Jesus, but to embrace it with abandon.[18]

18 In this way, the essay might be thought of as a small note appended to Kierkegaard's great *Postscript* to the *Philosophical Fragments*. A post-postscript, then, by a lesser hand.

Part One

CULTIC SPEECH

Catachresis or Recognition?

1

Ernst Troeltsch and the Cult of Neo-Protestantism

Pausanias describes the cave sanctuary of "Black Demeter," *Deméter Mélaina*, a few miles from Phigalia in Arcadia. He has much to say about a semihuman cult image, a horse-headed Demeter who had somehow perished even from the memory of the people in the place.

Walter Burkert | *Structure and History in Greek Mythology and Ritual*

I.

In the middle of March 1911, around 130 German-speaking university students gathered in the town of Aarau, midway between Basel and Zürich, for the annual Swiss Student Christian Conference.[1] The address on the last day of the meeting was, it might be presumed, especially anticipated. The topic was the theological and religious connection between faith as a salvific relation to God and the historical factuality of Jesus of Nazareth. This was a timely choice given the commotion caused by the sensational argument of Arthur Drews that "Jesus" was no historical figure but an entirely mythical construct.[2] The speaker, too, was a draw: the Heidelberg theology professor

1 Paul Gruner, *Menschenwege und Gotteswege im Studentenleben: Persönliche Erinnerungen aus der christlichen Studentenbewegung* (Bern: BEG-Verlag, 1942), 433, 435.

2 On Drews see Albert Schweitzer, *The Quest of the Historical Jesus: First Complete Edition*, ed. John Bowden (Minneapolis: Fortress, 2001), 381–89. Chapters 22 and 23 of Schweitzer's book (355–436) present an overview and penetrating critique of the entire debate in those years concerning Jesus' historicity.

Ernst Troeltsch was known as one of the towering intellectuals of the turn of the century, though a source of theological controversy. To the mounting discomfort, one imagines, of many in the audience, Troeltsch's lecture patiently and forcefully made the case that a truly modern Christian belief in the forgiving and redeeming presence of God in human hearts cannot any longer be seen as necessarily or essentially dependent upon the existence some two millennia ago of Jesus Christ.[3]

How had Troeltsch arrived at this position? The assumption of such a necessary dependence, shared by the ancient Catholic faith and the great mainstream reformers alike, had been rendered unbelievable, Troeltsch argued, in light of modern historical consciousness. Though not dependent upon any particular natural scientific conclusion or metaphysical system, this consciousness provides the sometimes-hidden but ever-present framework of presuppositions underlying contemporary educated culture, an entire worldview; it is "the modern attitude of man to his memories and accounts of the past which has been achieved on the basis of thousands of penetrating reflections and justified by thousands of successes" in reconstructing what has gone before.[4] Troeltsch formulated in authoritative fashion the methodological principles demanded by this attitude: "the methodical criticism of sources, the reconstruction of facts by analogy with events otherwise known to us or at least frequently attested, and finally the construction of a causal scheme which binds together all the phenomena."[5] The colossal advance in critical understanding of the past made possible by this approach was, indeed, undeniable. But the consistent application of these principles in theology could only mean that miraculous interruptions or disruptions of

3 Ernst Troeltsch, "Die Bedeutung der Geschichtlichkeit Jesu für den Glauben," in *Kritische Gesamtausgabe*, vol. 6: *Schriften zur Religionswissenschaft und Ethik (1903–1912)*, ed. Trutz Rendtorff (Berlin: Walter de Gruyter, 2014), 820–852. Troeltsch quotations will follow the English version, in this case Ernst Troeltsch, "The Significance of the Historical Existence of Jesus for Faith," *Writings on Theology and Religion*, trans. and ed. Robert Morgan and Michael Pye (Louisville: Westminster John Knox, 1977), 182–207. Page references for Troeltsch will be made to the German edition, followed in parentheses by the corresponding pages of the English translation.

4 Ernst Troeltsch, "Was heisst 'Wesen des Christentums?" in *Gesammelte Schriften*, vol. 2 (Tübingen: J. C. B. Mohr, 1913), 397. Quotations follow Ernst Troeltsch, "What Does 'Essence of Christianity' Mean?" in *Writings on Theology and Religion*, trans. and ed. Robert Morgan and Michael Pye (Louisville: Westminster John Knox, 1977), 133.

5 Troeltsch, "Was heisst 'Wesen'?" 394 (131).

the causal regularity (physical or psychological) of nature can no longer serve as plausible validations of the founding events of any religion, or of the normative authority of its tradition.[6]

As a vast, multiform, and always changing historical phenomenon, the defining identity and perennial meaning of the Christian religion can no longer be determined for believers today dogmatically, by appeal to Scripture, doctrine, or ecclesial authority. The discernment of its essence, Troeltsch had argued elsewhere, requires the continual exercise, for each generation, of the most factually informed and delicately discriminating historical judgment.[7] On the basis of his own reflections along these lines, Troeltsch concluded that an enormous shift within Christian self-understanding, at once necessary and salutary, has taken place since the dawn of the modern era. A new logic of Christian belief has established itself, according to which "real religious faith has severed its connexion with the old belief in a redemption that divinized history."[8]

The Christian's transformative faith in the loving, forgiving creator, whatever its factual roots in a long tradition, has finally unveiled itself as a genuine possibility granted by God to individual spirits; it is in no way logically or effectively dependent upon the past existence or present influence of Jesus or the church as supposedly "divinized" realities within the historical world. Though he claims to find it already adumbrated in a figure like Meister Eckhart, Troeltsch traces the basic prehistory of this awareness back to the humanists (like Erasmus) and the radical wing of the Reformation (Socinians as well as mystics like Sebastian Franck), through the enlightened Christianity of Locke and Leibniz, up to the generation of Idealism (Lessing, Kant, Hegel and his followers). As Troeltsch saw it, after Protestantism had revolutionized the ancient faith, it later experienced in turn its own transformation, though in accord with its own internal dynamic. So dramatic has been the resulting break with the classical Reformation that Troeltsch christened the modern religious logic "Neo-Protestantism" (*Neuprotestantismus*).[9]

6 Troeltsch, "Was heisst 'Wesen'?" 395 (131–32).

7 Troeltsch's discussion of the dimensions of this problem are a perceptive, nuanced, and still relevant set of reflections on the unavoidable intertwining of objectivity and subjectivity in the reconstructive imagination of the historian. See Troeltsch, "Was heisst 'Wesen'?" 432–40 (163–70).

8 Troeltsch, "Geschichtlichkeit Jesu," 825 (186).

9 Ernst Troeltsch, *Die Bedeutung des Protestantismus für die Entstehung der modernen Welt*, in *Kritische Gesamtausgabe*, vol. 8: *Schriften zur Bedeutung des Protestantismus*

Thus the legacy of modern historical consciousness, in company with modern science, has been a fundamental and permanent alteration of the shape of Christian faith. Though contested within authoritarian Christianity (fundamentalism or Catholicism) and often hardly conscious in much mainstream Protestantism, Neo-Protestantism was deemed by Troeltsch to be at least the implicit framework of belief for all his reflective and responsible contemporaries. He sought to make it explicit, and to apply it consistently. It demands a rejection of the classical (premodern) view of redemption as "something achieved once and for all in the work of Christ and then appropriated by individuals" through the extension of Jesus' incarnation "in the divine humanity of the Bible and of the church as the institution of salvation." There remains for the honest modern believer not an historical work of salvation accomplished in Jesus and applied via the church but an ever new "operation of God upon the soul" that effects in Christians "faith in [God] as a holy will that forgives sins," with "sins" cast in ethical terms.[10] As evidenced in his Aarau lecture, one area most urgently in need of consistent application of the new principle was Christology.

Neo-Protestant faith demands a breaking-up or disintegration of what classical Christology held together. For historical consciousness strictly enforces what Troeltsch held to be the basic presupposition of all authentic belief under modern conditions, a presupposition that had found its classic formulation in "the Hegelian school": the essential detachment of the "principle of Christianity" from the "person of Christ."[11] This means that, whatever the historical connection between the redeeming and morally transformative faith in God animating the Christian communion on one hand, and the life, preaching, and personality of Jesus on the other, the former cannot be made radically dependent, either conceptually or efficaciously, upon the latter. For all the scandal the suggestion of such a separation had provoked in the early nineteenth century (deftly avoided by Hegel himself but positively courted by his left-wing progeny), it is

---

für die moderne Welt (1906–1913), ed. Trutz Rendtorff (Berlin: Walter de Gruyter, 2001), 224–32. Ernst Troeltsch, *Protestantism and Progress*, trans. William Montgomery (Philadelphia: Fortress, 1986), 34–40. The English version renders "Alt-" and "Neuprotestantismus" by "early" and "modern Protestantism."

10 Troeltsch, "Geschichtlichkeit Jesu," 824 (185).

11 Troeltsch, "Geschichtlichkeit Jesu," 826 (186).

now, said Troeltsch, the common assumption not only of most academic theology but even of considerable numbers of ordinary churchgoers.[12]

Theology, however, had until now failed to carry through this disintegration. The most influential recent dogmaticians, such as Albrecht Ritschl and Wilhelm Herrmann, had grasped and accepted the basic premise of Neo-Protestantism that faith is not the appropriation of an act of redemption effected in Christ but is itself God's act of redemption. Yet they maintained a relic of the old faith in their insistence that this saving faith is still somehow connected to the efficacious presence of Jesus Christ. Even the great Schleiermacher himself, whom Troeltsch deeply admired as the pioneer who had best understood the implications of the new faith for theological method, still clung stubbornly to this essential connection between faith's power and the presence of God in the Jesus of history.[13] With the keen insight and courageous honesty that characterized his thought, Troeltsch sought to force the choice between Neo-Protestantism and the classic faith, and to show that the Christological "halfway house" erected by Schleiermacher and maintained by liberal theology was uninhabitable.

What, then, of the positive question which Troeltsch sought to answer for his hearers in Aarau? Did not this separation of principle and person render the historicity of Jesus Christ simply irrelevant to Christian belief today? Once its logical independence of ancient "saving" facts had been granted, it might seem to be the case that religious faith was now freed for an ongoing self-development, drawing upon its own contemporary spiritual resources without constraint from the influences of the past, even from its past founder, since the latter could assume only "pedagogical and symbolical significance."[14] But Troeltsch insisted this was not so. In the final parts of his lecture, he argued with care and precision for an ongoing

12 Troeltsch, "Geschichtlichkeit Jesu," 825 (185).

13 Troeltsch, "Geschichtlichkeit Jesu," 827–29 (187–88). To address the impending breakdown of the reigning but compromising liberal consensus in dogmatics, and to heal the yawning breach between the latter's half-hearted traditionalism and the ever-more independent and triumphant exegetical and historical disciplines within theology, Troeltsch hoped to revive those programmatic insights of Schleiermacher which had never truly been implemented since his death. See Ernst Troeltsch, "Rückblick auf ein halbes Jahrhundert der theologischen Wissenschaft" [1908], in *Gesammelte Schriften*, vol. 2 (Tübingen: J. C. B. Mohr, 1912–1925), 193–226, esp. 221–26; English translation: Ernst Troeltsch, "Half a Century of Theology: A Review," in Troeltsch, *Writings*, 53–81, esp. 76–80.

14 Troeltsch, "Geschichtlichkeit Jesu," 834 (193).

and quite vital orienting role for the historical figure of Jesus even among modern Western Christians.

Sociological study of how human religiosity functions has shown, he argued, that a tradition of belief cannot flourish and undergo a healthy development simply by relying upon the spontaneous inspirations of individuals. It requires, on the one hand, a reciprocal exchange of religious insight and cultivation of feeling within the context of some kind of structured collective of believers. On the other hand, that collective itself can only find stability by "gathering around" a single figure, venerating and celebrating a great religious personality who embodies the religious ideals of the community. The full depth and complexity of "higher" religious truth can never be reduced to abstract teachings; it can only impress itself on persons in a vital and ever-self-renewing way through its instantiation in the life of some fontal religious hero.[15] For Troeltsch this, in fact, had always been the true religious significance of Jesus for Christianity, and it continues to be so.

Here, finally, is where the historical question enters in, for Troeltsch argued that only the critically assured factuality of such a figure ensures the community of the reality and human practicality of its guiding ideal: a fictional portrayal, no matter how skillful, cannot do this.[16] So for the twentieth-century inhabitants of the West, he concluded, the historical figure of Jesus can and must continue to be the inspiring central icon of the Christian religion, at least as long as that faith itself remains a living force shaping European civilization.[17] Jesus will play this role not as a miraculous savior, not as God incarnate, not as an "absolute" occurrence somehow exempt from the historical relativity of all facts and events. Rather, he remains the center of faith as (for us) the most inspiring of religious geniuses and as the rallying point of religious communion: not an exception to the laws of history and sociology, but their highest (for us) exemplification.[18]

II.

Troeltsch's Aarau proposal of a truly Neo-Protestant Christology, for all its ingenuity as a response to modern challenges, still claimed authenticity as

15 Troeltsch, "Geschichtlichkeit Jesu," 835–37 (194–95).
16 Troeltsch, "Geschichtlichkeit Jesu," 839–40 (197–98).
17 Troeltsch, "Geschichtlichkeit Jesu," 849–50 (205–6).
18 Troeltsch, "Geschichtlichkeit Jesu," 837 (195).

an expression of the Christian faith practiced from the beginning. But this claim to genuine continuity rested on foundations whose weakness was already being probed in Troeltsch's day. The current essay seeks radically to rethink the kinds of connections that Troeltsch established between faith, history, and Jesus, in a way that preserves a more classical or orthodox theology of incarnation and redemption, but that at the same time honors the demands of historical consciousness (a feat judged impossible by Troeltsch for any such theology). Initial clues for the way forward can be found by considering some forms of the skepticism with which his project was met by his contemporaries.

Troeltsch's case for the fidelity of his Neo-Protestant Christology to the historic faith rests precariously on the idea of "cult." That is the bridge-concept that must bear much of the weight of the claimed continuity between Jesus' significance for ancient Christianity and for modern, in face of his analysis of the profound displacement of meaning suffered in the interim by the basic notions of "faith" and "redemption." How does this bridging function work? Troeltsch had to be able convincingly to show the abovementioned "gathering around," the collective veneration and celebration of Jesus upon which he pinned his hopes for the continual vitality of Christianity, to be in some sense equivalent to the worship paid to Jesus from the beginning by the premodern faith. Wherein lay the equivalence? The ancient worship and the present-day "centering" are both expressions, he claimed, of the same "motive," a "law of social psychology" that conditions the coalescence and maintenance of all vital and cohesive communities. In regard to religious communities, this law or motive decrees in general that individuals must be drawn together through their mutually reinforcing common investment in a central, concrete focal point; in regard to prophetic (monotheistic and ethically focused) religions in particular, this focal point will be provided by the "vividness and plasticity" of an imaged "personal concrete life" (typically that of the community's founder).[19]

For Troeltsch, this constitutes the authentic original meaning of the cult of Jesus, and such a cult, he insists, is still viable and necessary today. Granted, the difficulties inherent in this equivalence are considerable. For one thing, would the early Christians and Neo-Protestants be venerating the "same" Jesus? The latter are directed to a religious personality, and

19 Troeltsch, "Geschichtlichkeit Jesu," 837–38 (195–96).

this assumes reliable historical access to his life and teaching; the former were worshiping a savior, "a Jesus transfigured by belief in the resurrection." For another thing, are their expectations in regard to this figure at all analogous? It is hard to see how, for even if one grants his sweeping assurance (on unspecified grounds) that the original cult of Christ involved "no sacrifice and rites, no magic or mysteries," Troeltsch must still acknowledge that a cult centered like that of the ancient church on a "mystery of redemption" through Christ is no longer possible.[20]

In short, the unity provided by the concept of cult is far more a matter of function than intention; it will not be easy, however, to justify the extraneousness of intention (the identity of the cultic object and its subjective value for worshipers) in determining the real continuity of a given cultic phenomenon. Perhaps Christians, like the Phigalians in Pausanias, have maintained their cult but long ago forgot the original object of their worship? Troeltsch was certainly aware of the broader tensions here. It is presumably one more reason why he affirmed the urgent necessity in contemporary theology of a general philosophy or science of religion as a human, historical reality, one that could ground the posited unity of ancient and modern belief in spite of the apparent chasm between them (which he himself had so relentlessly brought to light). Only such a science or philosophy would be able to provide the general presuppositions enabling modern theology both to defend the historical knowability of Jesus' teaching and person and to articulate their prime religious significance for humanity (in terms of the faith in God they articulate).[21]

Troeltsch, always a sensitive and candid observer, could not have failed to realize that the terms in which he was attempting to maintain Christological continuity between the classic faith and Neo-Protestantism were already being put under pressure from various points. The most general objections were lodged against the prima facie plausibility of the general claim to continuity itself. Such an attack was made in the keenest terms by a prominent monist philosopher in the lineage of Schopenhauer, Eduard von Hartmann. Troeltsch summarized the latter's attack on the theologians of Neo-Protestantism:

> What they claim to be Christianity is their own modern religious conviction which is now only loosely connected with the real spirit

20 Troeltsch, "Geschichtlichkeit Jesu," 835–38 (194–96).
21 Troeltsch, "Rückblick auf ein halbes Jahrhundert," 222–23 (77–78).

> of Christianity, and which therefore clings all the more anxiously to a few fortuitous pieces of historical evidence, and especially to the proclamation and personality of Jesus which is really quite strange to us.[22]

Troeltsch's response to this accusation in his essay on the question of the "essence" of Christianity is telling in several respects. In the first edition he contented himself with brief remarks to the effect that Hartmann's rival reading of the meaning of Christianity in terms of his own philosophy simply exemplified Troeltsch's own insight that subjective factors necessarily shape the historical assessment of the meaning and value of any intellectual or religious movement. Revising the essay ten years later, however, the threat represented by Hartmann's charge had sufficiently rattled Troeltsch that he expanded the original dry paragraph into an energetic counterattack running several pages.

But in his refutation of Hartmann, he expends most effort not in defending his own threatened principles but in attacking Hartmann's (admittedly quixotic) attempt to make his own pantheistic pessimism the true meaning of Christianity. When he does finally come to state the real matter at issue, he simply reiterates the centrality of the Christ-cult.

> The importance of christology [sic] . . . lay . . . in the consolidation and justification of Jesus' authority and his position as an object of devotion in the cult, which in turn was and is only the presupposition and means of what is really essential, namely the recognition of the living, sin-forgiving and sanctifying Father in Christ.[23]

The wording reveals even more starkly the merely functional role of "devotion" to Christ's person as a medium of religious ideas, and ignores Hartmann's pertinent insinuation that historical retrieval of Jesus' "proclamation and personality" might well reveal, not Troeltsch's bland liberal pieties about "the Father," but something "really quite strange to us." Moreover, Troeltsch's position by 1913 on the central question of the continuity of Christianity itself has become rather wobbly. Whether his modern faith "is 'no longer Christianity' or 'still Christianity'" is, Troeltsch avers, a relatively uninteresting question. "[W]e can leave it to the future to decide whether we are producing a movement which moves

22 Troeltsch, "Was heisst 'Wesen'?" 441 (171).
23 Troeltsch, "Was heisst 'Wesen'?" 444 (173).

away beyond Christianity or one which remains in continuity with it."[24] His avowed personal consciousness of fidelity notwithstanding, the conceptual bridge provided by Troeltsch's proposed Christ-cult is showing signs of strain.[25]

This impression is only strengthened by the assessment around this time not of a theological dilettante but of one of the greatest figures in historical Jesus scholarship: Albert Schweitzer.[26] In the second edition of his great history of scholarship on Jesus, Schweitzer justly praises Troeltsch as one of the few contemporary theologians "able to think historically and philosophically at once," and rightly acknowledges the importance of his published Aarau address as rising above "the Jesus-scholasticism of modern theology" to forcefully grasp and state the real problem of the historical significance of Jesus for Christian faith today. Yet he concludes that Troeltsch's positive proposal miscarries, citing three problems. First, Troeltsch "fail[s] to go further into the questions which arise from the alien element in Jesus' character," and does not meet the objections raised by Hartmann. Second, he "deliberately choose[s] to work with an image [of Jesus] which is to some extent blurred and thus evade[s] many difficulties."

But the third and most important problem is his dubious claim that the cult of Christ was somehow a direct outgrowth from the person Jesus of Nazareth (a vital point enabling Troeltsch to assert that the ancient cult and the modern are "essentially" versions of the same phenomenon). "Historically this assertion is scarcely tenable, for the expectation of the kingdom of God and the Parousia which held the early church together is only indirectly linked with the historical personality of Jesus of Nazareth." In other words, the fervent worship of Jesus in the early church bears no real resemblance to the modern veneration of a (supposedly historically accessible) religious genius. Nor can there be a Christ-cult today on Troeltsch's terms because, once his vaguely outlined figure of Jesus is brought into sharper focus by consistent historical criticism, the result is not the inspiring proponent of the Neo-Protestant gospel, but a stranger to us, a personality and a message utterly steeped in the apocalyptic and eschatological ideas of a bygone period.

24 Troeltsch, "Was heisst 'Wesen'?" 445–46 (175).

25 Historical pressure is also mounting on the grounding of Christianity in Jesus, as Troeltsch, with his usual candor, acknowledges in the second edition of the essence essay. See Troeltsch, "Was heisst 'Wesen'?" 415–16 (148–49).

26 Schweitzer, *Quest*, 408–10.

Schweitzer exposed the dual vulnerability of Troeltsch's Christological project, pivoting as it does on rooting the general religious significance of Christianity in the teaching and personality of Jesus, and (consequently) requiring a critically reliable historical reconstruction of that teaching and personality. As mentioned above, Troeltsch hoped to ground both of these premises in considerations drawn from a scientific philosophy of human history, society, and religion. Indeed, his careful theorization of historicism, his magisterial survey of the development of Christian social forms, and his pioneering work as one of the founders of emerging sociology were only high points in an almost superhuman effort to realize such a philosophy for his own time.[27] But within a few short years of Schweitzer's negative verdict from the standpoint of liberal Christianity, a completely different protest arose against Troeltsch's Neo-Protestant project, in fact, a protest against the deeply immanentist and evolutionary philosophical presuppositions of liberal Christianity itself.

III.

One of Troeltsch's unhappier listeners at Aarau was a twenty-four-year-old assistant pastor in Geneva named Karl Barth. The former, though striving to present an alternative to the currently fashionable historical skepticism about Jesus, forcefully reminded his audience that this historically retrievable figure could only have the effectiveness granted him by historical and psychological causation. Even such a towering influence might eventually have to vanish along with the civilization inspired by it. The young Barth, decidedly on the liberal wing of theology though he was, even then suspected that Troeltsch's historicist relativism was heading toward a Christological cul-de-sac. Vividly recalling the Aarau talk, Barth wrote in 1920, "I listened to him . . . with the dark foreboding that it had become impossible to advance any farther in the dead-end street where we [i.e., Barth and his fellow liberals] were strolling in relative comfort."[28] Rudolf

27 Ernst Troeltsch, *Der Historismus und seine Probleme: Gesammelte Schriften, Dritter Band* (Tübingen: J. C. B. Mohr, 1922); Ernst Troeltsch, *Die Soziallehren der christlichen Kirchen und Gruppen* (Tübingen: J. C. B. Mohr, 1912); English translation: Ernst Troeltsch, *The Social Teachings of the Christian Churches*, trans. Olive Wyon, 2 vols. (London: Macmillan, 1931); Ernst Troeltsch, *Aufsätze zur Geistesgeschichte und Religionssoziologie; Geseammelte Schriften, Vierter Band*, ed. Hans Baron (Tübingen: J. C. B. Mohr, 1925).

28 Karl Barth, "Unerledigte Anfragen an die heutige Theologie" [1920], in *Die Theologie und die Kirche* (Zollikon-Zurich: Evangelischer Verlag, 1928), 1–25 at 8;

Bultmann, too, another leader of the postwar decade's revolt against the previous century, singled out Troeltsch's Christological proposal for sharp questioning.[29]

Both young scholars were unimpressed with Troeltsch's attempt to prop up Jesus for contemporary faith by appeal to an historical retrieval of cult; it appeared to them a desperate accommodation that could only obscure and muffle the hard Neo-Protestant dichotomy of person and principle that remained intact in the center of his Christology. The "dark foreboding" that this dichotomy might prove fatal to the Christian faith eventually drove Barth, Bultmann, and the other proponents of "dialectical theology" to the conclusion that it was this disintegration itself that had somehow to be overcome, along with the direct connection drawn by Troeltsch between it and modern historical consciousness.

A forceful impetus toward that conclusion was provided by the cultural upheaval consequent upon the World War (which erupted the year after Schweitzer's own critique of Troeltsch). The seemingly meaningless devastation of Europe threw a glaring light on the extent to which Troeltsch's entire Neo-Protestant project seemed to lean heavily on a narrative of historical progress. The latter's essay on the idea or essence of Christianity predicated the survival and flourishing of the faith upon the continued effort of cultured and historically informed individuals reenvisioning the essence of its past anew, for each future moment.[30] This heroic task is best left to the experts ("Most people have nowhere near sufficient materials to do it."), but the ongoing success of the endeavor is ultimately rooted in the ability of these thought-leaders "to align [themselves] through correct intuition with the creative course of world teleology."[31] Precisely this was what many in the postwar generation found so hard to stomach: a scarcely acknowledged merger between faith in God's work in Christ and faith in a "world teleology," a confusion between salvation and the supposed

---

English translation: Karl Barth, "Unsettled Questions for Theology Today," in *Theology and Church*, trans. Louise Pettibone Smith (New York: Harper & Row, 1962), 55–73 at 60–61.

29 Rudolf Bultmann, "Die Liberale Theologie und die jüngste theologische Bewegung" [1924], in *Glauben und Verstehen: Gesammelte Aufsätze I*, 9th ed. (Tübingen: J. C. B. Mohr, 1993), 1–25 at 3ff. English translation: Rudolf Bultmann, "Liberal Theology and the Latest Theological Movement," in *Faith and Understanding*, ed. Robert W. Funk, trans. Louise Pettibone Smith (London: SCM Press, 1969), 28–52 at 30ff.

30 Troeltsch, "Was heisst 'Wesen'?" 428–29 (160).

31 Troeltsch, "Was heisst 'Wesen'?" 437 (167); 435 (166).

"inner necessity" of history in which "the Kingdom of God is realized as it matures towards its perfection."[32]

But for the dialectical theologians, Troeltsch's ideology of progress (with its accompanying immanent, psychological soteriology) was only the presenting symptom for a deeper Christological malady. At Troeltsch's hands, historicism understood as a heuristic tool or methodology for critically and reliably reconstructing the past had become entangled with, or elaborated into, an entire metaphysic claiming to determine the mode and limits of the divine spirit's engagement with the world. He made no attempt to mask or soften the constraint thereby placed upon Christology.

> The doctrine that human development in and outside Christ is unable to find power and certainty, and is raised to a higher stage of development . . . only through Christ . . . has had no influence upon modern thought in general on account of the inner contradiction between the two interests which are united here. It contradicts the idea which lies at the foundation of all modern thinking—a development of spirit which emerges at different nodal points [*Knotenpunkten*] from the depth of the divine life, and a possibility of future developments which can never be circumscribed in advance.[33]

Confined within this metaphysical iron cage, the cult of Jesus Troeltsch proposed as the answer to the religious crisis of his day appeared no more than the solemn yet fervent memorializing of a deceased hero. And even that only for the time being: "[W]e gather around him unconcerned whether in a hundred years religion will still be nourished on Jesus or will have some other centre."[34] Seeing this as the real danger lurking in the Neo-Protestant separation of person and principle, the dialectical theologians experienced more than Troeltsch's "slight shiver" [*leises Frösteln*] at its risks: their "dark foreboding" consequently demanded more than his recommended palliative, the socio-functional cult.[35]

As was the case with Schweitzer's critique of Troeltsch's proposal, that of the dialectical theologians suggested that the cult so conceived failed in its essential task: to anchor the identity of the community in a continuous history of venerating Jesus that could resist the pressure

32 Troeltsch, "Was heisst 'Wesen'?" 417 (150).
33 Troeltsch, "Geschichtlichkeit Jesu," 834 (193).
34 Troeltsch, "Geschichtlichkeit Jesu," 850 (206).
35 Troeltsch, "Geschichtlichkeit Jesu," 835 (193).

of historical consciousness. For them, the bridge-concept breaks down because the Jesus it commends has only the limited and fragile human significance allowable to any entity by the elevation of historicism into a metaphysical system. His significance rests exclusively on his relative position in history, for any fact finds its place defined for it by all others, woven into the complete texture of causal circumstance. The background assumption is that God's work in history just is history. But can such a figure be the object of cultic veneration in any but the most equivocal sense of the term? Troeltsch in his Aarau talk and elsewhere had energetically and insightfully exposed the great liberal Christocentrisms as hopeless compromises, inhabiting an impossible "halfway house" that tried to retain an anomalously premodern position for Jesus as the universal necessary condition mediating a nonetheless modern soteriology of faith.[36] Yet, ironically, from their arguably more radical point of view, Barth and Bultmann came to see Troeltsch's Jesus-cult "pending the next ice age" as itself an awkward and unsustainable marriage: Christ as sociologically necessary (for the time being) yet metaphysically dispensable. Such a figure cannot be made the object of a cult except by bending the meaning of that term completely out of shape.

What did the dialectical theologians propose in response? Resistance to Troeltsch's historicist metaphysic, no longer a "regional" methodological ontology of events and their interconnections but a generalized account of worldly reality, prompted the rediscovery among Barth, Bultmann, and others of the principle of eschatology. God's presence in Jesus, and hence a genuine cult of Christ, depends on reasserting divine power over (without violation of) the historical process. In their differing ways, these theologians wanted a theology of God's Spirit in history, a pneumatology, that refused to reduce the effective presence of deity to the universal, immanent dynamics of historical causality as such. Rather than a purely immanent or "weak" pneumatology (Spirit as history), they wanted a "strong" pneumatology: not transcendent instead of immanent, but immanent because transcendent, a genuinely historical presence such as only transcendence could achieve. Ironically, Troeltsch's eloquent commendation of Neo-Protestantism, in all its purity, over against its incorrigibly premodern alternative was having its effect. The demand to choose

36 Troeltsch, "Geschichtlichkeit Jesu," 827–29 (187–88). For a broader and more detailed critique, see Troeltsch, "Rückblick auf ein halbes Jahrhundert," 200–21 (58–76).

rather than settle for halfway houses was compellingly presented; only the dialectical theologians, without ceasing to see themselves as modern, chose for the ancient faith: "a redemption that divinized history."[37]

The critiques of Schweitzer and of dialectical theology each suggest, from diametrically opposed theological directions, that Troeltsch's cult of an historically available Christ cannot perform the role he assigned to it. Otherwise put, historical thinking fails to bridge the crevasse between person and principle which historical thinking itself, according to Troeltsch, had forced open. For Schweitzer there can be no cult of the historical *Jesus*, as the Jesus retrieved by history cannot appeal directly to our religious values. For Barth and Bultmann there can be no *cult* of the historical Jesus, as the Jesus defined by historical immanence is only one more created fact, however exceptional or inspiring. Interestingly, both of these very different critiques locate Troeltsch's weakness in a failure to take eschatology seriously: for Schweitzer, a first-century eschatological prophet cannot be an object of our direct veneration; for dialectical theology, a human being cannot be an object of worship unless eschatology in some way absolutizes his history.

These results orient all that follows in two ways. For one thing, this essay shares the general realization of Barth and Bultmann that only a strong pneumatology can justify the cult of an historical human being. The actual proposal as to how this works, however, will differ from theirs. Both theologians theorized, under the rubric of eschatology, a "divinization" of history; it can be argued, however, that the epistemic and existential centrality for both of a Protestant version of justification left little space in their respective models for the essential role in history of time and of human agency. With Barth, divine sovereignty over history results in a "pointillist," recurring event of divinization that is carefully shielded from human subjective-psychological and cultural dynamics; with Bultmann, the event of divinization is too immersed within and conditioned by the inherent possibilities of those same dynamics. The pneumatology to be outlined in this essay will try to tread a middle course by preferring a more catholic scheme of created "supernatural" grace. Part 2 will be given over to outlining such a scheme.

But that discussion must be deferred, for the remainder of part 1 must analyze in more detail the "Neo-Protestant" separation of person and

37 Troeltsch, "Geschichtlichkeit Jesu," 825 (186).

principle in Christology. If this separation is a direct and unavoidable result of modern historical consciousness, then a strong pneumatology can conjoin ultimate religious truth with the human reality of Jesus only by breaking with that consciousness. Seeking to avoid such a break, our discussion must now devote more careful attention to this question: How, exactly, is the modern separation of person and principle driven by historical thinking? This is the second area where a critique of Troeltsch informs the course of this essay, for his Christology finally obscures the details of the Neo-Protestant disintegration he himself insisted upon. This is what Schweitzer showed: Troeltsch's bid for a cultic continuity between ancient and modern faith in Christ inevitably reconstructs Jesus historically in a way that "fudges" his religious intractability for us even as it fails to account for the gap between his original personality and the "transfigured" object of early Christian worship. So, before the essay can pursue the construction of a strong pneumatology, it must press deeper into the investigation of the disintegration of Christology, beyond Troeltsch's generalities. To discern in greater detail the exact conceptual connection between historical thinking and the Neo-Protestant person/principle dichotomy, the next chapter turns to the thinker Troeltsch credited as among the first to fully and classically formulate that connection: David Friedrich Strauss.[38]

38 Troeltsch, "Geschichtlichkeit Jesu," 826 (186).

2

The Weight of Historical Consciousness and the Disintegration of Christology

So Christ, as a human being, with a human brain-structure, was at the same time omniscient and omnipotent? Indeed, even as an embryo he could know all and rule the world?
David Friedrich Strauss | *Die christliche Glaubenslehre*

Within the sphere of what is historically perceptible, Jesus as the Christ can be understood only as problem, *only* as myth.
Karl Barth | *Epistle to the Romans*

I.

When the young D. F. Strauss published his epoch-making *Life of Jesus* in 1835, he was a Hegelian.[1] This meant, first of all, that he was committed to

1 A broad overview of Strauss' life and writings, with some attention to the shifts in his Christology and his Hegelianism over time, can be found in Horton Harris, *David Friedrich Strauss and His Theology* (Cambridge: Cambridge University Press, 1973). The major exposition of Hegel's philosophical interpretation of Christianity is to be found in his lectures on the philosophy of religion, which he delivered four times during his academic career. We await the presumably definitive German edition in forthcoming volumes of the *Gesammelte Werke* (Hamburg, 1968 ff.); until then the standard remains volumes 11 and 12 of Hegel's *Werke*, in the 2nd edition edited by Philipp Marheineke and Bruno Bauer (Berlin: Duncker & Humblot, 1840). The invaluable English edition, with much useful editorial material, is *Lectures on the Philosophy of Religion*, ed. and trans. Peter C. Hodgson, 3 vols. (Berkeley: University of California Press, 1984).

the claim that Christianity was the ultimate *religious* manifestation of the final truth of all reality. Religion represented that form of human culture in which this ultimate truth initially had to become evident to human consciousness in history; in this way the truth entered as a shaping factor into individual minds, but by means of a preconceptual vehicle: images and narratives transposing the rational to the plane of the sensibly perceptual. Eventually, reason in the form of philosophy arrives at sufficient maturity and self-understanding to decode these images and narratives and process them into conceptual form. All cultures with their religious views represent stages and partial apprehensions on the way to philosophical truth, but Western Protestant Christianity is the final station along this road, where religion has reached its fullest development because its representations finally reach back upon itself, making central to religion an insight into its own ultimate meaning, namely that human religiosity is a revelation of God that is necessary to, a necessary aspect of, God himself, culminating in the historical appearance of the "God-man."

This most advanced religious content, in turn, is ripe for the most encompassing philosophical decipherment, presenting philosophy with its own final truth about reality. God, or the absolute, is himself not only ultimate substance but also the highest instance of the dynamism of subjectivity, and hence necessarily unfolds himself, unveiling as absolute subject his own limitless truth to himself by positing and working through his "other": a play of multiplicity and limitation in dialectical process, i.e., the world. In its development the world gives rise to finite subjectivity (humanity), whereby the world becomes aware of itself as a part of God's own progressive self-awareness, eventually (in philosophy) coming to grasp the culmination of human development as identical with the consummated identity of God. Thus God is the truly infinite reality that does not exclude the finite but contains it as a moment of its own constitution.

It is just this scheme of truth that first emerges historically in the Christian religion, in the representational or symbolic form of Christology. For what religion confesses and experiences as the incarnation of God in Jesus is actually the conceptual truth that finite spirit is necessarily one with infinite spirit; their apparent sundering through human frailty and failure is in principle, eternally, already overcome, already sublimated into the concrete identity of the absolute. The path of human history grasped in Christian faith is also God's living path to his own self-knowledge and self-actualization: an eternal redemption into a new life that encompasses death as one aspect of the absolute itself, so that concrete life is always already a resurrection, the surpassing of limitation through the rational recognition of both its necessity and its non-ultimacy. Hegel argued that this truth, this unity of God and humanity, actually had to appear to religious consciousness in the form of an individual person, and did so in Jesus.[2] But Hegel's own writings and lectures never finally cleared up a crucial ambiguity clouding the terminology of "appearance." Does Jesus of Nazareth "appear" to Christian belief as the unity of infinite and finite spirit, as the "God-man," because that is what he really is? Or rather is this association with an actual individual itself part of the sensuous medium of religiosity, such that Jesus' "appearance" as the God-man was just that, the subjective apprehension of religious enthusiasm? For if the truth is the unity of God and humanity, why cannot the historical individual Jesus simply be the occasion seized by the history of Spirit to insert this truth into religious consciousness?

This ambiguity, perhaps with Hegel's own connivance, opened a space for an initial wave of Hegelian dogmatic theologians who thought that he had shown with philosophical rigor the necessity and actuality of Jesus' divinity. In the midst of this comforting assimilation of Hegel to the Christian tradition, Strauss' *Life of Jesus* was a bombshell. The young Strauss accepted the entire structure of thought outlined above, but he balked at the conservative way of resolving the ambiguity of the truth's historical "appearance." Both in his book and in the polemical writings that he authored in its defense, Strauss argued with considerable effectiveness that the moment of negation in the rational appropriation of the religious truth of Christianity demanded not only the translation of incarnational language into the conceptuality of spirit, but also the dissociation of its truth from the facticity of an individual human life. Yes, this truth had to appear in association with a particular personality, and in fact it was Jesus who provided the occasion for its appearance, but this association is itself a figment of the religious mentality. The truth of the reconciliation of finite with infinite spirit, the redemption of humanity,

2 Hegel argues that the rational truth of humanity's substantial unity with God, precisely because it transcends immediate consciousness, could only appear to the sensible consciousness or intuition of human individuals as "over against" their immediacy, i.e., as "another" human individuality confronting their own. See Hegel, *Lectures on the Philosophy of Religion*, 3:313–14.

is actually instantiated in the entire developmental span of the human species. The dogma is true, God has indeed entered into human form, but this is only relatively true for any given individual, including Jesus; absolutely speaking, only finite spirit as a totality in the course of its history is the proper subject of incarnation.[3]

In short, Strauss showed that it was a necessary condition of the dialectical translation of religious dogma into conceptual truth that the dogmatic investment in the human individual Jesus had to be *negated*. And the means for this negation were already at hand: the tools of historical criticism perfected in the previous half century. With extraordinary patience and consistency, Strauss in the *Life of Jesus* subjected every episode in the canonical Gospels to historical critique, showing how the accounts of Jesus could not be read as eyewitness reports but only as faith-confessions of his unity with God in narrative form. The stories as they stand are not for the most part factually credible; to an unprejudiced historian's eye, they are filled with inconsistencies, implausible scenarios, special pleading, and, above all, fantastic tales of impossible events. The narrative structure, and much of the content, is the product not of reliable historical testimony but of the collective mythical imagination of the community that developed the stories as witnesses to their faith in Jesus' divinity.

The widespread cultural scandal Strauss' book caused is well known. More narrowly, he also caused a crisis among the followers of Hegel and helped usher in the era of his so-called left-wing interpreters.[4] And in fact,

3 Strauss made his initial case in the "Concluding Dissertation" (*Schlussabhandlung*) of *Das Leben Jesu, kritisch bearbeitet*, 2 vols. (Tübingen: C. F. Osiander, 1835–1836), 686–744 (Eng. 757–84). Attacks soon assailed the *Life of Jesus* from every point on the German theological spectrum; Strauss replied with wit and brio in a series of polemical treatises. His penetrating response specifically to the attack of the Hegelians that appeared in their journal *Jahrbücher für wissenschaftliche Kritik* is found in the third volume of his *Streitschriften zur Verteidigung meiner Schrift über das Leben Jesu und zur Charakteristik der gegenwärtigen Theologie* (Tübingen: C. F. Osiander, 1837), 57–126. For an English version with useful introduction, see David Friedrich Strauss, *In Defense of My Life of Jesus against the Hegelians*, ed. and trans. Marilyn Chapin Massey (Hamden, Conn.: Archon Books, 1983). The translator had earlier provided a helpful analysis of this Christological dispute within Hegelianism: Marilyn Chapin Massey, "David Friedrich Strauss and His Hegelian Critics," *Journal of Religion* 57 (1977): 341–62.

4 Strauss, *In Defense*, x. Massey mentions in this connection especially Arnold Ruge, Ludwig Feuerbach, and Karl Marx. The Left- or so-called "Young" Hegelians loosely designates the younger generation of Hegel's followers who, after his death, took advantage of the ambiguity of many of the master's statements to

as time went on Strauss, though (apart from a brief episode) he retained his basic interpretation of Jesus and the Gospels, gradually abandoned his Hegelian orientation.[5] But his initial Hegelian assumptions were crucial because they midwifed the Neo-Protestant logic of Christology in a particularly rigorous form, that separation of principle and person later championed by Troeltsch. But the latter's dichotomy is resolved by Strauss into something more structured: there are three terms, not just two, in the precise formulation of the Neo-Protestant logic, as the following lines from the *Life of Jesus* show.

> That [the absolute content of Christology] appears connected to the person and history of an individual has only the subjective ground that this individual, through his personality and fate, was the occasion for the elevation of that content into the general consciousness, and that the mental stage of the ancient world, and of the people of that time, could intuit the idea of humanity only in the concrete figure of an individual. . . . As the God of Plato formed the world by gazing at the ideas: so the community, occasioned through the *person and fate of Jesus*, while it projected the *image of its Christ*, unconsciously had in its mind the *idea of humanity in its relation to divinity*. The science of our time however no longer suppresses the consciousness that the relation to an individual belongs only to the temporal and popular form of this doctrine.[6]

---

insist on a new and radical interpretation of what his philosophy really meant. Over against the establishment consensus that saw in Hegel a philosophical apologist for ecclesial Christianity and a bulwark of the reactionary Prussian regime, they read his philosophy as in fact providing the rationale for the continuation and inevitable triumph of the emancipatory ideals of the French Revolution, and for relocating "transcendence" from its false alienation as the possession of a God abstracted from the world to its true home as an attribute of concrete, historical humanity.

5 Harris, *David Friedrich Strauss*, 242, cites Feuerbach's materialist and anthropocentric philosophy as a crucial influence eventuating in Strauss' abandonment of Idealist metaphysics in general, and Hegel in particular, in favor of a radically immanent, evolutionary worldview drawing upon Schopenhauer, Darwin, and Haeckel. This would suggest that Strauss' Hegelianism eventually succumbed to the radicalizing ferment among Hegel's heirs that he himself had done so much to initiate.

6 Strauss, *Leben Jesu* [1st ed.], 2:735–36, my translation (emphasis added). This passage had been dropped in the third edition and, probably due to an oversight, was not restored in the fourth edition; hence, it did not appear in the English version.

Strauss' early Hegelianism assured him that the "popular" doctrine of a God-man was indeed a necessary moment on the human road to truth, the positing of a rational idea in representational garb, and that this idea (the logic of infinite spirit as the positing and sublating of finite spirit) was definitive of humanity in its universality. Later, when these philosophical assumptions eventually dropped away, the structure of his Christological position was left untouched.

The three elements comprising this structure are highlighted by the italicized phrases in the quote. First there is "the person and fate of Jesus," that is, the embodied individual Jesus "of Nazareth" (presumably), along with his history, the totality of his thoughts, words, acts, and relationships distributed over the events he initiated or which happened in and to him during his biological lifespan. Second, there is "the image of [the community's] Christ," which means the identity, roles, and ultimate significance bestowed upon the individual Jesus by the groups revering him as their savior, the agent of their heavenly hopes (however envisioned); these would be culturally transmissible notions, whether oral or textually inscribed. Third and finally we have "the idea of humanity in its relation to divinity." The terminology in this case may be Hegelian, but by it Strauss means the actual metaphysical state of affairs obtaining with regard to God and human beings, as in reference to Jesus; this is the overarching claim or assertion about reality in terms of which are interpreted both the fact of Jesus and the meaning of his appearance to faith. For the remainder of this essay, we will denominate these elements, respectively, as the "fact" of Jesus, the "appearance" of Jesus, and the "truth" of Jesus.

What really defines the logic of Neo-Protestant Christology as classically formulated by Strauss is not in itself this (perceptive) resolution of the Christological question into three elements, but rather their dialectical configuration, i.e., the characteristically oppositional way in which the elements are related to each other. What is essential is that Strauss *juxtaposes* the three elements composing the history of Christ; they function in combination but only as extrinsic to one another, through the tension of their mutual negation. Neo-Protestant Christology takes off from the supposed insight that, in regard to Jesus, fact, appearance, and truth do not, in fact cannot, coincide, but operate via a double opposition. The first opposition is between the fact of Jesus and his appearance. One of the necessary assumptions built into the scheme is that the ancient communities revering the historical person of Jesus expressed their reverence using concepts that were finally incompatible with his genuinely human factuality. Though prompted by an authentic apprehension of his religious significance for them, the cultural terms available to them involved an intrinsic *misrecognition* of the historical nature of that significance. One of the most offensive things about Strauss was his bald insistence on the full extent of this misrecognition; Jesus of Nazareth, whoever he was, simply could not have been what the early church and the Gospels said he was: a miracle-working divinity in human form. Cultic speech is inherently a form of misspeaking, for it renders Jesus' humanity unspeakable. For Strauss, historical-critical investigation cannot help but disclose this opposition between the cult, the way Jesus appears to belief, and the merely human facts behind that appearance.

The second opposition dis-integrating the Christological elements is between the appearance of Jesus and his truth. Grasping what is shared by the varied Christological conceptions developed in early Christianity, several of which have left their traces in the New Testament, one might speak abstractly of the ultimacy or absoluteness of the fact or historical actuality of Jesus. If the highest deity is acting immediately in and through Jesus with final decisiveness for every human existence, then his importance is not merely historical—that is, his human value can never be relativized as one instance among others, nor can his role vis-à-vis others fundamentally differ in accord with variations of their culture or historical epoch. But for Strauss the very notion of an absolute fact is intolerable to modern historical consciousness, refused both by our sense of the reciprocal conditioning of all events as well as by our more sophisticated grasp of God's activity in the world: "[T]he immutable Being could not operate on the world first in this manner, then in that, at one time mediately, at another immediately, but . . . must always have operated on it in the same manner, namely, in himself and on the whole immediately, but for us and on individuals mediately."[7] Fortunately for Strauss the young clergyman,

7 Strauss, *Leben Jesu*, 2:680; *Life of Jesus*, 765–66. Cf. Strauss, *Streitschriften*, 3:97; *In Defense*, 40:

> Looking at the whole broad plain of events and at the strokes of the divine on the entire vast painting, critique cannot persuade itself that it is correct to cut a piece out of this canvas anywhere and encircle it with a tiny gold frame. . . . We have a concept of the relation of the infinite and the finite whereby that which is present in the infinite and in the divine idea, ideally and collected into one, exists in finite reality

Hegelianism provided a way of relating the appearance of Jesus to his truth that affirmed this necessary opposition but rendered it harmless: the Christian attribution of ultimacy to Jesus, though literally (historically and conceptually) false, was nonetheless the religious-representational form, required at that stage of history, of the rational truth of divine-human unity eventually to be deciphered by philosophy.

These are the specific ways in which Strauss came to dis-integrate or oppose the Christological elements. This three-part dialectic now provides an opportunity to propose a more nuanced statement of the way modern historical consciousness supposedly forces the distinction between the person Jesus and the religious principle of Christianity. Harking back to Troeltsch's own authoritative enumeration of the canons of historical apprehension, a rough-and-ready distinction can be drawn for the purposes of the remainder of the essay between historical criticism and historicism. The former comprises the way Troeltsch's third canon, the demand to construct a causally connected narrative that accounts for the testified phenomena, is conditioned by the first, the demand for a systemic critique evaluating the reliability of sources and testimony. The latter comprises the way the same third canon is conditioned in a different way by the second one, the demand that historical reconstructions must only posit events analogous to those typical and observable in the present. (This latter demand need not be metaphysically grounded; it can be regarded as a necessary and fruitful heuristic for methodologically imagining the past.)

In historical practice critique and analogy cannot, of course, be separated. But distinguishing them helps to identify the two distinct ways historical consciousness drives Strauss' Christological dialectic. Roughly speaking, the opposition between the fact of Jesus and his appearance as a deity can be treated more as a demand of historical criticism; the opposition, in turn, between the deified appearance of Jesus and his (merely

---

> and in the real world, dispersed into multiplicity. . . . [T]his is not to deny that there are certain nodal points [*Knotenpunkte*] in the realm of finite being in which a number of the otherwise dispersed threads of the divine life run together.

The imagery, even down to the "nodal point" terminology, reappears in the Troeltsch quotation above, highlighting the roots of Troeltsch's historicist metaphysic in the Idealist philosophy of *Geist*.

human and relative) reality or truth can be regarded more as a demand of historicism, even taking the latter in merely heuristic terms.

Strauss' conception of modern Christology in terms of a three-termed dialectic now makes it possible to state in more precise terms the course of the upcoming argument. The key disruptive moment in Strauss' dialectic is played by the *appearance* of Jesus, the way he takes shape in and is identified by the community that worships him, namely as a transcendent, divine, or more-than-human savior. As just suggested, there are two components of modern historical consciousness, each informing one of the disintegrating oppositions at play around that appearance. On the one hand, historical criticism of the records of Jesus seems to demand a rupture between his transcendent "appearance" as savior in the myths of his cult (including the Gospels) and the historical "fact" of his humanity; on the other hand, the assumptions of historicism seem equally to rule out the very possibility that his "appearance" could be "true," for that would mean bestowing ultimate or universal significance upon a relative phenomenon.

Taken together, both oppositions necessitate a radical redefinition of the truth of Jesus away from the impossible terms in which his initial appearance was expressed and toward a general salvific state of affairs between God and humanity that Jesus merely exemplifies or effectually instantiates. Thus Strauss' dialectic forces a divorce between the person of Jesus and the religious principle of the Christian faith; Neo-Protestantism has found its only acceptable Christology. To overcome this dialectic in the name of a reassertion of a more classic doctrine of incarnation, but without simply repudiating the two dimensions of historical consciousness, would mean theorizing relations of coalescence, not of dialectical opposition, between appearance, fact, and truth. This sets the course of the rest of this essay.

The proposals to be made identifying Jesus' cultic "appearance" with his "fact" on the one hand and with his "truth" on the other (the outcomes of part 1 and part 2, respectively) can be encapsulated by the phrases "cultic recognition" and "absolute fact." The former means that the "appearance" of Jesus to the early community as a transcendent savior (in fact a cultural process partially leading to and inscribed in the canonical Gospels) need not be construed on historical grounds as the semantically violent application to an inspired human teacher of quite alien categories, born of a fevered religious enthusiasm that mistakes a man for a divinity. Rather, that "appearance" can be understood as the result of a communal interpretive process, perfectly comprehensible in terms of the reigning cultural dynamics, that adequately and correctly grasped the religious significance of Jesus' activity, indeed in terms quite possibly continuous with Jesus' own understanding of that significance.

"Absolute fact," in turn, means that a "strong" pneumatology is capable of investing the contingent, historical-factual complex or event of Jesus and his cult with a direct and decisive significance in regard to other facts (especially in relation to other human beings) that quite transcends its influence in immanent historical terms. The saving truth of Christianity would then no longer, as with Strauss or Troeltsch, have to be metaphysically reconfigured into a generality about God and the whole human race, "true" in the sense of a principle only inadequately symbolized by or encoded within the transcendent conceptuality of his cult. Rather his truth would in some way, even in view of critical adjustments, be essentially and adequately conceivable in just those cultic terms. Stated otherwise, Jesus would somehow have to be, as an historical fact, at once relative and yet absolute. The historical overcoming of the first opposition, that of fact and appearance, and hence the formulation of cultic recognition as an historically possible and not implausible construal of Jesus and his early worshipers, will be addressed first. The reason for this order of procedure, and the proposed method for presenting cultic recognition as an historical-critical construal of Jesus, will be explained in the following sections of this chapter.

II.

Strauss' dual dialectical opposition structures the general division between the historical-critical and historicist challenges defining parts 1 and 2, respectively. But now specifically within part 1, Strauss' work initiates the remainder of the discussion because far more than that of Troeltsch, it allows the first Christological opposition (fact versus appearance) to come to view as a specifically historical-critical problem. It has been suggested above that Strauss' subtler analysis of the dichotomy between person and principle was obscured not just by Troeltsch's more general terminology, but also by the latter's bid to renew a supposedly perennial Christ-cult. This was because Troeltsch as a theologian was disturbed by the harshness of the opposition Strauss demanded between the fact and the appearance of Jesus. As Troeltsch surveyed contemporary religious movements in Germany, he found himself unable to greet with equanimity the enthusiastic calls for a new era of purely spiritual religion, freed from slavery to the dogmas of the past. However consonant all this might seem with the Neo-Protestant logic of belief that uncoupled eternal truth from the history of Jesus, he confessed distaste for the actual doctrines being propagated under the quasi-Joachimite banner of Lessing's "new gospel" or of Ibsen's "third *Reich* [!]."[8] The dizzying freedom of the present was giving birth to strange religious mutations; the solution for Troeltsch was the steadying influence of the Christian tradition, mediated by the communal cult of Christ. But this meant that religious belief had to take a vital interest in the historical retrieval of the central figure of Jesus.

Here especially Troeltsch needed to distance himself from Strauss, whose Hegelianism left his critical judgment dangerously unfettered by his religion. His reconstruction of the rise of Christology pictured the early communities retroactively attaching to Jesus mythical motifs derived from elsewhere and preexisting him.[9] In fact, Strauss' radical theological position left him free to critically pursue the evidence wherever it might lead him, even to the point of discovering a Jesus totally at odds with the New Testament accounts, indeed, a Jesus utterly alien to the assumptions and religious values of modern persons.

Troeltsch the believer was alarmed by the threats he saw opening up on this path; Troeltsch the historian (not surprisingly, given the necessary connection he acknowledged between subjective assumptions and objective judgments) tried to dismiss Strauss' account as critically ill-founded. He countered with the claim that the cult of Christ, even though a misrecognition of Jesus in literal terms, arose according to a recognizable socio-cultural dynamic as an authentic collective response to the impact of Jesus' teaching and charisma, organically rooted in his personality and functionally preserving its communal force.[10] To protect this position Troeltsch also had to appeal to the biblical criticism of his own day as putatively more mature and restrained than that of Strauss: a consensus was solidifying, he assured his hearers, that preserved "the factuality of the

8 Ernst Troeltsch, "Die Bedeutung der Geschichtlichkeit Jesu für den Glauben," in *Kritische Gesamtausgabe*, vol. 6: *Schriften zur Religionswissenschaft und Ethik (1903–1912)*, ed. Trutz Rendtorff (Berlin: Walter de Gruyter, 2014), 835 (193).

9 Troeltsch, "Geschichtlichkeit Jesu," 826–27 (186–87).

10 Troeltsch, "Geschichtlichkeit Jesu," 838–39 (197–98).

total historical phenomenon of Jesus and the basic outline of his teaching and his religious personality." The spiritual demand driving this historical judgment is frankly confessed: "This *must* be capable of being established as historical reality by means of historical criticism if the 'symbol of Christ' is to have a firm and strong inner basis in the 'fact' of Jesus."[11]

Strikingly, the lifeline Troeltsch was hereby throwing out to the assembled students at Aarau as the fortunate result of the latest scholarship hardly differed from an option Strauss himself had toyed with seventy years before, only to reject as a lame compromise. There was a brief period when the latter, stunned by the universal ferocity of the reaction to his book and hopeful of salvaging an academic career, made some tentative concessions that softened his original conclusions as to the religious unavailability of the historical Jesus. In his book's third edition (1838) and in related writings from the same period, he suggested that even the mythological analysis of the Gospels might discern in them an historical kernel that reveals Jesus as a great, perhaps the greatest religious personality; he added, too, that Jesus' life must remain central to our religious consciousness as the perfect revelation of the great truth of divine-human unity. This wavering position, which so clearly adumbrates a compromise similar to Troeltsch's at Aarau, evaporated within a couple of years. With some embarrassment at his own weakness, Strauss by the fourth edition (1840) had rightly retracted these claims as the result of a temporary confusion; he roundly reasserted, now and for the rest of his life, that his mythological interpretation of the Gospels can only deliver a skeptical verdict on the religious decisiveness of the historical figure of Jesus.[12]

Why "rightly" retracted? Because a compromise position like Troeltsch's, poised between the need for Christian veneration of Jesus on the one hand, and for unencumbered historical consciousness on the other, arguably ends up satisfying neither demand. That it can deliver only an equivocal "cult" of Jesus was the verdict of the dialectical theologians; sketching a theologically more satisfying alternative is the task of the second part, where attention turns to the second opposition within Strauss'

11 Troeltsch, "Geschichtlichkeit Jesu," 841 (198) (emphasis added).

12 For a good overview of this episode, see Harris, *David Friedrich Strauss*, 117–22. Cf. the editor's comments in Strauss, *Life*, xxxvi–xlv. Hans Frei situates these shifts within Strauss' complex relationship with Schleiermacher's thought. See Hans Frei, "David Friedrich Strauss," in *Nineteenth Century Religious Thought in the West*, ed. Ninian Smart et al., vol. 1 (Cambridge: Cambridge University Press, 1985), 245ff.

Christological dialectic, "appearance" versus "truth." But of preliminary concern here is the first opposition, that between Jesus' "appearance" as a deity among his worshipers and an (at least in principle) religiously unbiased historical reconstruction of Jesus as "fact." The comparison of Troeltsch with Strauss suggests that the former's Christ-cult, product of historical judgments informed by prior religious commitment to an "historical" Jesus, merely shrouds the opposition Strauss identifies but does not alter it.

That Troeltsch's obscuring of the opposition was itself dubious in historical-critical terms is a restatement of Schweitzer's verdict on Troeltsch's Jesus: his reconstructed "liberal" religious prophet has no relevance for the "transfigured" Jesus actually worshiped in the early cult, a fact only masked by Troeltsch's keeping the historical outlines of this prophet reassuringly vague. Indeed, the overall judgment of Schweitzer's massive chronicle is that the entire "liberal" quest for a usable Jesus consistently skewed critical appraisal, largely blocking from view the "stranger" actually presented in the Gospels, the radical eschatological preacher and wonder-worker. Strauss remains one of the great heroes of Schweitzer's account because as an historical critic, he was able to think outside the categories of this liberal quest. The sympathies do not stop there. Just as Troeltsch's modern cult could have satisfied neither, so also they would have concurred in Schweitzer's judgment that the early church's worship of the human being Jesus was a well intentioned but outdated superstition. Both would agree that the cultic language of divinization necessarily fails to account for Jesus' true significance. For both, historical criticism of the New Testament and the religious literature of early Christianity necessarily uncovers a yawning gap between the plausible life and teaching of Jesus and the cosmic *kyrios* ascended to heaven. This is the historical-critical opposition within Strauss' dialectic: fact versus appearance. The ideas animating the Christ-cult that deified Jesus must, according to historical criticism, be seen as a form of misspeaking, a misrecognition, a category mistake. This is the force behind Strauss' employment of the concept "myth."

Myth is the work of the religious imagination, formulating claims to spiritual significance in symbolic narratives rather than in philosophically or scientifically adequate concepts. For Strauss, the Gospels are mythic products, expressions of the cultic life of the early communities that apotheosized Jesus. More than anything else, the mythic character of early ecclesial confession signals for Strauss the opposition between the historical "fact" of Jesus the man from Galilee and his "appearance" as Christ the exalted Lord. The gap between the human being and the cult is filled by the backward projection of mythical ideas upon the real Jesus; his actual contours are only hidden by later cultic enthusiasm. Historical criticism *necessarily* discloses this process. If modern historical consciousness forces a separation between person and principle in Christology, this is one of the (two) modes in which that consciousness exerts its effect. And if the present essay seeks to rethink the doctrine of incarnation in a way maximally compatible with historical awareness, it must address this initial question to which Strauss directs us: must religiously unbiased historical criticism inevitably conclude that the language of divinization is a catachresis, that it fails to recognize its object, that cultic myth cannot speak the historical (i.e., evidentially retrievable and contextually plausible) Jesus?

Before setting up the following chapter as a way of answering this initial question, it should be pointed out that the rhetoric of myth already points indirectly to part 2. Following this hint will enable a specification of the relation of the first two parts of the essay, and in so doing clarify why the historical-critical problem (fact versus appearance) is for our purposes necessarily prior to the problem of historicism (appearance versus truth). It was the "strong" (i.e., non-immanent or eschatological) pneumatologies of Barth and Bultmann that gave each the theological courage to accept Strauss' historical insight into the fundamentally mythic character of the Gospels, where Troeltsch (still pursuing the liberal "quest") had to balk. Hence Barth's insistence that for historical perception, Jesus can only appear as a myth; hence, too, Bultmann's daring skepticism: "I have never yet felt uncomfortable with my critical radicalism. . . . [T]he Christ according to the flesh is no concern of ours. How things looked in the heart of Jesus I do not know and do not want to know."[13]

13 Karl Barth, *Der Römerbrief, 1922* (Zurich: Theologischer Verlag, 1940), 6; English translation: Karl Barth, *The Epistle to the Romans*, trans. Edwyn C. Hoskyns (Oxford: Oxford University Press, 1933), 30; Rudolf Bultmann, "Zur Frage der Christologie" [1927], in *Glauben und Verstehen: Gesammelte Aufsätze I*, 9th ed., Tübingen: J. C. B. Mohr, 1993, 101; English translation: Rudolf Bultmann, "On the Question of Christology," in *Faith and Understanding*, trans. Louise Pettibone Smith, ed. Robert W. Funk (London: SCM Press, 1969), 132.

Part 2 below will pursue a similarly strong pneumatology of incarnation, but differently: the mythical does not merely mark the limits of historical insight into Jesus (beyond which faith is necessary), nor is it primarily a demand for existential reinterpretation (demythologization). Pneumatology names that aspect of God's creative and providential action that turns history toward his saving disclosure by working in and through human minds and hearts, in and through their cultural generativity. The account to be developed, therefore, will propose that the mythical dimension that suffuses the accounts of Jesus and the conceptions of his worshipers expresses just those human cultural processes that the divine Spirit works through to effect the incarnation of the Son in (as) Jesus. The classical theologies of Trinitarian mission deem the human Jesus of Nazareth and the pneumatically formed community to be those created, temporal effects of the timeless act of creative omnipotence which "present" the divine persons (Son and Spirit) within history. Indeed, as will be proposed in part 2, the counterpart reality within the created order to the incarnation is not confined to the human personhood of Jesus, but in fact incorporates the communal cultural outworking that imaginatively "received" or "construed" Jesus as divine, i.e., the history of his cult. This means that the process of mythic imagination so central to Strauss' critical analysis of the Gospels is itself part of the created vehicle of incarnation itself.

This is the hypothesis at the heart of the essay, designed to face the modern historicist challenge that opposes the divine appearance of Jesus to his truth. But this demands at least a preliminary reckoning with the modern historical-critical challenge (appearance vs. historical fact). This is because such an incarnational hypothesis will gain in plausibility to the degree that the historical relations between Jesus and his worshipers can be constructed in terms of a single, semantically integrated process; not just in terms of historical effects, nor just a "socio-functional" unity such as Troeltsch posited, but a genuine community of meaning. If the incarnation of the Word in Jesus as an eternal theo-metaphysical act takes historical shape in the religious "divinization" of Jesus by his followers, in the "use" made of that divinization by the Spirit, then the divinizing process, precisely as a purely historical phenomenon, is properly pictured not as the arbitrary imposition of religious meaning upon Jesus by others (having then to be "overpowered" by the Spirit's work in order to connect with his person) but as a unified play of meanings shared between Jesus and others. For this reason, prior to the development in part 2 of a cultural pneumatology of incarnation (absolutizing the fact of Jesus), the essay must secure in at least a preliminary way the historical possibility of a genuinely human and historical "cultic recognition" of the religious meaning of Jesus by way of the mythic apotheosizing processes of late Hellenistic (Jewish and pagan) culture.

III.

Chapter 3 experiments with some of the cultural possibilities which might make plausible such a semantic unification of Jesus with his cult. The mere identification of such exploitable options will in itself form the preliminary answer to the first dichotomy within the Neo-Protestant dialectic, for it will suggest that history does not, in fact, demand a necessary opposition between the "fact" and the "appearance" of Jesus. Once this historical aspect of cult has been explored, then the next part can turn to the pneumatological "use" of this unified event (Jesus-in-his-cult) in the incarnation of the Word. But in order to set up that chapter, some further comments are in order concerning its intent and especially the rationale for its peculiar approach to the historical question.

What is needed is the excavation of certain potentially illuminating but underutilized interpretations of Jesus and the Jesus-communities, but only to note their standing availability and utility, not to claim that they define the essence of the phenomena or would be adequate on their own. If this succeeds, two goals will be met. First, resources will be isolated for a purely historical account (incorporating no claim to theological relevance in itself) that could plausibly and without critical violence connect a possible portrait of Jesus with the subsequent divinization of him into a single event, an event of collective meaning over time, comfortably situated within the ancient world. Second, the resulting historical picture of "cultic recognition" will anticipate the theological hypothesis to be developed in part 2, namely that the cultural divinization or cult of Jesus can be understood to play a structural role within a pneumatological model of the Word's incarnation, even as the extreme, anti-theological elements of the picture serve as a "test case" for that hypothesis. For if even so "unorthodox" an historical picture as chapter 3 will develop can be deployed for that orthodox theological end, then a reconciliation in principle can be envisioned between classical Christological claims and modern historical consciousness. In sum, the following chapter exhibits the historical possibilities; part 2 then develops the pneumatological hypothesis along lines structurally similar to those possibilities (though not dependent upon any particular factual reconstruction of history); part 3, finally, will have to tackle the difficulties for Christian belief arising from the hypothesis.

But what kind of historical scholarship is most likely to supply the interpretive resources conducive to a history of cultic recognition? The aim is to highlight certain cultural materials and mechanisms available in principle for multiple different reconstructions, but which enable the historian to portray Jesus in his context in such a way that the worship offered to him in early Christianity can be seen as an "appropriate" response in cultural terms, a genuine sort of "recognition" of who he actually was and claimed to be. For reasons which will become clearer as we go on, the most promising resources will most likely not be found by drawing on the current consensus among "historical Jesus" scholars, or the current range of "probable" reconstructions. In fact, the proposals soon to be introduced, though well-informed on the relevant historical material, have been marginal to mainstream conversations, and at any rate are distinctly out of date. But the two scholars of particular interest have been selected to ensure that the resulting picture of Jesus and his cult avoids three sorts of problem identified by Schweitzer in his critique of Troeltsch's Christ-cult.

Schweitzer's main material criticism of Troeltsch, it will be recalled, was that he did not succeed in providing a persuasive account for the cultic continuity he maintained between his reconstructed Jesus and the fervent eschatological communities that claimed him as their Lord. Underlying this is a second, more general methodological criticism indicated by Schweitzer's complaint that in its retrievals of Jesus "modern theology . . . is intent on tempering the historical with the unhistorical to a degree sufficient to retain a Jesus of whom it can make use of for its own religious ends."[14] In Troeltsch's case, Schweitzer suspected that his reconstruction of Jesus lacked precision and historical cogency because it was yoked to the former's religious interests.

Third, Schweitzer rejects in principle the possibility that theology can take comfort from history's supposed ruling out of "extreme" conclusions

14 Albert Schweitzer, *The Quest of the Historical Jesus: First Complete Edition*, ed. John Bowden (Minneapolis: Fortress, 2001), 405.

concerning Jesus, for the very nature of the problem forbids such comforting simplifications. Schweitzer's words ought to be prominently displayed above the desks of every theologian and exegete:

> [T]hese writers are faced with the enormous problem that strictly speaking absolutely nothing can be proved by evidence from the past, but can only be shown to be more or less probable. Moreover, in the case of Jesus, the theoretical reservations are even greater because all the reports about him go back to the one source of tradition, early Christianity itself, and there are no data available [about Jesus from non-Christian history] which could be used as controls. Thus the degree of certainty cannot even be raised so high as positive probability. So nothing is achieved by calling on sound judgment or on whatever else one likes to ask for in an opponent. . . . Modern Christianity must always reckon with the possibility of having to abandon the historical figure of Jesus.[15]

Although not an objection made directly in reference to Troeltsch, it throws a harsh light on the former's attempt to ward off Strauss' extreme skepticism concerning the gospel's evidential claims by appeal to a sober, supposedly more reliable scholarly consensus about them.

If historical resources are to be identified that can make possible a critical construction of Jesus and his cult that undermines Strauss' opposition of fact and appearance, they will work best if they embrace the three strictures forcefully identified by Schweitzer. These resources and how they work will come to light by retelling the early Christian mythos, reimagining its underlying history, in a way that, first, accounts in a culturally and contextually fitting way for the swift and spectacular "rise" of Jesus from charismatic folk hero to divine savior. Second, the proposed narrative should be manifestly free of Christian apologetic commitments, even unconscious ones. Third, the construction's effectiveness as a test case will be enhanced if it is imaginatively open to "extreme" consequences for the historical Jesus, moderated neither by the regnant scholarly consensus (always subject to change) nor by presupposed proximity to the canonical (scriptural) account. Therefore, the following chapter will introduce theological readers to two scholars who are well-versed in the history and cultural modalities of the relevant period but who are emphatically

15 Schweitzer, *Quest*, 402.

not theologians or even biblical scholars strictly speaking, who self-consciously and vigorously resist the encroachment of religious assumptions on their constructions of Jesus and his cult, and finally, who are perfectly comfortable with results that diverge as widely as necessary from traditional or contemporary majority assumptions.

The resulting picture could be called a "comparative" or "history-of-religions" Jesus, because Schweitzer's conditions invite consideration of the broadest array of potential cultural ingredients, with no privilege whatever granted to those theologically driven retrospective selections of material known as the Bible or the Old and New Testaments.[16] Ironically, such an abandonment of religious canons might prove promising in itself for addressing the historical problem at hand. The Christian reader of the Gospels has no difficulty understanding in the abstract the charge of blasphemy made against Jesus ("making himself equal to God," John 5:18), but faith and familiarity dull one's sensitivity to the sharp historical and religious scandal here. Pliny's famous puzzlement is more apt: How could this bizarre superstition maintain the infamous Jewish intolerance of rival deities and yet "sing to Christ as to a god" (*Epistles* 10.96.7)? The picture to be developed centers on just this question of the rise of Jesus as a cult figure.

The issue is not how soon Jesus came to be worshiped, as if cult was a "late" development. It can be as early as one likes, for the issue is how he came to be worshiped at all. Adopting the theological apparatus of the Gospel writers (messianic prophecy fulfillment, eschatological scenarios, etc.) actually reinforces the historical critic's inclination to see in Jesus-worship a blatant misrecognition of Jesus. The more the mental world of early Christians is assumed to be confined within the conceptual horizon of the Old Testament writings and priestly or proto-rabbinic ideologies, the harder it is to see by what religious logic the notoriously strict centralization of worship on YHWH came to be suspended to such an outrageous degree in the case of Jesus of Nazareth. Even the wisdom speculations of preexistent Sophia and the apocalyptic visions of the Son of Man really do not get us very far toward an actual cult of Jesus.

16 To be clear, Schweitzer himself found the eschatological traditions of late Judaism, rather than supposed pagan parallels, to be the primary cultural resource for understanding Jesus. But his reasoning is historical and specific, and in no way rules out, indeed, demands in principle, the serious consideration of the entire range of contemporary influence.

Christian faith thus conceals the historical conundrum that is built into it. The very attempt at a reconstruction of the ancient history along the lines demanded by Schweitzer's critique helps unveil and address the paradox that is hard to see from the standpoint of believing exegesis. Jesus may indeed be, for faith, necessarily a real, historical figure; yet precisely what makes him the savior may not be accessible to history at all. Conversely, the theological framework of Scripture which does make him apprehensible and accessible as savior may be exactly what hides or misdirects attention from those aspects of his story that make him intelligible as an historical figure in his original context. The point is that those cultural aspects are not at all new discoveries, but have been present all along as the nontheological remainder, the residue present throughout the Gospels themselves, but hidden from view until they are read using the "spectacles" of the history of religions. Overcoming Strauss' historical-critical opposition of fact and appearance will, in other words, come at a price: a picture of the historical Jesus that is in painfully sharp tension with the *Tendenz* of the Gospels. As Barth said, apart from faith, only a problem.

To positively commend the probability on historical grounds of the "comparative Jesus" sketch to follow is, fortunately, not at all necessary for the Christological purposes of this essay; for it is beyond the author's scholarly competence, and at any rate it could not be supported by briefly summarizing some anomalous, thirty- or forty-year-old research, no matter how insightful one takes it to be. The "comparative Jesus" is not the book's hypothesis, but it is indirectly a test case or experiment in service to that hypothesis. It is not an "*experimentum crucis*," that is, the incarnational model developed in part 2 does not succeed or fail based on the relative probability of the reconstruction in the following chapter. Rather the latter is a kind of mock-up providing what the engineers call a "proof of concept." If the elements proposed in the next chapter have even a modicum of historical plausibility, then Strauss' first opposition is shown up as contingent rather than necessary, and the later pneumatological hypothesis for dealing with his second opposition will be granted a compatibility with history that renders it at least feasible. And, as already mentioned, there will be an added, unsought-for bonus in these elements: the form of "cultic recognition" of Jesus they reveal will suggest (though not provide evidence for) the semiotic model of "epiphany-through-constructive interpretation" that drives the pneumatological hypothesis of part 2.

In sum, if the following experiment with the "comparative Jesus" is deemed successful, it will, first, bring to light certain cultural forms and possibilities available for the historical integration of Jesus and his cult as an organic (semantic) complex, resources likely to be overlooked or undervalued by a theologically or even just scripturally oriented approach. The goal is not to present the full historical picture, but rather to foreground certain cultural elements that, in one way or another, could well be incorporated into such a picture. The picture presented will be, second, usefully exaggerated in form, a "blowup" focusing specifically (grotesquely to some eyes) on the neglected elements in order to make their cultural workings more visible. The picture will be, third, radically unorthodox (incompatible with the Gospel portraiture *taken literally*), thereby suggesting that the incarnational hypothesis elaborated in part 2 could be sustained even under extreme historical conditions. The picture presents a story: how a magician became God. Troeltsch dogmatically asserted that the "earliest form" of the "Christ cult" had "no sacrifice and rites, no magic or mysteries."[17] Who says?

17 Troeltsch, "Geschichtlichkeit Jesu," 837 (195).

3

Return of the Sorcerer
The Comparative Jesus (A Thought-Experiment)

[Bruno] Bauer transferred [the suprapersonal aspect of Christ] to the historical plane and made the Roman empire in its death-throes the "body of Christ."

Albert Schweitzer | *The Quest of the Historical Jesus*

On the next day, they tell the tale that [Adonis] is alive, and send him into the air.

Lucian | *On the Syrian Goddess*

I.

The nineteenth-century historical Jesus scholars expended much effort trying to answer the question as to whether, and if so, when, Jesus came to believe he was the Messiah of Israel. The question posed in this way is almost certainly unanswerable in historical terms, but it points indirectly to a different question, one more amenable to historical treatment. Whether Jesus thought of himself as the Messiah or not, how can one account for the most striking aspect of what is blandly referred to as his "public ministry"? Not, that is, those aspects which have usually been of most interest to modern theologians and believers (Jesus' parables and discourses, his scandalous unconventionality, his relations to public authority, etc.), but his continual performance of healings, exorcisms, and other miracles. In the Gospels these are presented as famous and characteristic activities; the problem is that neither the traditions of the Messiah nor those of the various eschatological harbingers necessarily associate these figures with such behavior. So the question arises for the historian: unless these are all fabricated reports, how would Jesus have come to assume or become aware that he should and could do such things? Otherwise put, what contemporarily available "cultural script" was he following?

In the summer of 1977, Morton Smith (henceforth "MS") recorded with evident satisfaction that he was putting the finishing touches on his book *Jesus the Magician* in the Tübingen *Stift*, the same building where David Friedrich Strauss had written his *Life of Jesus* almost 150 years before.[1] The feeling is understandable: MS could rightly claim Strauss as an illustrious forerunner to his own project of employing the same historical principles used elsewhere in ancient history to reconstruct, without any tender regard for the sensibilities of contemporary apologists and churchgoers, a contextually plausible Jesus. MS in several publications, of which this would be the last, argued that a critical gleaning of ancient data attesting to Jesus helps to identify the stereotyped persona or role available in his cultural setting that most adequately accounts for the reports on his activity and self-presentation. As his book's title indicates, he had found that persona not among the comfortably familiar confessional identifiers employed by the Gospel redactors, nor among the innumerable, rather

1 Morton Smith, *Jesus the Magician* [1978] (San Francisco: Hampton Roads, 2014), xiv. As the two scholars drawn upon in this chapter will be relatively unfamiliar to most theologians, capsule descriptions will be provided. Smith (1915–1991) received a Ph.D. from Hebrew University and a Th.D. from Harvard. He taught at Brown and Drew before taking up in 1957 the position in the History Department at Columbia University that he would occupy for almost 30 years until his retirement in 1985. The author of seven books and over one hundred articles, he was an acknowledged expert on the history of ancient Israel and Judaism, early Christianity, and magic in antiquity. His work, though igniting fierce disputes, was internationally known and deeply respected by numerous distinguished researchers, as testified by the remarkable four-volume collection of studies produced in his honor: *Christianity, Judaism and Other Greco-Roman Cults: Studies for Morton Smith at Sixty*, ed. Jacob Neusner (Leiden: Brill, 1975). There were forty-five contributors, biblical scholars and ancient historians from the United States, Canada, the United Kingdom, France, Holland, Germany, Austria, and Israel, including Helmut Koester, James Sanders, Tjitze Baarda, Wayne Meeks, Robin Scroggs, Marcel Simon, S. G. F. Brandon, Elias Bickerman, Geza Vermes, Zwi Werblowsky, Kurt Rudolph, Robert M. Grant, et al. The two-volume set of his collected essays contains an overview of his scholarship with full bibliography: Morton Smith, *Studies in the Cult of Yahweh*, ed. Shaye J. D. Cohen, vol. 2 (Leiden: Brill, 1996), 257–85.

modest variants on gospel portraiture continually recycled by mainstream biblical scholarship on the "historical Jesus" ("a rabbi, a philosopher, a pacifist, a revolutionary, a moral reformer, a prophet of the coming end of the world," etc.).[2] Rather, MS's conclusion was just as readily imaginable within Jesus' own past context as it was discomforting within our own: the cultural profile of Jesus' reported activity would have been instantly recognizable to his contemporaries as that of the wonder-worker, the thaumaturge, the skilled trafficker in daimonic forces. For MS the historian, Jesus was probably a magician.[3]

MS was quite conscious that this judgment, though reached through historical reasoning, lined up with the charge most frequently made by the ancient critics of the Christ-cult. From the earliest period the church's traditions about Jesus had invited gleeful satirical exploitation on any number of points, wonderfully evoked by Tertullian:

> Son of a carpenter or a prostitute, profaner of the Sabbath, a Samaritan and one who had a demon, bought [by the high priests] from Judas . . . beaten with a reed and slapped, disgraced with spittle, given gall and vinegar to drink . . . [a man] whom his disciples spirited away [from the tomb] so that they could say he had risen, or whom the gardener hauled off, lest his lettuces be damaged by the crowd of sightseers.[4]

2 Morton Smith, *Clement of Alexandria and a Secret Gospel of Mark* (Cambridge, Mass.: Harvard University Press, 1973), 201.

3 MS does not present this as a new discovery. Not only was Jesus' status as a magician a relatively common assertion in the polemical literature of the first Christian centuries, MS recounts how, beginning in the early twentieth century, some scholars began to defend this same claim as a perfectly legitimate historical hypothesis. The Hellenistic ideology of the "divine man" (a revelatory wonder-worker to admirers, a magician to neutral or hostile observers) had already been used to illuminate New Testament material in pioneering works like Richard Reitzenstein's *Poimandres* (1904), Eduard Norden's *Agnostos Theos*, and Wilhelm Bousset's *Kyrios Christos* (both 1913). Gaining impetus from this consensus, Swedish scholar Gillis P. Wetter's *Der Sohn Gottes* (1916) argued that the gospel of John's Jesus falls unambiguously within this "sociological type." Following on this MS discerns a fluctuating but definite line of comparative research that firmly situates the gospel accounts of Jesus by similar appeal to this Hellenistic typology: from Windisch and Bieler in the 1930s up to Hans Dieter Betz and Dieter Georgi more recently. See the survey in Morton Smith, "Prolegomena to a Discussion of Aretalogies, Divine Men, the Gospels and Jesus," in M. Smith, *Studies in the Cult of Yahweh*, 2:18–24.

4 M. Smith, *Jesus the Magician*, 83–84.

But it was more particularly the interpretation by these ancient skeptics of Jesus' characteristic *actions* that appealed to MS as in fact likely to be reliable, and indeed as affording a plausible explanation for the fervid early following that attached itself to this dubious man from nowhere. The answer is right there in the Gospels, staring one in the face: he was a magic act, and apparently a pretty good one. Faced with accounts of Jesus' miracles, the typical "outsider" quite naturally, as Origen complains about Celsus,

> puts them on a level with the works of the *goetes* on the grounds that they too promise marvelous things, and with the tricks done by those who have learned from Egyptians, who sell their revered teachings in the middle of the market for a few obols, and drive demons out of people and blow away diseases.[5]

The point is that the itinerant wonder-worker was a well-known "type" in Jesus' cultural setting. For MS, it was this social type that made the best sense of the historic data on Jesus.

His reasoning is too complex to trace in detail, but a few salient points can be made. Early in his career MS was struck by the centrality to the canonical Gospels of the miracle pericopes. Evidently, the Gospel authors made no effort to conceal that Jesus' public reputation rested not solely upon his explicit teachings, but at least as much upon his personal charisma, and especially upon his wondrous feats of power. The numerous stories of his healings were deeply established in the tradition about Jesus; MS surmised that they circulated in the stereotyped format associated with tales of salvific interaction with a deity or supernatural person; and they seem to have coalesced from an early date into collections of linked episodes. For all these reasons, as early as 1955 MS proposed that the oldest extant Gospel, that of "Mark," was best understood as a local variant of Aesculapian, i.e., healing-oriented, aretalogy.[6] Aretalogy is a postulated literary genre recounting serial spectacular encounters with a numinous figure, a chain of vivid anecdotes, perhaps loosely linked within a vague overall narrative, presented as epiphanies to provide religious propaganda for the protagonist's divine status and

5 M. Smith, *Jesus the Magician*, 113.

6 *Morton Smith and Gershom Scholem, Correspondence 1945–1982*, ed. Guy G. Stroumsa (Leiden: Brill, 2008), 81.

capabilities. By 1971 MS was able to bolster this interpretation through an erudite essay retailing an extensive range of evidence for this cultural format and expertly applying it to the Gospels.[7]

MS was not a New Testament specialist, but an ancient historian; the adventurously skeptical proposal of an outsider to the guild for the most part invited a prudent neglect on the part of "mainstream" biblical scholarship and might have quietly faded from the consciousness of all but a few strong-nerved admirers. But MS was to gain unusual notoriety through a remarkable accident, a discovery that was to direct and deepen his nascent interest in reconstructions of Jesus. In 1958 at an Orthodox monastery a few miles from Jerusalem, he found an eighteenth-century transcription of a letter from Clement of Alexandria; the letter mentioned, and quoted from, an esoteric version of the Gospel of Mark closely held by the Alexandrian clergy. Clement's letter was responding to revelations of the content of this gospel by a rival Christian group ("Carpocratians"), attempting to answer what he saw as their distortions of it. Careful investigation, including the solicited judgments of numerous experts, confirmed to MS's satisfaction that the Clement letter was authentic, and that the heretofore unknown Markan passage was of the same age and provenance as material preserved in canonical Mark. But what particularly intrigued MS was that the quoted passage itself, a variant of the episode of the raising of Lazarus, concluded with a nocturnal initiatory encounter between Jesus and the raised "young man" where he "taught him the mystery of the kingdom of God." The text struck MS as most likely the narrative mis-en-scène for an arcane and very early ritual practice, perhaps even providing primitive evidence for the understanding of baptismal rites operative within some of the earliest Christian communities. Indeed, this baptism's origination with Jesus himself seemed a genuine possibility. And, to one as conversant with the literary context as MS was, its magical character immediately suggested itself.

Though announcing the find at the 1960 Society of Biblical Literature meeting (it was even reported, and immediately contested, in *New York Times* articles from December 30 and 31 of that year), MS meticulously labored over the manuscript for a number of years until ready to publish what he regarded as satisfactory reconstructions of its setting,

7 Morton Smith, "Prolegomena," in M. Smith, *Studies in the Cult of Yahweh*, 2:3–27.

transmission, and meaning.[8] The unavailability of the original (left in the monastery and later removed), combined with its challenging content and implications, early on invited a few scholars to raise questions as to its authenticity. Unhappily (and, surely not coincidentally, after MS began promoting the discovery to a popular readership), the cautious insinuation floated by one or two scholars that MS might have been taken in by a forgery was dramatically escalated. Eventually, with MS's death preventing any rebuttal from his side, a number of writers (including some outside of the field, evidently provoked by his well-known religious skepticism) made the outright accusation, on eminently contestable evidence, that MS himself was the forger.[9] The controversy ended up ensuring a far greater

8 The monograph *Clement of Alexandria and a Secret Gospel of Mark* provides Smith's detailed analyses and is directed to a scholarly audience. Photographs of the fragment itself, with transcription and translation, are found at 446–53. In the same year the monograph was published, Smith also composed for a popular audience an entertaining prospectus concerning the fragment's discovery and implications. Morton Smith, *The Secret Gospel* [1973] (Middletown, Calif.: Dawn Horse Press, 2005).

9 The issue is still being debated, though not necessarily with profit. This is not the place to enter into the properly professional discussion or the more extensive (sometimes vitriolic) popular literature, though it should be pointed out that some of the most widely read publications "proving" that Smith is a fraud have been written by people who are not scholars of the Bible or of ancient history, or who clearly have an axe to grind. For Smith's own brief and characteristically pungent survey of his discovery's reception (prepared for a 1982 reprint), see Smith, *Secret Gospel*, 139–43, with select bibliography up to 1979 at 151–53. Guy Stroumsa comments intelligently on the controversy, with a few references to literature up to 2007, in the preface to his edition of the Morton Smith/Gershom Scholem correspondence. Another interesting account, cautious but likewise inclined toward Smith's veracity, is to be found in Anthony Grafton, "Gospel Secrets: The Biblical Controversies of Morton Smith," *Nation* 288 (2009): 25–30. An admiring obituary written by a classics scholar of equally pugnacious temperament leads one to conclude that MS would have reveled in the pious fury evident among many of his detractors: see William M. Calder, "Morton Smith," *Gnomon* 64 (1992): 382–84. Probably the most persuasive arguments that Smith forged the Clement letter are marshaled in Stephen C. Carlson, *The Gospel Hoax: Morton Smith's Invention of Secret Mark* (Waco, Tex.: Baylor University Press, 2005). No one consulting that volume should fail to attend to the detailed rebuttals of Scott G. Brown. Besides his own monograph on the Smith discovery (Scott G. Brown, *Mark's Other Gospel: Rethinking Morton Smith's Controversial Discovery*, Studies in Christianity and Judaism [Waterloo, Ontario: Wilfrid Laurier University Press, 2005]), he has taken issue especially with Carlson's arguments, alongside those of others: Scott G. Brown, "Reply to Stephen Carlson," *Expository Times* 117 (2006): 144–49; "The Question of Motive in the Case against Morton Smith," *Journal of Biblical Literature* 125 (2006): 351–83; "Factualizing the Folklore: Stephen Carlson's Case against Morton Smith," *Harvard Theological Review* 99 (2006): 291–327;

popular hearing for MS's theories about a magical Jesus than he might have expected. More important for the present discussion, the find and its investigation was a watershed for MS's scholarly career; it prompted him to reexamine all the early Christian materials and the ancient reception of Jesus in order to fully construct a fresh and untraditional account of his role. The case MS built for this account of Jesus did not (and does not) rely on the authenticity of the Clement fragment, but the find did catalyze MS's reconstruction of Jesus and encapsulate its crucial elements.

Three of these elements, the most important for this chapter's experiment with the "comparative Jesus," are as follows. First, MS's reconstruction suggests a predominance of esoteric practice both by Jesus himself and among significant segments of the communities venerating his memory. This is notable because it invited the early proliferation of widely divergent opinions among practitioners of his cult as to his actual status and the nature of the salvation he brought. If, as MS suggests, the central practices both of Jesus and of many of his earliest followers were secret, not committed to writing but passed on by initiates, this left a much broader and more open field of interpretation among rival groups, then and later. Indeed, for MS it is clear that the Christian groups that eventually became dominant exerted considerable interpretive effort in reframing and reshaping the form of Jesus' original religious impact. This was all the more inevitable if, as MS argued, the circles preserving the esoteric side of Jesus' practices were also associated with libertine sexual customs.[10]

The second element of MS's account that possibly recovers a discounted aspect of the cultic history of Jesus is the essentially magical character of the latter's teaching and practice. As more than one scholar has argued, there can be no hard and fast distinction between magical and religious belief and practice, in spite of the usual (sometimes apologetic) attempts

---

"The Letter to Theodore: Stephen Carlson's Case against Clement's Authorship," *Journal of Early Christian Studies* 16 (2008): 535–72. This is only a sample of the controversy. Indeed, the very number and detail of exchanges threatens to turn Smith's claimed discovery into a Rorschach blot: partisanship on one or the other side of the dispute is likely to reveal more about the predilections and sympathies of particular scholars rather than the weight of the evidence. At any rate, it is simply not the case, logically speaking, that the merits of MS's reconstruction of Jesus rest upon a resolution of the forgery debate; the evidentiary warrants for his claims are not connected with the authenticity of "Secret Mark."

10 On the issue of esotericism, see M. Smith, *Clement of Alexandria*, 91f., 197–202, 283f.; on sexual libertinism see the same work, 254–65.

to define and enforce one.[11] Some considerable overlap seems undeniable. Both religion and magic are basically concerned with effecting a person's (proximate and/or ultimate) well-being through favorably disposing transcendent powers by means of a properly receptive mental and behavioral stance combined with formulized, repeatable symbolic actions. What marks out practices deemed "magical," then, is first and foremost the demarcation itself: magic is disreputable religion, which leads to "the one, universal characteristic of magic—it is illegal."[12] This is clearly linked to another typical trait of magic: it is religion undertaken as a private practice, lacking communal sanction and transparency.[13] Elaborating a bit, it can be said that "the social and religious role" of the magician is "one of *mobility* . . . frequently expressed theologically by the charge that the magician is heterodox or politically by the charge that he is a foreigner or a subversive."[14]

This subversive character of Jesus is a significant point, although not so much from the political point of view (contemporary theological enthusiasms notwithstanding). It is true enough that, given the delicately balanced local power arrangements, any unpredictable demagogue with an avid following could be inflated into a threat that warranted (in the eyes of both the Roman garrison and their Jewish clients charged with peacefully administering the sanctioned religion) capital punishment. But more interesting for this thought-experiment is the *religiously* marginal character of the magician, especially in a predominantly Jewish setting. On one hand, this is important because of the inherently syncretic nature of magical practice. As problematic as the notion of "normative" Judaism in the first century already is, Jesus' status as postulated by MS automatically positions him in an especially awkward way with regard to any traditions promoting strict monotheism or a supposedly pure ancestral religious identity.

11 On the relation of religion and magic, MS cites the German classical philologist Friedrich Pfister (in his Pauly-Wissowa entry under "*Kultus*"), and his own admired Harvard teacher Arthur Darby Nock, who favorably cites Pfister's language in his own 1933 essay on "Paul and the Magus." See M. Smith, *Jesus the Magician*, 258–59.

12 Jonathan Z. Smith, "Good News Is No News: Aretalogy and Gospel," in *Map Is Not Territory: Studies in the History of Religions* (Leiden: Brill, 1978), 190–207 at 192. Cf. M. Smith, *Clement of Alexandria*, 220.

13 "[P]rivate dealings with supernatural beings make up most of what we call 'magic' as well as what we call 'private religion.' There is no clear line between the two." M. Smith, *Jesus the Magician*, 94–95.

14 J. Z. Smith, "Good News," 192 (emphasis in original).

For MS the key to comprehending the "radical difference between Christianity and other forms of first-century Judaism" lies in acknowledging "the Graeco-Roman culture *and* the continuing Semitic paganism of first-century Palestine."[15] At the fountainhead of this alternative Judaism of the Jesus-enthusiasts stands the inherently hybrid culture of magical practice embodied in the founder. On the other hand, the religious marginality of Jesus as magician is also suggestive because the "heterodox" ideas that must have suffused his clientele might have helped force an opening even within the hostile mental setting of Judaea for that most dangerous of deviations from a "normative" Jewish perspective: the worship of a human being. The intimacy with the high gods or God typically claimed by the magician could then have assumed in Jesus' case a troubled but nonetheless recognizably Jewish character as a proximity to the creator confessed by Israel.

The third and final aspect foregrounded by MS's reconstruction of Jesus and useful for our comparative experiment is a special constellation of elements whose trace might arguably be discernible in primitive Christian sacramental usages. MS speculates that the earliest strata of the Jesus tradition, though obscured by later layers, presuppose a link between Jesus' promise of admittance to the heavenly kingdom and the two rituals associated with him in the Gospels. Although later tradition, presumably for some apologetic purpose, was at pains explicitly to deny that Jesus practiced baptism in spite of its prevalence among his disciples, MS thinks it inherently more likely that it sprang from a magic initiatory rite used by Jesus himself (hence the suggestiveness of the "Secret Mark" passage). So understood the immersion rite has no real analogue in Jewish baptismal practice.

Even more striking in this respect is the Eucharistic meal of later tradition, in this case positively affirmed as instituted by Jesus himself; the ritual's potent associations of cannibalism and blood-drinking seem almost calculatedly revolting to Jewish sensibilities. The point is that both of these rites privilege identification of the initiate with Jesus himself, indeed with his very body: he is to be put on, he is to be consumed. To what end? MS argues that in both cases we have symbolic actions the distance of which from Jewish religious custom signals their magical provenance, and the efficacy of which lay in their power to grant Jesus' followers a share in his

15 M. Smith, "Prolegomena," 23 (emphasis in original).

personal access to the divine realm, the heavenly sphere where the divine presence reigns. This proximity to the divinity would be both the source of Jesus' own wonder-working power and the prize awaiting those inducted into his mysteries.[16]

The presence of many points of contact between the Gospel portrayals of Jesus and the widespread Hellenistic motif of the "divine man" is an old exegetical insight, though its applicability has been variously assessed. MS's privileging of Jesus' reputation as a wonder-worker continues in a way this scholarly tradition, but the three elements just enumerated, which result from situating Jesus more explicitly within the milieu of magic, add some notable touches to the Hellenistic picture. First, the occult nature of Jesus' most important practices and teachings about the divine kingdom would help ensure that no strong line of open transmission could secure their presence amid the traditions about him that eventually became authoritative. The consequent degree of incomprehension left the field clear in the earliest period for quite distinct interpretations of his significance to quickly proliferate, opposing each other or coalescing in different communal settings. Second, exacerbating this later clutter of readings of Jesus is the religiously subversive character of magic, its inherently syncretic and heterodox nature. It is just this social dynamic which might have eased the blasphemy of a human with divine honors into the forbidding environment of Jewish cultic purism. Third, the embodied, sacramental aspect of magic suggests that ritual association with Jesus' own bodily presence might have been an original, even a central aspect of his cultural impact; this would be in contrast to the rather peripheral and symbolic role assigned it in portrayals that privilege Jesus' role as teacher, prophet, or sage.

An extraordinary exercise in cross-cultural comparison, MS's critically informed application of the category "magician" might enable historians of the Jesus phenomenon and the rise of his cult to lay new eyes upon the Gospels; we might then recognize for the first time elements we had always seen but not really noticed. MS urges the historical interpreter to focus on what Jesus actually *does*, and not to be mesmerized by the confessional armature giving shape to the canonical narratives. In fact, the categories deployed by the Gospel writers themselves scarcely seem able to integrate his activity with his confessedly unique status. The Gospels

16 M. Smith, *Clement of Alexandria*, 209–51.

readily see in him "more" than a prophet; yet their vague attempts to name this "more" are curiously unsatisfying.

> He is generally represented as an advance agent, sent to proclaim the coming of the kingdom and to exemplify its presence, to manifest its power in his miracles and its requirements in his preaching. But all this could have been done by any prophet, let alone by the Baptist. . . . So what did Jesus' followers think that he could do, but the Baptist couldn't?[17]

Perhaps it was the force of just this question that pushed the gospel traditions to centralize the singular title of "Messiah"? But MS sharply exposes the ineptness of the appellation.

> [T]he stories of the Gospels are mostly stories about things a magician would do. They are not mostly stories about things the Messiah would do. (Who ever heard of the Messiah's being an exorcist—let alone being eaten?)[18]

Who indeed! This mismatch in the Gospels between the stories of Jesus' activity they preserve and the dominant categories of the interpretive framework within which they (re)present them possibly points to a suppressed dimension in his history, that of magic. This dimension, at once obscured yet preserved in the Gospels, commends itself to the historian of the Jesus movement as a potentially illuminating, even if not exhaustive, element in his story.

Concluding this section, it could be said that two resources have been released by MS for the historical imagination of Jesus as a cult figure. First, the critic must reckon with the possibility that Jesus seized public attention and a growing following at least in part through magical operations. This immediately shifts the emphasis away from his exemplification of moral or social ideals or his wise utterances and focuses it squarely upon his unique person with its characteristically "divine" acts. It also problematizes his connection with tradition; his relation to Judaism in its various contemporary incarnations is not at all severed, but is set at something of an angle. Jesus is authorized by no communal institution: there is no

17 M. Smith, *Secret Gospel*, 86.
18 M. Smith, *Clement of Alexandria*, 227.

church of magic.[19] Who is it who can claim not only saving intimacy with divinity, but even the power to bestow this privileged access upon those who submit to him and his practice? Who will make such claims relying neither upon prophetic ecstasy, nor priestly caste, nor scribal learning, nor in fact any communal ordination? The claim to magical power is precisely one way of accounting for this authority, this freedom.

And it should be noted that this highly personal charisma fits with those suggestions recorded in the Gospels that somehow connect the divine reign with his very presence; the kingdom is near not because of his stories or sayings, but because he himself, his living body as conduit of transcendent forces through his theurgical performances, is its point of access. The Jesus "fact" is then to be read not so much as a propagation of ideas about God or of a new morality, but as a locus of a peculiar sort of divine *agency*. Here was someone who did not just talk about the Kingdom, but was in a position to *do* something about it. What he could do was based on who he was, on the divine power and influence directly operative in and through his bodily person. It thereby becomes more understandable how his invitation to initiates to share in his numinous authority could possibly be elaborated into a kind of worship or cult, even in a Jewish setting.

Why has this aspect of Jesus' history been so hard to see? Because, MS argues, of the confusing and overlapping layers of categorization present in the Gospels. This points to the second result of the "fact" of Jesus as read by MS. In the wake of the selectively repressed memory of it, there ensued among the communities inspired by Jesus a conflicted and lengthy process of identifying and explaining him. The Gospels present traces of this multifarious process even as their redaction fixes its results in particular ways. MS points out the tensions between the different Christological interpretations even within the single Gospel of Mark.[20] His explanation is that Mark is a palimpsest: continually becoming visible beneath the "official" text confessing his messianic status are the faded but decipherable letters of the thaumaturgical script Jesus was following. To return to the paragraph opening this chapter, this might mean his miracles predate his "messianic" status.[21]

19 A formulation of Durkheim's, cited by J. Z. Smith, "Good News," 192.
20 M. Smith, *Jesus the Magician*, 53–54.
21 M. Smith, "Prolegomena," 25.

In fact, MS speculates that much of the later tradition informing the Gospels is a kind of retrospective "Judaizing" of Jesus, an attempt to situate this anomalous figure more securely with regard to Jewish religious ideas. (On such a reading Paul, too, would have played a big role in this process: he would not be, as usually portrayed, the "Hellenizer" of Jesus the simple Jew, but rather the moderate "Judaizer" of Jesus the complicated magician.) Some of the interpretive "noise" found in the Gospels might bear witness to this inability of his tradents to satisfactorily "speak" him in a direct way, utilizing a single readily available set of cultural resources. For example, the actions of Jesus are often those of a god, but Jewish traditional reflexes would necessarily censor any straightforward attribution of divinity, maybe blurring the issue with the expression "son of (a) god."[22] For MS such a title marks the truly successful magician, one whose devoted following graduates him from the "market quack" peddling spells to the divine man possessing "his own spirit who has only to be ordered and will at once obey."[23] The point is simply that Jesus may well have started as a "son of god," but other categories, such as that of "messiah," had to accrue to him by means of mostly posthumous communal processes.

If MS's insights are even partially valid, the critical historian of Jesus and his movement now has two neglected resources for use in their imaginative reconstruction: personal participation in a divinely powerful agent, and a syncretic cultural figure whose "unspeakability" forces the gospel to superimpose Jewish prophetic and apocalyptic tropes upon an aretalogical substructure. To see how both of these elements could have undergone a natural semantic extension, connecting the historical Jesus with his nascent cult, it will be helpful to direct attention to another Smith.

II.

The picture of Jesus that has emerged locates him at the tense intersection of two cultural circles: as a Jew, he owes fealty to the unique God of Israel; as a powerful and successful magician, he readily assumes quasi-divine status within a pagan cosmic arena crowded with gods of lesser or higher grade. According to MS the gospel genre, especially in the seminal instance of Mark, reveals to close inspection the original lineaments of

22 M. Smith, *Jesus the Magician*, 140.
23 M. Smith, *Clement of Alexandria*, 227–28.

aretalogy, but also the marks of a process whereby Jesus' original "divinity" as master of daemons began to jostle together with other categories that complicated his status, inflating it and moving it toward a vexed but unmistakable proximity to Judaism's sole deity of creation and covenant. The veneration originally accorded to him as serial healer, exorcist, and gateway to the heavens, his singular, pragmatically, or "locally" ultimate religious status within the circle of his original enthusiasts, has by the time of the multiple Gospel compositions somehow edged decisively closer to the worship due a figure of cosmic significance within a monotheistic framework.

The work of cultural historian and ritual theorist Jonathan Z. Smith (JZS) on late antique Mediterranean religion reveals that this astonishing cultural ascent of the figure of Jesus need not be seen as an anomaly, but would have been deeply rooted within certain large-scale cultural mutations undergone by a number of archaic religious motifs during the Hellenistic and Roman centuries.[24] JZS in effect takes the notion of the "magician" applied to Jesus as a somewhat perennial category by MS and historicizes it, putting it into a moving landscape, so to speak. He thereby makes it possible to see an unexpected semantic and conceptual continuity between Jesus the magician and the worshiped Christ whose growing cult solidified its self-understanding through literary productions within an innovative genre, that of "gospel." In light of the picture JZS provides, the "mismatch" discerned by MS in the crucially generative Gospel of Mark between the categories identifying Jesus and the magical profile implied by his wonder-working agenda, instead of being straightforward evidence that the process of Jesus' "appearance" was a simple misrecognition of his

24 Jonathan Z. Smith (1938–2017) obtained his Ph.D. from Yale University. After brief stints at Dartmouth and the University of California at Santa Barbara, he joined the faculty of the University of Chicago in 1968, where he taught the history of religions for over forty years, retiring in 2011. His areas of expertise included ritual theory, Hellenistic religious cultures, and the methodology of comparative religion. In addition to publishing two monographs and editing the *HarperCollins Dictionary of Religion* (1995), he produced three essay collections; the last of these contains a bibliography up to 2003 as well as a splendid intellectual autobiography: see Jonathan Z. Smith, *Relating Religion: Essays in the Study of Religion* (Chicago: University of Chicago Press, 2004), 1–60, 391–401. A Festschrift was published in honor of his seventieth birthday: Willi Braun and Russell T. McCutcheon, eds., *Introducing Religion: Essays in Honor of Jonathan Z. Smith* (Sheffield: Equinox Publishing, 2008). There were thirty-one contributors from the United States, Canada, Belgium, Denmark, Greece, Northern Ireland, and South Africa, including Catherine Bell, Karen King, Burton Mack, Tomoko Masuzawa, Jacob Neusner, Donald Wiebe, etc.

original "fact," just as easily suggests that this process was a kind of conceptual extension and intensification of that fact. What if the language of the Jesus cult was no catachresis, but shared in fundamental respects Jesus' own self-conception?

As long as the historian of Jesus relies solely upon descriptive categories such as "inspired teacher," "ethical reformer," or even "eschatological prophet," it is extremely difficult to theorize such a continuity. But the reconstruction put forward by MS adds new cultural configurations that supplement and complicate the more standard categories. Jesus is seen chiefly as a powerful, charismatic actor (i.e., more agent than sage) whose lack of public association with an authorized doctrine left in its wake a relatively open interpretive space; moreover, his characteristic agency (master over demons, conduit of the divine "spirit," gatekeeper to the heavenly kingdom) was numinous, more than human, and yet remained identified with his very human presence (he offers his personal proximity as itself salvific, proposing to extend his physical embodiment to others through rites of bathing and eating). It is precisely this characteristic juncture of quintessentially divine and human agency attributed to Jesus as magician that, instead of being simply superseded in the following decades, is, wittingly or not, creatively furthered and indeed radicalized by processes of mythical imaginative construction undertaken by the communities for which he was an object of worship.

In short, the two factors drawn from MS give the historian grounds to anchor in the event of Jesus himself, perhaps even in his self-consciousness, both a "divinized" humanity and the resulting interpretive inadequacy demanding superimposed categorizations (gospel as palimpsest). The work of JZS will supply further historical elements for understanding the development of Jesus' explicit cult along these very lines; it theoretically captures the cultural forces that might well have been at work, extending and amplifying the two dimensions identified by MS which remain anchored in the historical person of Jesus.

In the writings of JZS, one finds the transformation of ancient religious ideas in Hellenistic antiquity thematized in terms of two broad developments which, simplifying for the purposes of this essay, will be labeled "anthropologization" and "eschatologization." In this chapter these two developments will be applied in order to understand the intensification of the dimensions of numinosity and unspeakability in the traditions venerating Jesus. Through the cultural impetus toward *anthropologization*, what began as the superhuman efficacy and proximity to the heavenly realm of a Galilean thaumaturge is heightened and transformed, such that he becomes a personalized embodiment of YHWH's temple or law, or even the anointed viceroy and head of that human community (Israel) in which is found the name and presence of the unique Jewish creator-God.

Through the other urge of the time, *eschatologization*, the saving decisiveness of Jesus' particular, human presence is enhanced to truly transcendent significance; he becomes the invading agent who is initiating the overthrow of the demonically infested, imprisoning structures of the cosmos. The scarcely defined but decisive fusion of human and divine agency in Jesus initially categorized as magical is not dissolved by this intensification but reframed and amplified. In the specific case of the Jesus-communities, both cultural developments play out as a steady aggrandizement of his individual human role, and consequently of the associated notion of divinity implied within the practice of his cult. Increasingly, what comes to be worshiped in Jesus is not a local epiphany, but the sole, inner-worldly representative and instrument of the one transcendent God of Jewish tradition. No longer just a healer or point of heavenly access, he is the unique agent of the creator-God who not only elected Israel from the nations but also is shortly to dissolve the entire world order. Some circles, such as those informed by Johannine speculation, end up seeing in him a kind of eternal living emanation of God, preexisting the world itself, i.e., God's timeless wisdom or *logos*. The "gospels" as theorized by JZS invite one to see them as the literary trace of this process; aretalogy is transformed such that the unspeakability of Jesus (the open interpretive field in the wake of his semi-divinity) becomes a matter of principle, a conscious literary strategy for depicting transcendence.

Looking in more detail at JZS's two hypothesized cultural trends will help make more intelligible this complex process of Jesus' exaltation. First, the trends are actually closely related: JZS speaks of "a new, utopian [i.e., eschatological in my parlance] religious situation with a concomitant shift from a cosmological to an anthropological viewpoint."[25] The latter, somewhat broader development is described in the following terms.

25 Jonathan Z. Smith, "Earth and Gods," in *Map Is Not Territory*, 104–28 at 128.

> The old, imperial cosmological language that was the major mode of religious expression of the archaic temple and court cultus has been transformed. Rather than a city wall, the new enclave protecting man against external, hostile powers will be a human group, a religious association or secret society. . . . Rather than a sacred place, the new center and chief means of access to divinity will be a divine man, a magician, who will function, by and large, as an entrepreneur without fixed office and will be, by and large, related to the "protean deities" of relatively unfixed form whose major characteristic is their sudden and dramatic autophanies. Rather than celebration, purification and pilgrimage, the new rituals will be those of conversion, of initiation into the secret society or identification with the divine man.[26]

The resulting "highly mobile understanding of religion" involves, in turn, a devalorization of "place," structure, and stability that resonates with the other (utopian or eschatological) trend, which JZS summarizes thus.

> One finds in many archaic cultures a profound faith in the cosmos as ordered in the beginning. . . . But it is equally apparent that in some cultures the structure of order, the gods that won or ordained it, creation itself, are discovered to be evil and oppressive. . . . [Such a] rebellion occurred in the Mediterranean world during the hellenistic period. Here the all pervasive structure of Gnosticism judged the cosmos, its gods, the human condition, and all structures of order to be evil and oppressive and sought to liberate man by annihilating or reversing these structures.[27]

The shorthand chosen here for this latter shift from "locative" to "utopian" categories, "eschatologization," does not intend to emphasize only the temporal motif of the imminent advent of the divine savior, but also the more basic spatial vision of salvation presupposed by that urgency: liberation from the world itself, a radical destruction and reordering on a universal scale, implying, of course, the cosmic transcendence of the saving agent. "Eschatological" thinking, in other words, can envision the subversion of cosmic structure either in temporal or spatial terms. A fine example of the

26 Jonathan Z. Smith, "The Temple and the Magician," in *Map Is Not Territory*, 172–89 at 187.

27 Jonathan Z. Smith, "Birth Upside Down or Right Side Up?" in *Map Is Not Territory*, 147–71 at 150–51. JZS memorably illustrates the phenomenon by citing incantations (*Map Is Not Territory*, 139–40, cf. 162) in which the celestial spheres themselves are personified as malevolent, imprisoning rulers.

latter is quoted from the pseudo-Hermetic *Poimandres*, where the primal, archetypal human is said to have "bent through the composite framework of the spheres, having torn off the covering, and showed to downward tending Nature the beautiful form of God."[28]

What concrete forms might these broad cultural shifts have taken in the multiple traditions that arose in the wake of Jesus? JZS suggests some possibilities. The impetus toward anthropologization would be most visible in the creative reapplication of established Jewish religious symbols to the phenomenon of Jesus. JZS points to examples of this "revalorization" of "the language and ideology of the [Jewish] cult": "the concentration upon mobile elements from the Jewish cultus, e.g., the *shekināh*, *kābôd*, and ark rather than the 'house'" and "the image of the temple as the community of believers and the 'body' of the divine man."[29] In other words, layered over the reminiscences of Jesus' rather anomalous, pagan-inflected relation to "correct" Judaism are later strata of tradition that associate him quite explicitly with the narratives of Israel as chosen people and Israel's God as elector. His followers become a single *ethnos*, a corporate entity unified in connection with his body, a newly configured "Israel"; his human body is the new temple, the dwelling place of YHWH's glory and "name." Perhaps it was just such creative symbolic identifications of Jesus with Israel's headship and with God's earthly presence that cemented an early connection of Jesus' name with the flexibly definable but traditional figure of God's anointed, the select individual empowered by God to lead, or, later, to reestablish and vindicate Israel: the "Christ." In short, the "anthropologizing" elevation of Jesus, especially visible in the developments issuing in the canonical Gospels, more closely attaches the figure of Jesus to Jewish traditions even as it remains in (increasingly unconscious) proximity to

28 J. Z. Smith, "Birth Upside Down," 167. This image of liberation through violent rupture of the ordering cosmic framework has its "from below" counterpart in the often-reproduced "Flammarion engraving": a human figure (the magus?) transgressively penetrates the rigid, outermost stellar sphere at the horizon line, thereby bursting through to attain a glimpse of the arcane (and presumably more fundamental) metaphysical wonders beyond. This early modern, humanistic confidence eventually wanes with the installation of the scientific worldview, which demands the repudiation of eschatological thinking and the inviolability, for some the solitariness and meaninglessness, of the nature-machine. Hence the antithesis of JZS's Hermetic savior might well be found in the famous atheistic nightmare from Jean Paul's novel *Siebenkäs* (1796–1797): "The address of the dead Christ from atop the world-structure, announcing that there is no God."

29 J. Z. Smith, "The Temple and the Magician," 188.

repressed dimensions of that figure's possible original form: the religious entrepreneur, the "holy man," the magician.

The "eschatologization" or utopian impulse of late antique society, too, contributes in its own fashion to the surge in Jesus' status. The motif of "resurrection," applicable both to Jesus himself and to the community united to him, imagines a translation to a radically new mode of existence, indefinable in terms of the existing cosmic order. It bespeaks a cultural situation in which "salvation is no longer a matter of 'walls and bulwarks' . . . but of breaking out or breaking free of all walls; sanctification is no longer the goal, but rather salvation as achieved through acts of rebellion and transcendence." The "archaic locative traditions of dead deities," including perhaps original venerations of Jesus as dead hero, give way in the early centuries of the common era to "utopian goals of salvation."[30] JZS cites Burton Mack's perceptive description of Paul's peculiar version of the utopianizing process:

> Paul . . . fastened on the Christ event as if it were a formula to be applied to every personal and social ill. . . . The process of application can be viewed as a dislodgment of the Christ event from its originally 'historical' placement, to become the sign marking every community event of exchange.[31]

The Gospel of Mark, too, proves a crucial precipitator of the more general trends later to become victorious. Again following Mack, JZS indicates how in this Gospel the transition is visible from Palestinian "Jesus-traditions which either do not focus on his death, or conceive of his death without attributing . . . saving significance to [it]" to more utopian traditions in northern Syria and beyond that focus on resurrection "as having saving significance for the members of the community."[32]

Elsewhere JZS associates the utopian trend with the application to Jesus of the category of "the savior, the paradigm of [religious success in] the Hellenistic world," the one who succeeds in "escaping the tyrannical [cosmic] order."[33] If the "origin of this perverse world is the establishment

30 Jonathan Z. Smith, *Drudgery Divine: On the Comparison of Early Christianities and the Religions of Late Antiquity* (Chicago: University of Chicago Press, 1990), 133.

31 Burton Mack, *A Myth of Innocence: Mark and Christian Origins* (Philadelphia: Fortress, 1988), 122. Cited at J. Z. Smith, *Drudgery Divine*, 141–42.

32 J. Z. Smith, *Drudgery Divine*, 138.

33 J. Z. Smith, "Birth Upside Down," 162.

of the astral and planetary *archons*' rule over the cosmos," then the advent of Jesus in effect turns the world upside down.[34]

> It is this sort of cosmic reversal wrought by a savior such as Jesus which would give to circles of his devotees their mood of "freedom now" and the confidence to assert: "We are exalted above Fate and in place of the planetary daimons we know but one ruler of the cosmos."[35]

These assumptions are prevalent not only in Mark but also in John, and are glimpsed as well in the Pauline and deutero-Pauline writings (e.g., Colossians).

These considerations suggest that under the influence of eschatologizing trends, just as much as with anthropologizing ones, some of the most influential later Jesus traditions maintain an effective semantic fidelity to Jesus the magician even as they reframe him within Judaic religious assumptions. The cosmic "wrongness" of the utopian savior-from-the-world strongly echoes the "threatening aspect" of the sorcerer or witch, who in many traditions walks backwards or upside down: both are at cross-purposes to the "normal" course of things.[36] On the other hand, however, it might seem as if eschatologization in its typical manifestations would be a poor promoter of Jesus' "re-Judaization," given its hostility to the created order and hence to the creator God (cf. JZS's reference above to Gnosticism). But remarkably, the Jewish apocalyptic literature could be read as the key pathway by which utopian impulses were accommodated within Jewish tradition: the transcendent savior need not be opposed, as in Gnosticism, to a lower demiurge, when the power of the savior to transcend the fallen order lies precisely in his identity with or representation of the original founder of that (only later perverted) order.

This leads to a more general observation concerning the shape taken by both of JZS's identified trends in the case of the Jesus communities. What is striking is that the cultic exaltation of Jesus as driven by and exemplifying anthropologization and eschatologization involves both the intensification of Jesus' deification with a concomitant Judaification of identity. That is, the retrospective Judaizing of Jesus visible according to MS in the Gospels turns out to provide the symbolic equipment, as it were, by means of which the twofold development traced by JZS takes place. In each case,

34 J. Z. Smith, "Birth Upside Down," 164.
35 J. Z. Smith, "Birth Upside Down," 165.
36 J. Z. Smith, "Birth Upside Down," 157–58.

through the process of manipulating Jewish cultic and apocalyptic symbols, the awkward "fact" of Jesus the magician is not really effaced, but is resituated into a securely (if scarcely "orthodox") Jewish setting.[37]

The focus in the immediately preceding paragraphs on the way Christian literary productions track the enhancement of Jesus' transcendence leads to a discussion of the intensification in Jesus' cult traditions of his "unspeakability." The canonical examples can be read as weaving together three different transcendent "roles" for Jesus; the original thaumaturgic figure, with its Hellenistic/semitic pagan overtones, is complicated by the "re-Judaizing" addition of messianic and eschatological functions. These roles might be symbolized by his three filial titles: son of (a) god, Son of David, and Son of Man (Dan 7:13, RSV: the apocalyptic savior is "one like a son of man," i.e., human in appearance). But clearly, at least by the time of John's late Gospel yet already adumbrated in the earlier canonical texts, Jesus warrants in the eyes of his communities some kind of unique status that is not fully represented merely by this clustering of traditional honorifics; we might, somewhat inadequately, mark off this status by capitalizing the first title: he is "the Son of God." JZS once again provides tools for understanding the cultural process whereby this leap to a higher transcendent status works; these come to view in his reflections upon the literary form called "gospel."

The gospel genre is precisely the theater, at least for our later eyes, in which is played out the imaginative construction of Jesus' full deity, the process by which the original "fact" of Jesus comes to "appear" to his cult in a socio-culturally efficacious or socializing literary form. But this now demands a "failure" of speech concerning him that is not adventitious but a matter of necessity. MS, as was mentioned earlier, saw in the Gospels an instance of the broader category of aretalogy; he also emphasized how "Mark," testifying to the Jesus worshiped in his own community, found it necessary to sift, arrange, and finally combine various current religious ideal figures and titles to do justice to his transcendent status.[38] None of these readily available categories of exalted being quite "worked." JZS, in a significant tribute to MS and his suggestive work on aretalogy, begins

37 None of these possible interpretations, it should be added, imply that Jesus himself was anything other than Jewish in ethnicity or self-consciousness. Neither MS nor JZS construe Jesus as initially a purely "pagan" phenomenon only later rendered significant in Jewish terms.

38 M. Smith, *Jesus the Magician*, 54.

from this categorial inadequacy to introduce further nuance into the former's account.[39] It is especially in this scholarly compliment paid by one Smith to the other that a new way of linking Jesus' posthumous "appearance" to his original "fact" is suggested.

The gospel genre (which in JZS's usage here extends well beyond Christian texts to embrace a range of Hellenistic religious biographies) effects a peculiar twist within the aretalogical tradition. This new variant of the genre not only bears witness to the eschatological trend already discussed, but is further evidence for that feature of the Jesus traditions remarked upon in the last few paragraphs: the preservation of his divine power, his wonder-working human agency, as central to the picture of Jesus, even as the theoretical or symbolic identification of the divinity assigned to his presence is elevated and intensified. The insights of JZS so far discussed have focused on the way in which specifically Jewish quasi-monotheist motifs are captured and put to work to retrospectively reconnect Jesus' divinity with the unique deity of Israel's God, the elector of a world-paradigmatic people and the cosmic consummator. With JZS's discussion of the Gospels in his contribution to the Festschrift for MS, another side of this process becomes visible; the deification of Jesus utilizes the utopian impulse to heighten his transcendence into a deliberately problematic and linguistically elusive zone.

JZS wishes to reserve the broader term "aretalogy" to indicate "those collections of model hagiographies and paradoxographies which are so widespread in the period of Late Antiquity." Within this more general category, the special case of the "gospel" appears as a kind of immanent problematization. Gospels are

> works in which the adequacy of a magical or divine man interpretation of a son of god . . . is relativized by the motif of misunderstanding and through the depiction of the protagonist as sui generis, as enigmatic and estranged. *A "gospel" is a narrative of a son of god who appears among men as a riddle inviting misunderstanding.*[40]

JZS describes this internal complication of the aretalogy as a "reverse aretalogy" because it functions as a sort of "polemical parody" of the genre.[41]

39 J. Z. Smith, "Good News."
40 J. Z. Smith, "Good News," 204 (emphasis in original). JZS proposes as prime examples Mark, John, Philostratus' life of Apollonius, and Iamblichus' life of Pythagoras.
41 The phrase is borrowed from Norman Peterson Jr. See J. Z. Smith, "Good News," 204.

The typical aretalogy, described earlier, collects wondrous incidents to attest the excelling worth of the deity or supernatural figure being celebrated. The reverse-aretalogy or gospel, a response to the reshaping of the religious imaginary under the pressure of progressive utopianization, internalizes the apologetic thrust of the aretalogy. That is, in a reverse-aretalogy the incomprehension of the deity displayed by those who encounter him is made constitutive of those encounters; the failure to grasp the true nature of the hero's divinity characterizes not just hostile outsiders but dedicated followers as well, and not just the recalcitrant but even the best intentioned. Indeed, JZS suggests it is these misidentifications by insiders that are the hallmark of the genre. The dullness of the chosen disciples in Mark, as well as their displays of naiveté in John, come immediately to mind.[42]

What of the central figure of the reverse-aretalogy, the hero/god? The genre highlights three characteristics repeatedly exemplified in the Christian Gospels. First, the status of the hero's miraculous deeds becomes ambiguous. In aretalogy these astonishing feats of power clearly registered for believers the religious efficacy and the relevant, "local" divinity of the hero; in reverse-aretalogy the miracles are pointless, and indeed misleading, unless they lead to recognition of the unexpectedly exalted identity of the hero.[43] That is, the extraordinary deeds in themselves, the stock in trade of every magician and demigod, remain all too ordinary, stunts in fact, unless they lead beholders on to grasp the mysteriously unique transcendence of their author. The genuine mystery lies in who he is, not what he does. The true disciple is not the one who gawps at "wonders," but who understands them as "signs" of an overwhelming noumenal presence.[44]

Second, it follows from this that not just the deeds but even the words of the hero, representations and enactments of divine truth though they may be, no longer fix the attention of the true disciple. In fact, if the words often seem designed to induce bafflement, it is because the true content of divine "revelation" turns out to be the figure himself. His transcendence

42 J. Z. Smith, "Good News," 204.
43 J. Z. Smith, "Good News," 201.
44 J. Z. Smith, "Good News," 194. The deliberately induced narrative tension is perfectly captured by Jesus' mocking rebuke at John 6:26 (RSV), following his wondrous feeding of the five thousand: "Truly, truly, I say to you, you seek me, not because you saw signs, but because you ate your fill of the loaves." The one who "seeks" Jesus rightly is moved not by the inexplicable physical multiplication and satiation, but by the disclosure of Jesus' transmundane dignity.

is not in service of communicating divine oracles and benefactions, but is itself the focus of disclosure. He himself is the message; revelation, as JZS says, is here without independent content, for the point is precisely the very enigma of the hero's transcendence.[45]

Third and finally, the cultural process that produces the reverse-aretalogy is a continuation of the mythic imagination of the communities reverencing the hero, but it displays a more self-aware and aggressive manipulation of the religious categories it utilizes to express his transcendence. It has already been pointed out that the Christian Gospels are a kind of record of different communal traditions in which such categories accumulate and mingle in their varied attempts to capture the unique status of Jesus. The discussion of JZS helps to clarify that in reverse-aretalogy, this multiplication and muddying of concepts shifts from a hapless pleonasm to a deliberate strategy, a conscious playing with inherited mythical notions in service of heightening the hero's transcendence above all received wisdom concerning divine beings. The perceived inadequacy of the available resources is shown initially by their very multiplication, but in the reverse-aretalogy this inadequacy of human language and conceptuality becomes not a problem to be solved but a necessary principle, a signal truth about the divinity of the hero.

> For mere mortals, a figure like Pythagoras [in Iamblichus' *Vita*] must remain a cipher. They will be "disturbed by his strangeness" but they cannot overcome it. They will either be reduced to misunderstandings or dark riddles or complex and paradoxical theories. . . . The only possible means of obtaining true knowledge is through the principle of like knowing like. Thus Abaris and Pythagoras [i.e., the priest of Apollo who was initiated directly by Pythagoras such that he could grasp that Pythagoras *was* Apollo]; or, in the Fourth Gospel, the Father and the Son.[46]

In short, the insight of the gospel genre is that the true god/hero is *unspeakable*. As JZS defined it above, in a gospel the "son of god" is a riddle, and part of the action lies precisely in the never-resolved interplay between the protagonist and others, with elusive disclosure meeting persistent misunderstanding.

45 J. Z. Smith, "Good News," 205.
46 J. Z. Smith, "Good News," 203.

III.

What has been accomplished for our purposes by foraging for resources among theorists of the "comparative Jesus"? The preliminary result can now be summarized. The history-of-religions speculations of the two Smiths alert the historian to important motifs in the milieu of Jesus and his (contemporary and later) followers. The point has not been to commend their picture of Jesus and Christianity as the true and adequate one. It has been to recover elements in the cultural context of these two factual complexes that could be incorporated into contemporary historical reconstructions in a way that undermines the necessity of Strauss' historical-critical opposition of Jesus' fact and his appearance. These elements point the way to a reimagining of the Christian past that construes both Jesus and his eventual cult in fully human and historically plausible cultural terms, but in a way that creates a purely "worldly" human space within which these two cultural assemblages can be envisioned theologically as in fact semantically continuous, as a single composite event of human meaning, unfolding over time. We will call this single event, integrating Jesus' own person and activity with the historically most effective trajectories of his religious reception, the "collective Christ-event." To repeat, the possibility of critically and non-apologetically constructing versions of this "event" is initially significant for this essay because it is composed of occurrences and elements that are fully explicable in purely historical, human, and cultural terms, and thereby evades the supposedly necessary opposition of fact and appearance posited by Strauss.

How is the Christ-event immanently explicable? The approaches of MS and JZS are premised upon the utterly generic character of Jesus' cultural performance and of his posthumous exaltation. That is, although the numinous status inchoate in Jesus' actions and elaborated in his cult is a unique configuration of detail (like every other historical event), the cultural terms in which this "divinity" is constructed were widely diffused and multiply instantiated. These terms, as MS and JZS never tire of reminding the reader, were not confined to the consciousness of Jesus or of the Christian communities but reflect broader trends throughout the late Hellenistic milieu: magic, anthropologization, eschatologization, and the refinement (the "reversal") of aretalogy into gospel. The concepts and traditions of divine, anointed, and eschatological figures were available to be "borrowed" from elsewhere and applied to Jesus by himself and by those seeking to interpret their own worship of him. One need not accept the crude older conjectures on these lines (e.g., of a widespread "dying-and-rising" deity based on the seasonal cycle) to take the basic point, and to see thereby Strauss' insight confirmed against the earlier mentioned criticism of Troeltsch: the mythic structures that might well have informed Jesus' self-understanding and his cult could have been annexed from various, initially unrelated traditions. JZS, following Burton Mack, goes Strauss one further: quite distinct Jesus-figures were in fact constructed by the earliest groups, only gradually coalescing. The speculated details need not detain us.[47]

The very possibility, in turn, of these historically explicable cultural dynamics gives the lie to the critic's supposedly necessary structural opposition between fact and appearance in the reception-history of Jesus. For the "collective Christ-event" is an event of cultic recognition. As was suggested above, reading MS and JZS together helps make imaginable not Troeltsch's merely socio-functional cult, but a continued act of semantic fidelity to Jesus on the part of his worshipers. What happens in the wake of Jesus is historically intelligible as an expansion of the original categories of the Jesus-fact, the magical individual and his liberative bodily act. The category of Jesus' divine "appearance" had since Strauss and Troeltsch been presumed to mark the rupture between the original Jesus and his followers, the sign of their misrecognition; the ideas of MS and JZS suggest a way that divinity can be said instead to mark their unity, a sign of genuine apprehension.

In the collective Christ-event the implied divinity of Jesus the magician organizing his original circle was mythically reconstructed and augmented in such a way that the initial fact, Jesus' embodied agency as intersection of heaven and earth, divine realm and quotidian, could be maintained and extended under late antique social pressures. If such a process is historically feasible, and if its dynamics are given place within a fuller presentation of Jesus and early Christianity, then the worship of Jesus need not be the violent imposition of alien, deifying categories upon Jesus the Galilean preacher, but might just as well be the continuation and extension of the assumptions and activities of Jesus the magician or thaumaturge. The prejudice of Strauss, and of Neo-Protestant Christology generally, is that Jesus of Nazareth understood himself and was received by his original

47 J. Z. Smith, *Drudgery Divine*, 134–43.

interlocutors in exclusively human terms. If this were not so, it seemed, he would have been either deranged or a deluded fanatic; a disaster for liberals like Troeltsch who sought to justify his continued veneration, but an historical embarrassment even for Strauss. This ingrained preconception made the opposition seem obvious: Jesus the man versus his worshipers. But read in the comparative terms of MS and JZS, divinization can be seen as a cultural dynamic that Jesus himself might well have actively participated in, providing terms for his own self-understanding as well as for the acceptance and deeper exploration of that self-understanding in his cult.

Hence the dialectical opposition posited by Strauss is seen to be unwarranted in historical-critical terms. The "comparative Jesus" experiment in historical criticism has accomplished its preliminary goal. There now remains the harder task, the specifically theological task undertaken in the remainder of the essay: the second and more daunting opposition formulated in Strauss' dialectical formula, that of Jesus' "appearance" as transcendent fact versus the "truth" (the metaphysical status) of his or any fact as assumed by historicism—utterly relative and exhaustively conditioned by other relative facts. It was suggested that the theologian must have recourse to a strong pneumatology to overcome this opposition. The experiment of this chapter has apparently removed a preliminary obstacle from the theologian's path (the historical unity of Jesus and cult is now imaginable), but at the cost of burdening her pneumatology with a singularly inhospitable picture of Jesus. The "collective Christ-event" becomes an extreme test case for what follows: could even *this* fact be made absolute by the divine Spirit? Could even *this* Jesus be the Word incarnate?

Part Two

THE CULT OF JESUS

Historical Matter and Pneumatic Form

4

The Risen Lord
Frampton Comes Alive (An Allegory)

[I]t is . . . the inner logic of the messianic idea that the
Messiah lives on in the symbolic transformation
of the "scandal" of his earthly life.
Jacob Taubes | "The Price of Messianism"

Frampton is God. | **Broadly diffused ritual inscription, circa 1977**

I.

The focal point of this essay now begins to shift: from one facet of modern historical consciousness to another, and from one of Strauss' dialectical oppositions (fact versus appearance) to the other (truth versus appearance). This does not mean, however, that what has gone before can simply be laid aside, the historical-critical problem dropped, so to speak, in order to pick up the new and quite distinct problem of historicism. This is because historical-critical judgments and an historicist framework of assumptions belong together and work together as different sides of the single reality of historical consciousness. For that reason Strauss' two oppositions as well, logically discrete though they are, must be connected conceptually at some level.

If the goal, then, of the essay is to develop an orthodox Christological hypothesis that nonetheless aims at maximal compatibility with historical consciousness, it cannot merely juxtapose disparate and unrelated answers to Strauss' different oppositions. Historical-critical judgment and historicist assumptions are inherently connected; therefore, the pneumatological Christological hypothesis to be developed in response to the latter cannot simply abandon the historical speculations already developed in response to the former. Especially if the same Jesus is supposed to be the common subject of both discourses, some thought must be given to the positive, systematic connection between the pneumatology of incarnation outlined in what follows and the cultural dynamics brought to light by the previous chapter's reconstructive experiment. If avoiding or deconstructing Strauss' oppositions cannot help but attend to the way historical reconstruction and historicism are affiliated, it might be helpful to consider how the latter are connected in Strauss' scheme.

A double disjunction of the elements of Christology (fact, appearance, truth) was judged in chapter 2 to be the hallmark of Neo-Protestant Christology, classically formulated by Strauss. Recall the quotation which first set out the terms of the Christological problem: "[T]he community, occasioned through the person and fate of Jesus, while it projected the image of its Christ, unconsciously had in its mind the idea of humanity in its relation to divinity."[1] The relation between fact and appearance indicated here is one of misrecognition so sharp as to amount to opposition. The "person and fate of Jesus" are merely the *occasion* for the community's religious imagination; that imaginative activity, taking off from the name and legend of Jesus, traced or designed (*entwarf*, projected) a picture (*Bild*) that, Strauss argues, *necessarily* had to be incompatible with the fact of Jesus because it bestowed supernatural or divine attributes upon a figure who, according to the critically sifted evidence, was demonstrably a mere human being. The characteristics of a transcendent savior, then, are "projected" back upon a man of the past whose own historical actuality, for its part, can only be hidden from view behind that projection.

But what if Jesus had been aptly construed by contemporaries, or even construed himself, as a kind of thaumaturge, initiating his intimates into the divine sphere via magical rites? And what if the later cultic communities proliferating after his demise did not simply invent a supernatural hero but, exemplifying broader cultural trends and creatively employing all manner of borrowed mythical motifs, elevated that same magician into quasi-

1 David Friedrich Strauss, *Das Leben Jesu, kritisch bearbeitet*, vol. 2 (Tübingen: C. F. Osiander, 1835–1836), 735–36; English translation of the 4th German edition: trans. anon. [George Eliot] as *The Life of Jesus Critically Examined*, 3 vols., ed. Peter Hodgson (Philadelphia: Fortress, 1972).

coincidence with the Jewish God by insightfully and fruitfully extending his original attributes? Otherwise put, the particular strategies gathered from MS and JZS for imagining the early Christian past afford the possibility (no more than that) of historically constructing the relationship between the "fact" of Jesus and his "appearance" in a continuous rather than disjunctive mode. In such a case, the sharp asymmetry of fact and appearance insisted upon by Strauss (mere "occasion" imposed upon by "projection") cannot be regarded as the inevitable result of applying critical (even religiously skeptical) historical imagination to the evidence. But more than skepticism was involved in Strauss' disjunction, for he had more than historical-critical reasons for sharpening the cultural variations between Jesus and his cult into a necessary opposition. Historicism played its role, too.

As discussed above, Strauss arrived at his Christological approach under the Hegelian conviction that philosophy had translated into conceptual thought the essential content of Christian dogma: the dialectically mediated unity of finite and infinite spirit. This truth had to make its initial historical appearance in the pictorial thought-forms of religious consciousness; in this supreme instance the thought-form was that of a divine human being, the "God-man" Jesus Christ. If Hegel were correct, then at length human thought would rationally pass from the sensuous immediacy of a particular individual-turned-cult-object to the philosophical truth symbolized by that state of affairs. This passage would follow the path of all rational processes, the dialectic of spirit wherein the initial representation is *negated* in order to be preserved in a higher and more encompassing conceptual form. But Strauss went on to apply this logic to a problem that Hegel had avoided. Drawing what seemed the consequence of the latter's dialectic for the critical reconstruction of Jesus' history, Strauss argued eloquently that the moment of negation demanded an outright denial of the actual identity of a single human individual with the universal truth of humanity as spirit. The relation of the fact of Jesus to his subsequent appearance as divine properly operates on the symbolic plane. It effectively performs its representative function within the historic dialectic of spirit, but only if its literal truth on the plane of history is negated. Conceptually, that is, the historian as such must conclude to a direct opposition between Jesus and his attributed divinity.

Strauss' philosophical assumptions, it could be said, forced his historical-critical judgment into a reconstruction of the past defined on dialectical grounds. But surely logical opposition is not the sort of relation that could possibly obtain between complex historical facts such as the human consciousness and activity of Jesus and the conceptions of his worshipers. Indeed, the considerations offered in the previous chapter render conceivable an interpretive continuity between the fact and the appearance of Jesus, just because they assume on the historical plane the interpretive freedom and flexibility of the human religious imagination and the fluidity of the cultural materials upon which it works. So as effective and insightful as Strauss' critical dissection of the Gospels and their mythical elaboration upon history undoubtedly is in itself, it claimed an exaggerated necessity by philosophically assuming an architecture of logical relations determining temporal events. This dialectical malfunction of historical criticism does not in fact depend strictly upon Hegelianism (which Strauss later abandoned and Troeltsch, for example, never avowed); it rests more broadly on a philosophical picture of the relation between God or the Absolute and history that can be called a "weak pneumatology."

Consider again the key sentence of Strauss quoted above. The individual "fact" of Jesus causally occasions the "appearance" (image) of Christ, but that image formally negates the fact (i.e., must be "projected" upon it). Why? Because the "truth" of this complex of events is already conceived to be the unconscious idea of *God's unity with humanity or human history in general.* In other words, the first opposition (fact vs. appearance) attains its peculiar logical sharpness only as already structured by the deeper assumptions of the second opposition (truth vs. appearance), and this second opposition is driven by metaphysical rather than historical considerations.

The appearance of Jesus as the transcendent Christ *must* be critically construed as an outright historical misrecognition of his fact because the critic already is certain *as a philosopher* that an absolutized fact could not be true. Strauss eventually abandoned the Hegelian dialectic of history that still allowed the God-man to function as the symbolic or representational mediation of the truth, but he did not abandon the metaphysical framework of the relation of absolute spirit to history. Recall the quote from chapter 2:

> Looking at the whole broad plain of events and at the strokes of the divine on the entire vast painting, critique cannot persuade itself that it is correct to cut a piece out of this canvas anywhere and encircle it with a tiny gold frame. . . . We have a concept of the relation of the

> infinite and the finite whereby that which is present in the infinite and in the divine idea, ideally and collected into one, exists in finite reality and in the real world, dispersed into multiplicity.[2]

Absolute spirit's relation to history on this understanding is "weak" not in the sense of being intellectually feeble, but in the sense that Spirit has no purchase on historical change but simply realizes itself within it. Strauss, like Hegel or Troeltsch, understands the work of God in history to be completely conditioned by, absorbed into, indeed identical with the unfolding dynamic of history itself, history as in principle perceptible to rational comprehension.

To repeat the definition laid down earlier, historicism can be regarded as an heuristic or methodological ontology of facts or events in which the historical efficacy and human significance of each is exhaustively determined by its causal interconnections with other, likewise relative events. Each event must be historically explained and evaluated as a function of this spatial and temporal location. That means that qua historical fact, Jesus could never be the bearer of that absolute efficacy assigned to him by religious faith in the Christ. As a limit on specifically historical judgments and explanations, this is indeed an essential methodological axiom, but to treat it as an unconditional definition of the temporally actual as such is to elevate a "regional" ontology of events into a universal metaphysical system. This is the quintessential gesture of "weak" pneumatology. If the task of part 2 is to hypothesize a broader reconciliation between the confession of Christ and historical consciousness, then it will have to reject this metaphysical aggrandizement of historicism and offer instead a "strong" pneumatology.

Let it be noted clearly that this entails a move from the experimental historical possibilities explored in chapter 3 to a discussion premised upon the explicitly metaphysical, in fact theological avowal of God's efficacy in history and of Jesus' deity. The task of the second part of the essay is to propose a hypothesis as to how the believing theologian might participate in the cultic confession of Jesus' deity while continuing to see in historical actuality the continuous causal network envisioned by historicist method.

2 David Friedrich Strauss, *Streitschriften zur Verteidigung meiner Schrift über das Leben Jesu und zur Charakteristik der gegenwärtigen Theologie*, vol. 3 (Tübingen: C. F. Osiander, 1837), 97; *In Defense of My Life of Jesus against the Hegelians*, ed. and trans. Marilyn Chapin Massey (Hamden, Conn.: Archon Books, 1983), 40.

This will inevitably involve a reconsideration of the relation between the latter as the heuristic ontology of human events assumed by historical consciousness and the more encompassing framework of metaphysical assumptions depicting the relation of God to the finite historical order.

The challenge can be conceived this way. On the one hand, "weak" pneumatology would have the agency of God in history as identical with the immanently driven emergence of historical change itself. On the other hand, the desire to recognize the proper integrity of that emergent process suggests that a "strong" pneumatology should not be a violent one. The Spirit has no need of arbitrary and direct "intervention" just because in its transcendence of history its causality does not compete with or impose upon historical causes, but establishes them and their agency from within, thus shaping through their very finitude, from moment to moment, their causal connections.[3] An interventionist picture, by contrast, is sheer arbitrariness from the immanent point of view. It cripples historical judgment in principle, at its source, thereby threatening to dissolve historical consciousness itself. A theology that realizes the loss this would involve for the contemporary conception and communication of the gospel will avoid it.

The validity of historical thinking with its associated presumption of the complete causal interconnection of events must be preserved even as it is situated within a broader regime of divine causal efficacy. Like Newtonian mechanics, which turns out to be a perfectly valid local and condition-specific regime preserved within the more universal domain defined by relativity theory, the autonomy of historically conditioned causality should be maintained even as the same facts are situated within a regime of unconditioned or metaphysical significance based on their relation to divine intention. Not new facts, not "special" miraculous facts, not an "interruption" of history, but an impress of transcendent efficacy by the creative or providential spirit working through and "using" history even as it creates it. This is arguably the sort of vision that motivated

3 Creative causality is uniquely prior to finite agency, even finite choice, hence infallibly operative through the latter's very immanent spontaneity: "[T]he will has its strip of autonomy, yet beyond this there is the ground from which free acts spring; and that ground God holds and moves as a fencer moves his whole rapier by grasping only the hilt." See Bernard Lonergan, *Grace and Freedom: Operative Grace in the Thought of St. Thomas Aquinas*, vol. 1 of Collected Works of Bernard Lonergan, ed. Frederick E. Crowe and Robert M. Doran (Toronto: University of Toronto Press, 1988), 147.

the dialectical theologians: a "strong" pneumatology that works in and through history but not as a directly visible and hence competitive historical causality. In the crucial test case of Christology, this demands that the dynamics of historical change themselves are not only left intact by the incarnation, but are taken up into and serve the becoming human of God. There is more than one way to conceive how this coincidence between divine and human causal regimes would work, however, and that is where the hypothesis motivating this essay seeks to make its contribution.

II.

The incarnational hypothesis of this essay takes off from a literalization of one of the many metaphors used in the New Testament to describe the advent and significance of Jesus as the Christ. God spoke in the old days through the prophets, but now God has spoken in the Son (Heb 1:1-2); what becomes flesh in Jesus and dwells with us is the word of intelligent discourse, God's *logos* (John 1:14). What if the idea of meaningful communication were not just enjoyed as a poetic image but employed as a model? To say that Jesus is God incarnate would mean that God speaks herself into, and is heard as meaningful within, the human, that is historical world. (That God is already eternally herself as also other is the Trinitarian background, the reason the eternal Word can also become historical word.) If the Word is what becomes historical as Jesus, then the Spirit is the omnipotent force of creation working within history to enable this new presence and, equally important, to create within history the "ears" to hear this utterance. No genuine incarnation without "strong" pneumatology!

Working out this hypothesis in more detail, the goal of the present part of the essay, presents a challenge (as do the difficulties for faith that will result, dealt with in part 3). A quick glance at two pneumatological modes within the dialectical theology tradition will highlight the narrow path that must be followed. Chapter 3 can be read as a sympathetic variant on Bultmann's reading of early Christian history. From the beginning Jesus attained significant historical actuality through his magical performance, and through the reception of that performance by others as an intimacy with and a command of forces from the realm of divinity. Posthumously, as Jesus-groups spread and diversified and then eventually began to stabilize around fixed interpretive forms, such as are exemplified in the narrative faith-confessions known as gospels, they generated a cultural process characterized by a progressive identification of his particular humanity with a more and more transcendent notion of his deity. In this process he attained a new kind of life in the communal interpretive activity of his worshipers; the Jesus who died, we might say, "rose" as the cultic savior.

Bultmann's famous claim, of course, was that Jesus rose in the kerygma, that is, he attained effective status as an agent even after his death by way of the collective faith of believers.[4] Some of the pious objections raised against this formulation fail to notice its dual function for Bultmann, both historical claim and theological confession at once. Of utmost importance to him as a penetrating and deeply learned historian of the Hellenistic world, there is visible in the records (quite apart from any faith-commitment of the observer) the traces of the purely human socio-cultural interactions through which Jesus came to be grasped and interpreted *as* the Christ, *as* the eschatological event of God in history. But as a Christian he also believed that just this effective agency of Jesus is indeed the power of God still at work in history, repeatedly recreating the possibility of authentic human existence through the ongoing proclamation of God's presence in the Jesus-event. Something like the same dualism animates the hypothesis to be developed here.

A question can be raised, however, about the specific way Bultmann envisions the connection between the historical kerygma and the eschatological act of God. Yes, Jesus really did rise in the kerygma; the proclamation of his divinity in worship was the cultural modality through which he came to live anew. (Theologically, one will indeed want to say more about the resurrection of Jesus than that, but one should certainly say no less.) But already on the level of historical reconstruction, Bultmann argues for a questionable kind of interpretive continuity between the original "fact" of Jesus and what has been called above his "appearance" amid the communities of faith and in their gospels. The cultural processes outlined above on the basis of MS and JZS in no way rely upon the sort of implicit, existentially

4 Rudolf Bultmann, *Das Verhältnis der urchristlichen Christusbotschaft zum historischen Jesus* (Heidelberg: Carl Winter Universitätsverlag, 1960), 27. Actually, the claim as so phrased originated not with Bultmann but with his critics. But in response to them, he defends the claim, though only if it is correctly understood, namely, as the claim that Jesus is alive, effectively and savingly present, in the proclamation of the gospel.

oriented readings of Jesus, history, and selfhood that Bultmann thought could already be discerned in the New Testament. The interpretive linkage between the human being Jesus and his proclamation as the Christ was, Bultmann argued, a nascent form of hermeneutic activity that came to be articulated through the modern concept of demythologization.

Bultmann's conviction that a discernibly "authentic" kerygma could hereby be interpretively isolated as one historically distinct element alongside other, still mythological elements in the New Testament was challenged early on by Karl Barth, during a famous exchange in the 1920s. For Barth, Bultmann's claim ("In [Paul's Letter to the Romans] there are other spirits speaking besides the *pneuma Christou*.") was not critical enough; instead, "what speaks in the Letter to the Romans is nothing but the 'others', the various 'spirits' which [Bultmann] adduces, such as the Jewish, the popular Christian, the Hellenistic, and others."[5] For Barth it was impossible to understand the work of the Spirit as emerging to direct historical view in a definable set of human utterances expressing the possibility of authentic *Dasein*, set over against a merely human or merely cultural remainder. The divine causality at work in human words operates on quite another level, taking up the entire authorial process of Paul or the other New Testament authors as a whole, so to speak. Bultmann's retort was that if only the "other voices" come to expression in the actual words, this wrongly supposes an inability of the Spirit to come to actual linguistic presence, its exile from the human and cultural possibilities defining the texts. Barth's position seems to forbid faith to judge the relative fidelity of different utterances; culture would become an undifferentiated linguistic surface, where testimony to Christ either occurred in every word equally, or in none.[6]

5 The passages are taken from the foreword to the 3rd edition (1924) of Barth's *Der Römerbrief* (Zurich: Theologischer Verlag, 1940), in response to Bultmann's review of the second edition (1921); English translation: *The Epistle to the Romans*, trans. Edwyn C. Hoskyns (Oxford: Oxford University Press, 1933). The review and the various forewords, along with other material relevant to the controversy surrounding Barth's famous commentary on Paul, are conveniently available in Jürgen Moltmann, ed., *Anfänge der dialektischen Theologie, Teil I* (Munich: Christian Kaiser Verlag, 1962), 77–151; English translation: *The Beginnings of Dialectic Theology*, ed. James M. Robinson, vol. 1 (Richmond: John Knox, 1968), 61–130. The specific quotations can be found in the German edition at 142 and 148; in the English at 120 and 127.

6 *Karl Barth-Rudolf Bultmann Letters, 1922–1966*, ed. Bernd Jaspert, trans. Geoffrey W. Bromiley (Grand Rapids: Eerdmans, 1981), 4–6.

This exchange is paradigmatic of both the possibilities and problems of the hypothesis of incarnation as the eternal Word spoken in history. Both Bultmann and Barth are rightly reacting to the "weak" pneumatology presupposed by Neo-Protestant Christology; both are seeking to avoid making God's word and work identical with (hence relative to) the total movement of history itself, opting instead to make central that particular moment within history in which transcendence appears, the Word uttered as historical event. Yet it is arguable that due to their justifiable nervousness over historicism, both fail, in interestingly complementary ways, to fully embrace the historicity of the event. Against Bultmann, Barth correctly insists on the transcendent, "noncompetitive" mode of the Spirit's work in history; but (as Bultmann suggests) this threatens to bypass the inherent "local" human possibilities completely, leaving the Word operative somewhere "above" history but never really incarnate within it. Against Barth, Bultmann rightly demands a more intimate interlacing of eschatological agency with the intellectual modes and symbolic resources actually available to the inspired authors; but (as Barth worries) this results in a dubious post-hoc selection of historically identifiable "authentic" or "existential" textual gestures as direct manifestations of the Spirit.

The difficulty outlined by this tension within early dialectical theology is that of striking the right balance between the transcendence of the divine act (the "strength" of pneumatology) and the immanence of historical causality (the "flesh" of incarnation). The hypothesis to be developed here is one where the Word's presence and the Spirit's act are not juxtaposed against the human dynamics of history but utilize just those dynamics, in their autonomy and fragility. God "speaks" the Word into history and is heard there, and the divine "meaning" is truly made humanly meaningful; but the humanly meaningful means the historically meaningful, and historical meaning occurs as culture. So the speaking and hearing of the eternal Word into history can only take finite, temporal shape as a cultural event. That is the working hypothesis of the incarnation here: divine semiosis in and through human semiosis. The special demands this would make upon a theology of incarnation in Jesus can be gathered from the elements and processes already offered for consideration in chapter 3, and especially from the way JZS conceives them as instances of the universal dynamic of human culture.

Recall Barth's complaint about Bultmann's reading of Paul. What his theological instincts rebelled against was precisely what is likewise rejected today by the secular cultural theorist JZS. It is impossible for a genuinely critical historical procedure to countenance a directly "eschatological" moment, meaning a "rupture" wherein the "transcendent" appears that somehow transforms Christian writing into a culturally "unique" and unprecedented form. For JZS, seconding observations by Burton Mack and Dieter Georgi, this would mean an "illicit transfer from the ontological to the historical," an improper attempt "to transfer the (proper, though problematic) theological affirmation of absolute uniqueness to an historical statement that, standing alone, could never assert more than relative uniqueness, that is to say, a quite ordinary postulation of difference."[7]

The point here is that Bultmann's legitimate insight into the new cultural "life" of Jesus, that is, the effective religious presence of this figure perduring within his circle of worship, needs to be carefully freed from any reliance upon an existential ontology that allows a direct intervention or manifestation of the absolute or transcendent within that historical dynamic. It is the virtue of the work of MS and JZS that it affords possible resources for the historical construction of a definable interpretive continuity between the Jesus-fact and the figure worshiped by the later Jesus-groups. Jesus "rises" in the kerygma, but in this case no hermeneutic of "authenticity" as eschatological rupture is invoked, merely concepts and practices securely situated within their period and uniformly comparable to like instances in other contexts.

Otherwise put, if the Word becomes historical, if the Spirit works through history, then what the New Testament reveals is exactly not an incipient (and putatively unique) process of demythologization but the cultural labor of myth itself. For, as JZS emphasizes, this labor is not at all a semantic imprisonment within age-old symbols, the repetition of fossilized patterns. Rather the mythic process, exactly as instanced in the development of Jesus in his cult, is a product of the creative imagination, working through inherited materials but with a certain distance and freedom. Myth is always, JZS argues, applicative, continually improvised to illuminate new situations; an awareness of its inadequacy or lack of perfect "fit"

7 Jonathan Z. Smith, *Drudgery Divine: On the Comparison of Early Christianities and the Religions of Late Antiquity* (Chicago: University of Chicago Press, 1990), 39, 41.

is implicit among the practitioners of the process.[8] Indeed, the particular instance of reverse-aretalogy displays a heightening of this self-awareness, where incongruity itself becomes thematic.

> We have need of a rhetoric of incongruity which would explore the range from joke to paradox, from riddle-contest to myth and the modes of transcendence, freedom and play each employs. The "gospel" as I have described it stands in the closest relation to the joke which has been recently described by Mary Douglas as: "A play upon form. It brings into relation disparate elements in such a way that one accepted pattern is challenged by the appearance of another which in some way was hidden in the first."[9]

The gospel hero is a riddle; the gospel itself is something like a joke.

What JZS is suggesting by the functional proximity of the reverse-aretalogy and the joke (and this is what is so fertile for our theological hypothesis) is the close relation between human cultural transcendence and the divine transcendence celebrated by the hero's cult. The freedom of the mythic imagination to alienate and relativize its religious concepts, to take an ironic stance (the repeated breakdown of culture that is constitutive of culture), is the necessary presupposition of the process in which the obscure magician Jesus, for example, is continually rediscovered by his followers as himself relativizing and transcending all religious concepts. The deepening or heightening of Jesus' divine status is thus not a passive, punctual "experience" discovered or fixed by the Gospel accounts. There is no "epiphanic moment" to be passively absorbed, only an ongoing process of intelligent and imaginative communal action.

The difficulties for theology of the letting go of Jesus as "epiphanic moment" (though not of the incarnation!) will be the topic of part 3. The emphasis for now, though, is the cultural dynamic stressed by JZS's analysis. Worship, and reflection thereon, is the historical path by which Jesus' posthumous appearance is joined to his original fact. The negative point has already been drawn: against Troeltsch, the Jesus cult should not be

8 The notion that mythical motifs are inexplicable apart from their communal deployment casts an intriguing light on the idea, developed in Burkert's profound work on Greek myth, that they are structured as repeatable "patterns of action." See Walter Burkert, *Structure and History in Greek Mythology and Ritual* (Berkeley: University of California Press, 1979), esp. 1–25.

9 Jonathan Z. Smith, "Good News Is No News: Aretalogy and Gospel," in *Map Is Not Territory: Studies in the History of Religions* (Leiden: Brill, 1978), 190–207 at 206.

seen as a sort of unconscious or naïve socialization spontaneously arising from Jesus' "personal" impact as religious teacher or moral exemplar. The positive point for now, in considering incarnation as a cultural event, is that the culture of Jesus-worship entails a construction of divinity through creative irony, using cultural motifs in a self-subverting way in the interest of maintaining fidelity to the object of veneration. The cultural metamorphosis of the magician, the son of a god, into God (which involves the genre transition from aretalogy to gospel) is the ironization of magic in service of the confession of transcendence. The hypothesis of incarnation itself, as a way of theorizing the ontological confession of the presence of transcendence within history, will need to be guided by the cultural dynamics on display in the historical "Christ-event," because the temporal and finite effect of the eternal act of incarnation will be defined by them.

There are three fundamental characteristics of the generation of cultural meaning that the work of JZS especially emphasizes, and these will accordingly need to inform the incarnational hypothesis. The first is that cultural meaning is a collective reality, never the function of an individual in isolation. If the incarnation of deity is inserted into the dynamics of culture, then it will not be possible to conceptualize the event theologically save as an event necessarily involving persons other than Jesus himself; his reception or "appearance" as deity is an integral part of his being deity, especially since he is deity essentially as Word, i.e., as communication from God to human beings in history. The second characteristic of cultural meaning is that it never simply presents itself to direct apprehension in the fashion of a sense-object; to be received it must be produced through human interpretive acts. The incarnation, therefore, will connect Jesus with believers not simply as a unilateral transfer of meaning or "data," but rather Jesus will appear as what he is, the eternal Word, only through the constructive work of the mythmaking imagination. The final aspect of cultural meaning is that it is necessarily a process; even if we speak of a unified "event," what is intended is literally not a sudden, punctual occurrence that is inherently finished once and for all, but a temporally unfolding series. Jesus indeed is the Word; but the incarnation in the fullest sense, as the Word being uttered and heard in history, takes its time, and in fact, due to the previous two characteristics, will in some dimensions be constitutively unfinished. As long as history lasts, so does the actualization of incarnation.

As this approach is explored in forthcoming chapters, it might profitably be regarded not only as a way of thinking about the relation between divine and human agency in the incarnation, but also as a way of coming to grips with the nature of human personhood. The Christian confesses that God has become a human person, or that the eternal hypostasis of the Son or Word has appropriated a human nature to its divine nature. But the elements that make up a human self are never entirely confined within the body or psyche of the individual. This must condition our picture of just what is "taken up" by God in the incarnation. Theologians have often cautioned believers not to regard "the incarnation" as an initial act completed, perhaps, at Jesus' human conception. It is the entire human lifespan of Jesus that is appropriated; as long as Jesus lives, the incarnation is the temporally continuing effect of an eternal act.[10] But this principle should be extended beyond Jesus himself, because all human selves are partly constituted by the horizon of their symbolic world, and that world is always shared. True, the human self is always developing and reimagining itself in its world, but its initial symbolic equipment as well as its stock of new resources are always supplied through intercourse (direct or indirect) with others. If the Word was truly made flesh, it was thereby made cultural flesh.

III.

JZS argues that for the historian as such, the "transcendent" can only function as a cultural category, a moment of only relative difference within the comparative field, and never as an ontological category marking the arrival of absolute difference. This supports Barth's critical insight into the problem with Bultmann's critical hermeneutic of Scripture, where the transcendent establishes a direct presence over against other merely human "voices." However, the just-completed discussion should also be read as a support of Bultmann against Barth. The former demands against the latter some kind of involvement of pneumatic agency in the historically conditioned interpretive work of human beings. With many of his generation, Barth recoiled from Troeltsch's Christological "dead end," but perhaps he learned his lesson too well. It seems as if he wants to make sure that human action specifically as human, inspired by human desires and

10 Kathryn Tanner, *Jesus, Humanity and the Trinity: A Brief Systematic Theology* (Minneapolis: Fortress, 2001), 25–28.

incorporating human efforts at understanding, is somehow never where "it" (revelation, the advent of the Word) actually happens. His overriding concern to maintain God as the only genuine subject or actor in revelation appears to leave divine agency in a purely contingent relation with worldly, human agency, screened off from it. In contrast with this, our hypothesis explicitly positions worldly causality as such to function as a vehicle of divine causality in the incarnation. This involves a delicate superimposition or layering of differentiated causal contributions. A rudimentary schematization of semiosis as oral communication, drawing from Thomas Aquinas, will lead toward a model.

Aquinas generally points out that instrumental causality (an agent using a tool, e.g., a person using a saw to cut wood) requires not only that both primary agent and instrument have a role to play in the unified act, but also that the specific structure and potentialities of the instrument be maintained and, indeed, necessary for the act to occur. The saw by itself could never cut wood, but the person doing the cutting depends upon certain features of the instrument (sharp edges, notched tooth pattern, the rigidity of the metal, etc.). There is complete subordination of instrumental agent to prime agent within the overall act, i.e., there is only one act and one agent properly speaking; yet within this complex event the instrument itself has its own special potentialities which, far from rivaling those of the user, are actually relied upon, potency taken up into higher potency. Aquinas' understanding of human speech will now helpfully differentiate and dynamize this general picture.

Voice (*vox*) presupposes sound (*sonus*); Aquinas, following Aristotle, correctly recognized that sound is vibration, a movement of air caused by percussion. Sound can either be noise, or it can be voice, that is, articulated sound created by a living being for communicative purposes.[11] The articulation, one might say, is what turns the movement of air into a signal; the basic physical reality remains the movement of air, but that movement is manipulated in order to become a carrier of meaning. Now more than mere physical force, movement, is involved; there is present, in and through the physical movement, what Aquinas calls "spiritual force" (*vis spiritualis*).[12] This requires the careful direction of the physical forces of the communicating medium (air, in this case), but the basic laws of

11 Thomas Aquinas, *Commentary on Aristotle's* De Anima, *lectio* 18.
12 Thomas Aquinas, *Summa Theologiae*, III.62.4 ad 1.

physical interaction are in no way altered. Indeed, the superimposition of meaning depends upon those laws, though the constitution of meaning is irreducible to them, following other rules entirely.

Picturing this kind of causal stratification is an important starting point for modelling incarnation as cultural event. The key features are, first, the integrity of levels within the total event; the rhythm of moving air and the meaningful signal are a single happening, yet the latter depends upon the former without changing the former's fundamental physical character or lawlike regularity. Second, differentiation is emphasized here, distinct types of causation. The pattern of meaning is not "another" kind of efficient causality working alongside the vibrations of air. Drawing again on Aquinas' terminology, the meaning residing in those vibrations is more like a kind of quasi-form or formal cause, for which the specified air movements are the matter. Three things work together: the speaker, the careful manipulation of the atmospheric medium, and the audible code or sign system conveyed by that manipulation but existing on another plane as part of a social convention of meaning. The speaker as efficient cause generates specified vibrations though control of larynx, tongue, and oral cavity; the air, obeying its own dynamics as instrumental cause, is thereby disposed to carry the selected sounds; the meaning itself, symbolized in words, is like the formal cause for which the aerial matter has been disposed. Finally, note that the model so far addresses only meaning, not truth; one can perfectly well understand a false utterance. Conversion of sound to meaningful word is one thing, but the truth of a word happens, as Aquinas says, "when someone brings forth with the mouth what is both carried in the heart [i.e., it is not intentionally deceptive], and that is in the nature of things [i.e., it accurately reflects what it is talking about, reality or the world]."[13]

All these elements are analogously in play in the incarnational hypothesis. God is the speaker, manipulating the medium which is history, but (uniquely) from within, as its creator. The specific providential manipulation in question (pursuant to the advent of the Word, hence attributed to the Spirit) produces, not vibrations in air but specific cultural transactions among human beings. In other words, human events of meaning themselves become the instrument for a higher, divine meaning; but this instrumentalization does not violate, indeed depends upon the rules of

13 Thomas Aquinas, *Super Evangelium Sancti Ioannis lectura*, ch. 8, lectio 6.

cultural dynamics, just as verbal communication depends upon the laws of fluid dynamics. Finally, the divine meaning is the self-presentation of the divine person, rendering itself present in and through the human presence of Jesus as embedded within the Christ-event (the fusion of Jesus and his followers into a single event of meaning or symbolic communication). God speaks herself as Jesus into history, and when this word is truly heard it takes the cultural form of the cult of Christ. To put it differently, the historical "Christ-event" is the matter providentially "disposed" by the Spirit to "receive" the quasi-form of the divine Son or Word.

There are some factors which complicate this relatively straightforward application of Aquinas' speech model. First, his discussion assumes the direct physical proximity of speaker and hearer, connected by the aerial medium. Remaining within the bounds of Jesus' physical lifetime, it is fairly easy to apply the model. The bodily existence of this man, its living flesh, and its meaningful connections to others in the shape of its words, actions, and relationships, all of these together would be the physical medium, the vibrating "air" which is the historical reality of any fact. But superimposed upon this historical medium, imprinted upon this local train of historical events that we call the life of Jesus, and in no way disrupting their lawlike interactions (indeed using and deploying them), would be the signal or communicated meaning, the voice that expresses the living utterer: the selfhood or person present to the world was not just that of Jesus himself, but existed as well in some kind of unity with the creator of all things. They speak as one, and their "voice" in history is just the actuality of Jesus' embodied life. But if the human being Jesus in his entire active existence was the living voice of God, how could he be heard once that physical existence ended? He could no longer be heard in real time, so to speak; the aerial medium no longer vibrated at the instigation of his living body.

What is striking, though, is not just that he was indeed posthumously still heard as God's word; it is also that only after Jesus' death could the voice of God be more and more clearly heard (recognized) in his life. This points directly to the second difficulty, which lies in the relatively simple image of word spoken and heard. If they share a common language, as a rule the hearer readily grasps the speaker's meaning; everyday interactions too easily invite the image of "normal" communication as a transfer of information from producer to receptacle, enabled by the quasi-automatic decoding of linguistic signs. But clearly even in everyday speech, much more interpretive work is involved, and the scope for misunderstanding is wider than this picture assumes. Even a brief remark may reveal hidden depths of meaning which only disclose themselves to continued interpretive effort, whether by one or by several. Much more is it the case that the reception of Jesus by his worshipers involved repeated exercises of understanding, communally situated and imaginative or constructive in character.

The issue of truth presents a final challenge: what does it look like in this context? The divine or eternal truth of the trajectory of meaning we are calling the Christ-event is God, self-spoken in Jesus and heard by the faithful. In other words, truth in this instance appears less as a passive correspondence to reality and more as the active emergence of a transcendent presence. In light of these three considerations, thinking about incarnation as a cultural event evidently is going to require a somewhat more sophisticated schematic. To take account of the complicating factors in this case, the simple picture of face-to-face speech will be traded for a more elaborate allegory, i.e., a presentation of the interrelation of different ideas in narrative form. Sticking with the imagery of aural communication, we propose a scenario drawn from the world of popular music.

IV.

Let us imagine a singer and guitar player, in a foreign land; he is talented and skilled, but his genuine presence as a performer, it is agreed, only comes to full fruition during live performance. He develops a following in this country, but it is small at first, and moderate in enthusiasm. After all, these people have not really "heard" him yet. There are photographs and anecdotes. People may have heard one or two of his songs on the radio, but only as recorded under antiseptic studio conditions; they have become aware of the ecstatic response to his performances by the relatively small body of earlier followers in the foreign country, but its meaning is lost on them. But then something momentous happens. An expert recording of an especially captivating live concert begins to appear and circulate. Now the full impact of his talent, something of the mystery of his musical personality, is communicated clearly to thousands, hundreds of thousands, millions. Rejoicing is general. Whence comes his apotheosis as rock-god.

But this is not mere popularity, the evanescent enthusiasm of "fandom"; in this timeless performance the performer has solidified a claim to some kind of greatness. He has authored an event of aesthetic truth. Artistic "greatness" has always involved the mystery of inspiration in the artist, i.e., the sense that a greater presence or spirit has somehow expressed itself through the creative genius, such that the latter can never fully account for her own achievement. It has also always demanded a proliferating multitude of profound yet always different imaginative receptions by others. These bear witness to, and in fact partly constitute, the inexhaustible richness of the original aesthetic production, establishing its permanent presence in the history of meaning; they are its necessary supplement, extending the particular incarnation of beauty in further echoes and unpackings of its significance, even to the point of later meanings becoming inextricably incorporated into the original. The guitar hero, in short, is not just a popular success, but one of the avatars of music itself, whose spirit truly speaks through him.

Does our admittedly labored allegory subsume the complications of incarnation listed above? The first problem was how Jesus as God's word in the medium of history can continue to "vibrate" in that medium after the removal of his physical presence. The answer must be a symbolic transformation of his life, the translation of his living meaning into another medium, allowing it to maintain its identity even as it gives rise to multiple variations and elaborations. The allegory treats this in terms of the re-transcription and distribution of an original signal. To be sure, prior to dissemination of the crucial recording there were various public media (as listed in the previous paragraph) which fed the constructive imagination of the rock star's fans. But these modes of information were too variegated, too muted, too abstract to shape and unite the manifold but scattered imaginings of the many. They could not communicate the living performance (though they continued to function as active elements in its reception). It is the advent of the recordings that changes the situation decisively. Suddenly the images and affections of a multitude are made to cohere around a concrete representation of the "voice" of their hero. They continue to invest their own creative envisionings of him in assimilating this representation, but his voice now has the initiative, focusing these constructions toward a central point, or bending them around it like iron filings in a magnetic field. This can happen only because the presence of the original concert is, in a real sense, extended and communicated into another medium, long after it has come to an end in its initial form. For the believer this possibility is that of Scripture and tradition as modalities of the worshiping community; these are not merely modes of transmission but real (if limited) guarantees of fidelity in hearing.

Wittgenstein tried to explain the relation of propositions to states of affairs by appeal to this same kind of communicative extension across differing media.

> There is a general rule by means of which the musician can obtain the symphony from the score, and which makes it possible to derive the symphony from the groove on the gramophone record, and, using the first rule, to derive the score again. That is what constitutes the inner similarity between these things which seem to be constructed in such entirely different ways. And that rule is the law of projection.[14]

Strauss spoke of the "projection" of an image by the Jesus-communities; for him this image was purely a product of the later mythic consciousness, thrown back onto a shadowy figure from the past named Jesus. The historical possibilities gleaned from MS and JZS grant a similarly necessary role to the constructive imagination in the "appearance" of Jesus, but they allow the historian to see in it a hermeneutic process combining, rather than (as with Strauss) simply opposing, the original historical persona of Jesus and the divine-human Jesus of Christian confession. Now, in service to a theological reconstruction of that confession, a new sense of the word "projection" has come into view. In our parable, the guitar hero not only lives but attains musical truth by means of the extension of his performative presence directly into the later imaginations of the multitude of worshipers; his genius took "voice" initially in the medium of the air of the concert stage, but was "raised" into later history, long after the echoes of the concert had dispersed into empty space, through the translation of that original signal into a different physical medium, the vinyl of LP albums. Only thus was the voice heard anew, alive, and the full impact of its aesthetic truth, its greatness, finally disseminated in the "hearing" of millions.

14 Ludwig Wittgenstein, *Tractatus Logico-Philosophicus* (London: Routledge & Kegan Paul, 1961), 20 [in Wittgenstein's notation, 4.0141]; cf. 11 [3.11].

The second complication centered not on the transformed (intermedial) continuity of the "signal" of Jesus, but on that just-referred-to necessary active role of later worshipers in creatively grasping and developing it, i.e., recognizing his divinity through his cult. The rock-god, too, required this constructive reception. It must not be thought that his "coming alive" was an event just passively registered by the hearers. Even before encountering the recording, most were already engaged in what Strauss called "projecting an image" of the living performer. They were familiar with his name, knew some of his songs, had seen pictures of him and his band performing, and had heard by word of mouth or advertising of his glorious presence in concert. They pictured mentally what it would be like to share in the experience, even before hearing the famous concert. More importantly, however, even afterward, in listening to that galvanizing recording, time and time again they continued to fabricate in their imaginations the full experience of the musician's magic. Such constructions were not temporary expedients eliminated once the "real" recording was heard; they were the essential stuff even of experiencing the recording itself. To be sure, the audible signal carrying the rock star's performance now took a commanding role in that experience, shaping and ordering the imaginative material of the listeners. But as with the reception of music or any other aesthetic artifact, the constructive, creative, and interpretive work of the recipient is a sine qua non of the aesthetic event. The recorded event was identically communicated, and entered into a focal, ordering relationship with the aesthetic experience of all hearers, and yet no individual "heard" or imagined exactly the same concert others would hear via the same recording.

The third complicating issue has already been emerging even in discussing the first two issues. The "comparative Jesus" motifs of chapter 3 taken together suggest that the collective mythic imaginings of the communities worshiping the human Jesus of the past constructed various models of his divinity in their present, and in so doing did not displace but actually perceptively continued and amplified his original significance. But this unified "Christ-event" is an immanent, merely human historical possibility; it is a matter of semantic fidelity within ancient culture. It does not touch in any way the theological issue, that of the truth of Jesus' divinity. The Christian confession is that some of these constructive efforts actually succeeded in making actual contact, so to speak, with the living reality of God in Jesus. They genuinely heard the divine voice that spoke in his life, by its speaking to them now in a different way, in a different medium, that is, in and through their own (traditionally or communally guided) mythic pictures of him. If this was indeed a true recognition and not just an adventitiously similar replication, then that voice which the divine presence inscribed into the mental and bodily existence of Jesus really continued after his death; the signal was "played back," heard with high fidelity, in the enactment of the later Jesus cult with its stories and rites. In short, the multiform projection *backward* of which Strauss spoke and upon which JZS elaborated was itself captured in some of its elements and controlled by the projection of God's voice *forward* from Jesus into the imaginative medium of the cult. The same divine voice performing through Jesus' human existence continued the performance beyond that temporally limited site. Thus Jesus could "come alive" as truly the divine Word in the hearing of those who might be living decades, or centuries, after his physical passing.

This is the most difficult issue, and the key to the remainder of this essay. If there is one communicative pattern that persists across two different media, or if the "fact" of Jesus himself (his embodied life story) and the "appearance" (or audibility) of Jesus within elements of the celebration of his cult form a divine signal, are the collective expression of eternal "truth," this can only be a pneumatological possibility. All that history could tell us is that the meaningful content encoded within the living flesh of Jesus might have been semantically mapped onto some of the imaginative constructions of his worshipers. But if this is more than simply cultural evolution, typical traditionalism along with unavoidable semantic drift, it must be tightly unified by what Wittgenstein calls the "rule" or "law of projection." The divine spirit must be appropriating this segment of cultural history for its own ends. Only then could this historical play of ancient interpretations convey the one inexhaustible divine truth.

This work of omnipotent Spirit through history will not itself be an historically determinable fact, cognizable to the uncommitted investigator. It plays out in the history, but its "rules" are those of grammar, not physics, not those of factual cause and effect but of superimposed meaning. Again the analogy with speech: mathematical description of the frequency and wavelength of regular fluctuations in a volume of air within a defined period of time, no matter how exacting, will never in itself determine if the pattern of vibrations is meaningful. It requires a mind attuned (via some form of socialization) to the particular articulated signs determining, and hence carried by, the underlying physical rhythm. Not surprisingly, then, only pneumatic socialization into the Christian body ultimately enables recognition of Jesus' humanity as God's self-vocalization.

At this point, the allegory has done all it can do for us: it has incorporated the historical elements of the previous chapter, shown how they might connect with a pneumatology of incarnation, and now points to what remains to be done in outlining such a pneumatology. It has already been stated that the utility of the elements identified in chapter 3 for helping the historical construal of a unified Christ-event does not require the complete accuracy or adequacy of the specific Jesus construals of MS or JZS. Neither, it can now be added, does the hypothesis of incarnation as God speaking through the "flesh" of culture require it. But the elements drawn from the "extreme" reconstructions of the Smiths emphasize the cultural (communal and interpretive) dimension of the cult of Jesus, and also present a usefully unorthodox historical narrative to test the flexibility and hardiness of our pneumatological hypothesis. As a personal existence, a self-uncoiling in the "scandal of his earthly life" and continuing in its "symbolic transformation" through the cult, Jesus' identity was in fact the transcription within history of divine selfhood. And in order to be God in this "alienated" sense, the entire course of his unfolding must have been the cultural matter disposed by omnipotence to be "formed" by the arrival or presence of divine personality. If the historical "matter" of Jesus' story includes even some of the elements suggested by the Smiths, elements quite alien to the canonical Gospel portraiture, and yet can still be disposed and formed into the incarnate Word, then the hypothesis shows some promise of reconciling orthodox Christology with a whole series of "hostile" historical reconstructions.

The allegory offers nothing more than a possible schematization of the components of the hypothesis and their interplay. But however acceptable as coordinating the elements of an aesthetic "advent" (inspired performer, multiple creative receptions, projection into new media), can the model implied here really encompass the historical advent of deity itself, absolute fact? Thanks to our pop-music fable, two salient points come to view that might seem in especially sharp tension with the imperatives of orthodox Christology. First, the rock-god is one thing, but can a human being as human, thoroughly enmeshed within finite historical causality, embody the absolute being of God, the infinity of the Word? Second, if a human event is so absolutized, what remains in such a construction of the constitutive role played in the allegory, and in the "comparative" or "history of religions" Jesus account, by his imaginatively constructed communal reception? The next two chapters must face these questions. To anticipate, the answer to the second question is, briefly, that an ongoing, differentiated, and creative reception is not an obstacle but is especially required in this case, just because the "performer" incarnates an *absolute* Word. But that means it must be approached by way of answering the first question, which is the very question posed and answered negatively by Strauss' opposition of Jesus' "appearance" to his "truth." Therefore, in the next chapter the discussion must turn back to Strauss, and to the theologian who for him provided the most brilliant and profound, if ultimately doomed, attempt to answer that first question positively: Schleiermacher.

5

The Absolute Fact
Strauss' Triumph and Schleiermacher's Revenge

Where in ancient Palestine would one find a man whose understanding of the world and of himself was not mythological?

Morton Smith | *Jesus the Magician*

The lofty propositions that come to us from speculative theology, that the divine nature is the truth of human nature, human nature the actuality of divine nature. . . . That is the escape route upon which I was supposed to have been seen; but it was only my spectre, my *Doppelgänger*.

Schleiermacher | *Sendschreiben über seine Glaubenslehre an Lücke*

I.

It is impossible to resist the temptation to begin this chapter with an often-repeated anecdote about David Friedrich Strauss. The twenty-three-year-old Swabian curate arrived for doctoral studies in Berlin in November 1831.

> Strauss attended Hegel's first two lectures and was elated by the excellent beginning. On the morning of the 15th, however, he visited Schleiermacher for the first time, and when Schleiermacher informed him that Hegel had died of cholera on the previous day,

> Strauss was unable to contain his deep disappointment and unthinkingly blurted out the words: "But it was for his sake that I came here to Berlin," which Schleiermacher took as a personal diminution of his own prestige; from that moment on Strauss was accorded cool treatment from the great theologian.[1]

Student: beware pricking a professor's vanity! And yet, in spite of the young Strauss' awkward divulgence of his true love, one thing that differentiated him from most of Hegel's other theological enthusiasts (and indeed from Hegel himself) was that he always found in Schleiermacher a great mind worthy of serious engagement.

Schleiermacher's entire project, according to Strauss, was driven by his sharp perception of the central problem of Christology in the modern age: to express the status of Jesus as the unique and completely efficacious author of redemptive consciousness in all others, but in terms acceptable to contemporary scientific and philosophical consciousness.[2] In Strauss' estimation, no one was more aware than Schleiermacher of the weakness of so many of the traditional assertions of the faith in light of rational critique; indeed, on any number of topics the latter perfected that critique.[3] But he drew the line at Christology: the universal savior had to be an historical human being. Schleiermacher could not accept the contemporary expedient of maintaining the universality of Christianity by making "Christ" a rational principle, a philosophical construct. In particular, no Hegelian "logic" of spirit can penetrate the mysterious "fullness of time" in which the historical consciousness of Jesus was filled with the almighty presence of the creator. What must remain hidden to reason is revealed only in faith's living experience of redemption through him. Schleiermacher remained, to the last, committed to what he took to be the heart of the ancient faith: the man Jesus as the transcendent savior of humanity.

This is just the point, of course, that Strauss believes to be utterly untenable, as demonstrated once and for all by his own work. Yet he has no patience with those who miss the tragic brilliance of this last-ditch

1 Horton Harris, *David Friedrich Strauss and His Theology* (Cambridge: Cambridge University Press, 1973), 28.

2 David Friedrich Strauss, *Das Leben Jesu, kritisch bearbeitet*, vol. 2 (Tübingen: C. F. Osiander, 1835–1836), 686–87; English translation of the 4th edition: trans. anon. [George Eliot] as *The Life of Jesus Critically Examined*, 3 vols. (London: Chapman Bros., 1846), ed. Peter Hodgson (Philadelphia: Fortress, 1972), 768.

3 Strauss, *Leben Jesu*, 2:679; *Life of Jesus*, 765.

stand on behalf of the church's savior. The Hegelian Karl Rosenkranz had sniffed that Schleiermacher's Christology was merely forced, a tortured creation from the beginning. Strauss' rejoinder was that it was an undeniably beautiful construction; a work of genius, it went as far as one could ever go in giving conceptual form to the unity of divine and human in Jesus.[4] If, in the end, Schleiermacher's apologetic on this point satisfied neither the traditional demands of faith nor the requirements of modern scientific consciousness, the cause lay not so much in some deficiency of the author's supreme intelligence as in the flat impossibility of the attempt.

In this chapter a brief account will be given of three different aspects of Strauss' critique of Schleiermacher's Christology (with no pretense, naturally, of being able to do justice to the latter). It will be argued that this undeniably formidable critique is nonetheless not equally effective in all three of its dimensions. There are aspects of Schleiermacher's conception that seem to hold up pretty well against Strauss' criticisms, and these aspects point to possibilities for further development, particularly along just the line Schleiermacher himself (as Strauss saw) pursued: the reconciliation of incarnation and historicism. In short, the encounter of Strauss with Schleiermacher will distinguish the Christological dead ends from the still-open paths to be pursued; it brings to light the specific problems whose resolution will allow the previous chapter's allegorical model to be stretched so as to cover the case of the absolute fact.

The first aspect of Strauss' critique to be discussed had as its target Schleiermacher's historical-critical reconstruction of the life of Jesus. By common consent Strauss' appraisal of Schleiermacher's achievement on this point was devastating. Perhaps in light of that bravura performance, however, it has been too quickly assumed that Strauss' further assessments of the conceptual foundations of Schleiermacher's procedure are just as conclusive. These foundations were the objects of the second and third aspects of Strauss' critique, targeting on the one hand the basic notions used by Schleiermacher to account for Jesus' salvific absoluteness (archetypal causality and transcendent psychology), and on the other the assumption (underlying both of those notions) of an immediate or "local," as distinct from universal, presence and agency of God in the world. As will be seen, in contrast with Strauss' triumph in the first sphere of his

4 Strauss, *Leben Jesu*, 2:690; *Life of Jesus*, 770. The English lacks the footnote containing Rosenkranz's language.

critique, the second and third spheres must be accounted a mixed bag: his arguments are only partially effective in the former, and lose all persuasiveness in the latter. Schleiermacher's approaches to Jesus' absoluteness (properly reshaped in light of the weaknesses exposed by Strauss) and to the special, localized presence of divine omnipotence provide key insights that will be further developed in the next chapter. Each of Strauss' three lines of attack must now be discussed in turn, with the rest of this section devoted to the first.

Strauss' first point of attack, as has been said, was his most successful: an assault on Schleiermacher's presentation of Jesus as a strictly historical figure. It is not often remembered that Schleiermacher's exegetical work gained him an early reputation as one of the pioneer "higher" critics of the New Testament, indeed as one working on the more radical side of the enterprise. Among the first to dispute Pauline authorship of 1 Timothy (1807), Schleiermacher bolstered his standing in 1817 with a large-scale *Critical Essay on the Gospel of Luke*. In 1819 he became the first to offer a university course on the "Life of Jesus," utilizing his own critical sifting of the Gospel materials.[5] A bold and progressive biblical scholar, then? As always, that is in the eye of the beholder. Two contrasting reactions to his work will offer proof (if any is needed) of the extreme relativity, temporal and cultural, of judgments of "liberalism" and "conservatism" in theology.

The Luke commentary was the first of Schleiermacher's works to appear in English translation; the 1825 rendering by Connop Thirlwall caused an uproar among the theologians, fixing in the minds of the English clergy the image of German infidelity.[6] Compare now Strauss in the German milieu, who reports of his encounter with manuscript copies of Schleiermacher's "Life" lectures around the same years as the English commotion:

> I found myself repelled by almost every aspect of these lectures. I owe to this aversion to Schleiermacher's perspective my ability to delineate more clearly my own view on many parts of the life of Jesus.[7]

5 Schleiermacher's critical achievements are noted and contextualized by Werner Georg Kümmel, *The New Testament: The History of the Investigation of Its Problems*, trans. S. McLean Gilmour and Howard C. Kee (Nashville: Abingdon, 1972), 84, 93; and by Jack C. Verheyden, introduction to *The Life of Jesus*, by Friedrich Schleiermacher (Philadelphia: Fortress, 1975), xxix–xxxii.

6 Stephen Neill and Tom Wright, *The Interpretation of the New Testament, 1861–1986*, 2nd ed. (Oxford: Oxford University Press, 1988), 9–10.

7 David Friedrich Strauss, *Streitschriften zur Verteidigung meiner Schrift über das Leben Jesu und zur Charakteristik der gegenwärtigen Theologie*, vol. 3 (Tübingen: C. F. Osiander, 1837), 60; English translation: *In Defense of My Life of Jesus against*

Two violent reactions, but based on directly opposed assessments: unlike the scandalized English, the German found Schleiermacher the critic too apologetic, too conservative for his own taste. Strauss' own *Life of Jesus* cited Schleiermacher's earlier published Luke essay many times throughout, but almost always by way of negative contrast with sound critical judgment. Even thirty years later, the belated publication of Schleiermacher's "Life of Jesus" lectures prompted Strauss to demolish it in a lengthy and impressive review.[8]

Strauss' difficulties with Schleiermacher's historical judgments can be quickly summarized. The latter's heavy reliance upon the Gospel of John and its discourses as a trustworthy source for Jesus' life and personality seemed a fatal error. Not only did it ignore troubling questions concerning the theologically driven and speculative character of this (evidently late) narrative, it betrayed a nonhistorical bias. Schleiermacher favored it due to the close fit between his own dogmatic conception of Jesus and John's portrayal.[9] Another issue was Schleiermacher's continual lapses, contrary to his own better judgment, into the most forced sort of "rationalist" interpretation of the miracle stories, mimicking scholars like H. E. G. Paulus. Although Schleiermacher well understood the weakness of this interpretive ploy, his need to safeguard the historical bona fides of the Gospel authors required him to discern misinterpreted mundane events at the base of most miracle reports. But, as Strauss always rightly complained, such readings wrenched interpretation away from the evident intentions of the Gospel writers themselves. Finally and most importantly, Schleiermacher's supposedly historical judgments could be shown time and again to be twisted by the need to ground his "uncritical assumption" of Christ

the Hegelians, ed. and trans. Marilyn Chapin Massey (Hamden, Conn.: Archon Books, 1983), 6.

8 David Friedrich Strauss, *Der Christus des Glaubens und der Jesus der Geschichte. Eine Kritik des Schleiermacherschen Lebens Jesu* (1865; repr., Waltrop: Hartmut Spenner Verlag, 2000); English translation: *The Christ of Faith and the Jesus of History: A Critique of Schleiermacher's "The Life of Jesus,"* trans. Leander E. Keck (Philadelphia: Fortress, 1977). On Schweitzer's expert assessment, the advent of Strauss immediately revealed Schleiermacher's historical Jesus work to be useless for tackling the genuine historical issues, though this was not generally recognized for some time. For his harsh but not unfair appraisal, see Albert Schweitzer, *The Quest of the Historical Jesus: First Complete Edition*, ed. John Bowden (Minneapolis: Fortress, 2001), 59–64.

9 The veracity of John's Gospel was still broadly accepted when Schleiermacher wrote, but Strauss' merciless demotion of that text as an historical source, though controversial at the time, eventually became a critical commonplace. See Schweitzer, *Quest*, 80–83.

as the unique redeemer. Thus he "proceeded from a construction of the person of Christ out of the Christian consciousness."[10]

Detailed investigation of these claims would have to explore Strauss' many individual references in his *Life of Jesus*, but for the purposes of this essay his point can be taken as granted. The needs of Schleiermacher's theological position manifestly and repeatedly compromised his putatively historical reconstruction.

II.

But Strauss went further, opening a second line of attack by turning to Schleiermacher's dogmatic system (the *Glaubenslehre*) to probe the theological notion of Jesus that underlay the exegetical bias. In this second aspect of Strauss' critique, he echoed the arguments of other theologians like H. J. T. Schmid and C. J. Braniss that Schleiermacher's version of the Christological dogma not only marred his historical portrait, but was itself conceptually incoherent. Schleiermacher's theological reappropriation of the classic account of faith failed to do what it claimed, namely to conceive Jesus' uniqueness in terms reconcilable with modern historical assumptions.[11]

Strauss singles out for critique two strategies by which Schleiermacher tries to conceptualize and rationalize Jesus' absolute salvific character. The first of these conceptions is that of "archetypal" status (*Urbildlichkeit*); the *Urbild* is the being measuring and defining all the instances of some type by perfectly fulfilling its concept or notion. Whether the archetype of some class of thing or some kind of quality or capacity, it is not an abstract generalization or ideal but the real existence that informs all other instances, each of which have merely the character of the archetype's exemplification (*Vorbildlichkeit*).[12] For Schleiermacher, Jesus was the archetype of the essential human quality of "God-consciousness." This, the highest human state, is the pre-reflective awareness, incorporated into and conditioning everyday experience and action, of the conscious self and its world as dependent absolutely speaking—dependent,

10 Strauss, *Streitschriften*, 3:60; *In Defense*, 6–7.

11 Strauss, *Leben Jesu*, 2:690–93; *Life of Jesus*, 770–72.

12 Friedrich Schleiermacher, *Der christliche Glaube*, 2nd ed., ed. Martin Redeker, vol. 2 (Berlin: Walter de Gruyter, 1960), 34–73; English translation: *The Christian Faith*, ed. H. R. Macintosh and J. S. Stewart (Edinburgh: T&T Clark, 1928), 377–80.

that is, upon God. The human subject is always-already "presented" with its being as a locus of possible activity within, and actual conditioning by, a causally interwoven world-system that for its part, like the subject, is not self-originated but rests entirely upon divine power. Jesus brings human blessedness by sharing his archetypal God-consciousness with others; the socialized and habituated resistance to living and acting within this consciousness, universal fallenness or sin, is thereby overcome.

Strauss' general argument against such a conception is that in the natural order of things, the archetype is never itself a single instance; the "concept" of a type of entity or of one of its perfections is never concretely realized in a single individual but only in the totality of individual instances of the species or in the partial appearances of the essential quality.[13] This is a strong response which might well disable any straightforward use of "archetype" as an historical category; however, from the perspective of this essay it is important to understand the Christological reasons Schleiermacher insisted upon it. First, the ideal of God-consciousness must exist in the form of an historical individual because the human species, unlike lower, "more limited" types of living being, undergoes development not through the sheer cumulative multiplication of exemplars of the species, but through the free exercise of potentialities, the capacity for which resides only in each individual. If God-consciousness is an essential human quality, then humanity as such only appears in the world (its creation is only fully realized) when an individual freely embodies God-consciousness to its fullest extent; as a perfection precisely of the free individual it could not really be actualized even through an infinite number of approximations or partial instances.[14] This does not obviate Strauss' general objection, but it does point up the failure of his critique of Jesus as archetype to advert to the uniqueness of human subjectivity or free intentionality as a potential complicating factor in judging the possibilities of the divine appearance under historical conditions.[15]

13 Strauss, *Leben Jesu*, 2:691; *Life of Jesus*, 770–71.
14 Schleiermacher, *Christliche Glaube*, 36; *Christian Faith*, 378–79.
15 Strauss shows in a later context his awareness of Schleiermacher's focus on human subjectivity, but precisely misses the dimension of freedom. See below on his comparison of Schleiermacher's understanding of divine presence in the world to that of Spinoza.

Schleiermacher's second reason for insisting on the archetypal status of Jesus has to do with his role as redeemer; Christian faith locates in him the universal *cause* of the liberation of the God-consciousness of every other human being from sin (i.e., from its continual impairment and suppression by sense-oriented self-consciousness). Mere exemplification even of the highest God-consciousness would imply no such unlimited causal range, nor indeed any extension beyond Jesus himself. Such an efficacy is only possible on the assumption that Jesus is the archetype of humanity's perfect God-consciousness.[16] The *Urbild* as the maximal reality of a class of things or range of qualities works as a sort of "species" or natural general formality in the Aristotelian sense. Its effective reality is the determination of all lower or partial instances; their degree of approximation to it is formally derivative of its completeness. Thus Jesus' ideal God-consciousness conditions every other instance of human God-consciousness, and enables every emancipation from sinful self-consciousness. But how? Schleiermacher claims that his *urbildlich* causality is propagated solely through his historical influence, which initiates a developing growth of redeemed consciousness among more and more people that, in effect, constitutes a new, final stage of humanity, a progressive augmentation eventually encompassing the whole species (thereby fulfilling its creation).

Strauss quickly saw the tension here between the concept of archetype and the appeal to historical influence. He appeals to the very nature of progressive perfection itself with the following dictum: "[I]t would be contrary to the laws of all development to regard the initial member of a series as the greatest."[17] Schleiermacher, aware of his vulnerability on this point, had tried to adduce a parallel from physics, namely the mysterious initiation within a cloud of material elements scattered in empty space of a condensation and rotation that leads to the formation of cosmic bodies.[18] The appeal is to something like what is today called emergence: the sudden appearance within a physical system, as in a phase transition, of a new causal regime of larger-scale structure and interaction apparently

16 Schleiermacher, *Christliche Glaube*, 34–35; *Christian Faith*, 377–78.

17 Strauss, *Leben Jesu*, 2:691–92; *Life of Jesus*, 771.

18 Friedrich Schleiermacher, "Über die Glaubenslehre. Zwei Sendschreiben an Lücke," in *Kritische Gesamtausgabe, Erste Abteilung*, vol. 10: *Theologisch-dogmatische Abhandlungen und Gelegenheitsschriften*, ed. Hans-Friedrich Traulsen (Berlin: Walter de Gruyter, 1990), 351–52; English translation: *On the Glaubenslehre: Two Letters to Dr. Lücke*, trans. James Duke and Francis Fiorenza (Atlanta: Scholars Press, 1981), 64–65.

irreducible to the collective activity of lower-scale constituents, hence manifesting a new and unsuspected creative possibility within the natural order. The absence of an explanatory covering law suggests a truly basic quality of reality, grounded immediately in "nature" (or nature's source), hence attributable directly to the creative agency (though not necessarily "intervention") of God. Strauss, not surprisingly, rejects Schleiermacher's "vague analogies" as the unworthy exploitation of science's temporary ignorance to invoke a divine miracle.

Once again, there are promising possibilities within Schleiermacher's thinking at this point, but they are insufficient to override the genuine problem Strauss uncovers: too much weight is placed upon the notion of historical development in order to account for the dogmatically determined relationship of Jesus as redeemer to later human beings as redeemed. Schleiermacher insists that, granted God's direct action in constituting Jesus' perfect God-consciousness, everything else, his psychological development and human life, as well as the redeeming influence he releases into humanity and the consequent proliferation of communities of the redeemed, unfolds according to the strict laws of immanent historical causality.[19] The difficulty is whether the conditioning power of Jesus' person with its dramatic shaping impact upon the consciousness of Christians could really plausibly be mediated by a purely finite, historical causal mechanism. And, as Strauss clearly saw, fusing "archetypal" with developmental thinking tempts the theologian to derive the factual qualities of Jesus' person nonhistorically, from the general shape of redeemed consciousness among the faithful as the latter's putative condition of possibility.[20]

Strauss' objections are well taken, but Schleiermacher's insights remain promising. As long as a fontal, determining role for Jesus as the author of redemption is to be maintained, a role that Schleiermacher rightly sees as essential to the classical Christian system, the requisite connection of Jesus to believers will have to be conceived (contra Schleiermacher) according to a model that invokes some factor operative beyond the sheer immanence of historical development. Arguably, he was on the track of such a model with his "nebular" analogy.

19 Schleiermacher, *Christliche Glaube*, 1:86–90, 2:22–23; *Christian Faith*, 62–64, 365.

20 Strauss, *Streitschriften*, 3:60; *In Defense*, 6.

Even more auspicious elements will be found by turning to Strauss' arguments against Schleiermacher's other concept for conceptualizing the savior's absolute redemptive status: Jesus' "transcendent" psychology. Faith classically affirms an unsurpassable indwelling or presence of God in Jesus; Schleiermacher construes this presence in terms of his analysis of the structure and dynamics of the human ego or psyche, i.e., as a function of Jesus' perfect God-consciousness. The details of this fascinating proposal, Schleiermacher's reconstruction of the ecclesial doctrine of hypostatic union, are too complex to enter into. But the essential point is readily visible: the "being" of God as unconditioned or absolute act had to be "received" or registered and expressed within Jesus' capacity for immediate self-awareness, the grounding element within every human's psychic structure.[21]

One important corollary of this subjective incarnation is the necessarily sharp line that must be drawn between the perfect God-consciousness of Jesus and the merely relative, historically conditioned aspects of its temporal expression in his mediated awareness and activity. The linguistic and cultural elements of first-century Hellenistic and Jewish society, for example, formed the inevitable media for his public persona and even, to a certain degree, the spontaneously presented material of his own conscious thoughts. But at no point does this given matter touch the transcendent core of his unique personal identity; it is part of the "organism" mastered and reshaped, at every point of Jesus' developing experience, by the true ego or self defined by the immediate presence of deity in him.[22]

Schleiermacher requires this strong dividing line to ensure the right kind of dependent or derivative connection between the individual Jesus and the continual stream of development and refinement of ideas that ensued among his followers. Isolating Jesus' "inwardness" in this way would make it possible for faith to grasp and be influenced by the abiding significance of his words and acts, the triumphant, sin-conquering presence of God at the heart of his selfhood, abstracted from the mere trappings of his historical circumstances.

> [I]f Christianity in its progressive advancement in doctrine and practice, rejects more and more of those temporal and national limitations by which the actions and teaching of Jesus were circumscribed; this is not to surpass Christ, it is rather to give a more perfect expression of his inner life.[23]

21 Schleiermacher, *Christliche Glaube*, 2:45–46; *Christian Faith*, 386–87.
22 Schleiermacher, *Christliche Glaube*, 2:40–2; *Christian Faith*, 382–84.
23 Strauss, *Leben Jesu*, 2:692; *Life of Jesus*, 771.

Strauss' skepticism in face of this is hardly a shock, and is well grounded. For him, no such line of division can be drawn, at least not one that will serve Schleiermacher's purposes. This idea of stripping away the temporal husk to reveal the eternal identity of God in Christ is a psychological fantasy, in fact a form of docetism. The selfhood of a human being could never be detached in this manner from the complex of linguistically and culturally conditioned thoughts that constitute consciousness. Thus "the condition of [Jesus'] age and nation are a part of his individuality." If one abstracts from this complex, one does indeed arrive at an abiding identity; but it is not the selfhood of Jesus, it is rather generic humanity. "[W]hat lies beneath this phenomenal existence as the essence, is not the nature of this individual, but the human nature in general, which in particular beings operates only under the limitations of their individuality, of time, and of circumstances."[24]

Strauss' expressions at this point cast a light on the common strategy behind his distinct criticisms of Schleiermacher's two-pronged account of Jesus' absoluteness (archetypal status and transcendent psychology). In each case he sought to force a separation between what Schleiermacher was trying to hold together: on one side, Jesus' supreme and universal redemptive power, his divinity in fact, and on the other side, his complete historicity. Jesus as archetype overthrows the logic of temporal development; Jesus as transcendent psyche assumes an abiding zone of personality impossibly insulated from historical, cultural conditions. Either way, the point is the same: if such a redeemer were an historical actuality he would amount to a miracle in exactly the older sense of that term Schleiermacher wants to avoid: a divinely caused rupture of the continuity of natural and historical cause and effect. Schleiermacher did not want to assume such a causal disruption; the analogy of nebular star formation, for example, was intended to avoid this by indicating a creative impingement of total divine causality marking a mysterious elevation of human nature itself, working its way out from an initial point (Jesus) on the analogy of an unknown but nonetheless quasi-natural law. Strauss would have none of it.

To sum up this second line of his overall critique, Strauss presents Schleiermacher with a forced choice: either an absolute Christ or an historical Jesus, but not both. His first point of attack had uncovered the untenable critical foundations of Schleiermacher's historical Jesus; this second now argues that the latter's Christological concepts, quite

24 Strauss, *Leben Jesu*, 2:692; *Life of Jesus*, 771.

contrary to their intentions, deliver only an "ideal" Christ. That is, the image of a human being in perfect relation to God may well have a definite validity on the conceptual plane, but Schleiermacher was deluded to believe "that the Christ, as construed by him, really lived."[25] Christ is no historically actualized creative archetype, as Schleiermacher thought; he is a mental notion, reason's projected ideal of a perfected humanity, not *urbildlich* but *ideel*. This ranges Schleiermacher's Christ, Strauss says, right alongside those of rationalists like Kant and De Wette. All share the same weakness: their Christ as a human ideal floats unattainably above the sphere of real life, with no plausible way of attaining historical actuality. Strauss, at least when he wrote his *Life of Christ*, relied upon Hegelianism to overcome this impotence of the ideal. The "speculative Christ" in his sense is the rational principle of the ultimate unity-through-diremption of finite and infinite spirit; history, and supremely the history of the human race, is the true incarnation, the temporal actualization of the eternal truth of this unity.

III.

Strauss later lost faith in this speculative Christology, but he never abandoned his conviction that any attempt to locate ideal perfection in a single human life must assume a miraculous rupture of history. The "being" of God in a person could only destroy their humanity. But the very idea raises a bigger question: Does the "local" presence of divine omnipotence even make sense? This was the third and final aspect of Strauss' case against Schleiermacher. To reiterate: the first and most successful dimension of Strauss' critique of Schleiermacher was the religious bias and implausibility, the insufficiently critical handling of the sources, in his reconstruction of the historical Jesus. The second dimension of his critique touched on the concepts used by Schleiermacher's Christology. Although in this case Strauss did not do full justice to the complexities of the latter's thinking, overlooking certain possibilities which will be exploited in the following chapter, he did uncover two serious difficulties: the inadequacy of immanent historical development as a model for the efficacy of Jesus' archetypal redeeming influence, and the impossibility of explaining the divine presence in Jesus through an analysis of psychological structure,

25 Strauss, *Leben Jesu*, 2:695–96; *Life of Jesus*, 773.

locating in him a transcendent zone of "pure" (transcultural) inwardness or consciousness.

Strauss had good reasons for assuming that neither of these difficulties could be resolved without introducing the kind of direct or immediate divine involvement in the constitution of Jesus' selfhood and in the transmission of his efficacy to other human beings that (contrary to Schleiermacher's intentions) would undermine the genuine humanity and historicity of these phenomena. But for Strauss all this was problematic not only because the world's integrity was violated but also because it assumed an unworthy and mythical view of divine action. Strauss clearly assumed that the very notion of a spatiotemporally delimited area of special divine activity is unthinkable for a properly modern metaphysical theism. On this score he found Schleiermacher's Christology to be really no better than any number of more traditional notions of Jesus and redemption. But is this assessment justified?

Strauss' major philosophical presupposition was that all attempts to isolate any particular event or process within the natural-historical order as representing in itself a direct expression of divine creative will or power fail thereby to account for the unique mode of divine causality.

> It is impossible that the perfect God could have created a natural order that from time to time required an extraordinary assistance from the creator, especially not a human nature unable to achieve its destiny through the unfolding of its inherent faculties. It is impossible that the immutable could work upon this world now in this, now in another mode, at one point mediately, at another immediately, but [it must work] only and always in the same way: immediately in itself and upon the whole, but for us and upon the individual [only] mediately. To accept an interruption of the interconnection of nature and of the development of humanity through an immediate incursion of God would mean the abandonment of all rational thinking.[26]

There is a sound metaphysical instinct behind Strauss' protest here. The radical dependence of the entire finite and temporal order upon God strictly implies a disposition of divine activity toward it that is comprehensive, timeless, and not strictly representable in inner-worldly terms. It simply will not do to parcel this act out into separate "adjustments" and

26 Strauss, *Leben Jesu*, 2:680. Translation mine; cf. Strauss, *Life of Jesus*, 765–66.

"interventions" on behalf of special interests somehow unrelated to the overall flow of reality.

One must immediately be struck, however, by the degree to which the target of his critique shares Strauss' own inclinations on just this point; indeed, Schleiermacher develops his entire dogmatic system, including his Christology, in light of the utterly unique logic of an eternal divine creative act equally and utterly grounding the being of all things. This consistency is one aspect of his greatness as a theologian. In particular, he elaborates with extraordinary care the relation of universal divine activity to the particular divine incarnation in Christ. The details of his impressive treatment are beyond the scope of this essay.[27] However, some indications must be given in order to reveal the inadequacy of the assumptions driving Strauss' critique here. For the latter, everything turns on two considerations: first, the universal scope of the divine activity grounding the world rules out any direct manifestation or effect of that activity in a particular event; second, such an "immediate" presence of creative causality could only involve a rupture at that site of the established causal interconnections of the entire worldly process.

But Schleiermacher is quite aware of these potential objections. It appears that he could readily meet both of them from within his own scheme, maintaining a more "classical" conception of divine activity and thereby preserving the possibility of a direct and full "local" presence of the creator, as in the person of Jesus. Against Strauss' first consideration, he could reply that the universal and atemporal nature of the creator's causality cannot, in Strauss' fashion, be played off against the possibility of "local" manifestations, if such manifestations are in fact precisely the goal toward which the entire causal complex of the world is directed. The creative act is an intelligent act; the scope of divine intention must be identical with the scope of its causal efficacy, which is defined precisely by its encompassing of every particularity. Thus, as Schleiermacher points out, the act whereby God unites himself with the being of Jesus is an inherent dimension of the atemporal creative act in its entirety, and "this eternal activity means for us simply a divine decree, identical as such with the decree to create man and included therein."[28] Strauss thinks he

27 For a fuller treatment, see Paul J. DeHart, "Ter Mundus Accipit Infinitum: The Dogmatic Coordinates of Schleiermacher's Trinitarian Treatise," *Neue Zeitschrift für Systematische Theologie und Religionsphilosophie* 52 (2010): 17–39.

28 Schleiermacher, *Christliche Glaube*, 2:62; *Christian Faith*, 401.

must divide God's creative work *on* the whole cosmos against particular effects *within* that cosmos as "immediate" versus "mediate" activity. But in so doing it is he, not Schleiermacher, who is failing to do justice to the concept of creation. For Schleiermacher sees that the perfect comprehension of divine intentionality means that God does not have to bring about particular effects through the "mediation" of a logically prior universal concept of the whole. Particular and universal are equally mediate and immediate with respect to the other. Neither in the divine intelligence nor in the divine act does either one enjoy logical priority.

Schleiermacher also has an answer to Strauss' second consideration. Strauss correctly assumes that the universal range of divine creative power indicates an equal dependence of all things and events, with their causal relations, upon that power. But he wrongly concludes from this that the divine presence within the world can only be grasped as a function of the entire causal complex in its contribution to the world-process as a whole; any particular, "special" event of creative meaning isolable over against this universal movement could only happen via an arbitrary and disruptive intrusion of divine power unconditioned by the given causal relations at that location. Not so, according to Schleiermacher. In discussing the omnipresence of the divine creative causality, he points out that the complexity and richness of finite causal interactions varies greatly across the spatial extent of the created cosmos. Creaturely causality reaches upward from the relative emptiness of "dead" interactions (collisions between forces and inertial masses), to the dynamic intricacy of living systems, and finally to the perspectival and imaginative (secondarily creative) reproductions of the cosmos via the intentionality of free human intelligence. The heightened interconnectivity and range of reference implicated in the more complex events must, for Schleiermacher, represent an analogous intensification of the disclosure at those sites of the infinite creative causality. "[N]o distinction in the almighty presence of God is hereby posited, but only in the receptivity of the finite being to the causal activity of which the divine presence is related."[29] Far from calling into question the continuous causal interdependence of all finite creatures, this position positively demands it; only if all forms of finite interaction (including the higher ones) are, precisely in their differentiation, equally dependent upon the

29 Schleiermacher, *Christliche Glaube*, 1:273; *Christian Faith*, 207–8.

omnipresent creative cause, can that differentiation itself more fully disclose the dimensions of God's unbounded causality.

This is a powerful conception, and its Christological application is not far to seek. "[T]he receptivity of humanity is greater for [the divine causality] than that of any earthly being, but amongst humans it is greatest in the religious."[30] Human God-consciousness, then, represents the most intense disclosure of the creator within the world. Hence Schleiermacher in his dogmatics can then proceed to an ingenious elaboration of the perfect God-consciousness of Jesus as the very pinnacle of this human reality. He will argue that this perfect intentional reception of the divine act must be called the very being or presence of God in Jesus.[31] Whatever the difficulties with this scheme on the human side (as seen above), it provides solid grounds for refuting Strauss' accusation that any local plenitude of divine presence can only take place via a miraculous interruption of immanent worldly causality.

This chapter's survey of Strauss' critique of Schleiermacher's Christology can end here. Where do things stand on balance? Schleiermacher's Christology intends to preserve, under modern intellectual conditions, what he took to be the heart of the classical ecclesial confessions: Jesus Christ was the unique and perfect incarnation of deity in the world, and the redemption of all other human beings happens through his individual humanity. The present essay shares this orientation. The goal of critically analyzing Strauss' arguments has been to identify Schleiermacher's chosen conceptual moves in service to this endeavor, but to acknowledge as well their limitations as revealed by this bruising encounter. The verdict on Schleiermacher must be a mixed one. On the negative side, Strauss rightly questioned the attempt to cast the human redemptive connection with Christ in terms of an immanent historical development; the attempt to define God's presence in Christ by means of a culturally quarantined psychological zone; and the attempt, equipped with these dubious presuppositions, to reconstruct the "real" historical Jesus, not on purely critical grounds, but as the answer to faith's demand for a unique redeemer.

On the positive side, however, there are ingenious elements of Schleiermacher's scheme that would, with some modification, stand up well to Strauss' assault. First, his concept of the archetypal status of the Redeemer,

30 Schleiermacher, *Christliche Glaube*, 1:273; *Christian Faith*, 208 (translation altered).

31 Schleiermacher, *Christliche Glaube*, 2:43ff.; *Christian Faith*, 385ff.

though saddled with an inadequate causal model of redemption through historical influence, intriguingly points toward a formal identity of Jesus' redeemed subjectivity and that of those united to him in faith. This identity would imply a redemptive influence operating along the lines of formal rather than (though in combination with) efficient causality. Second, his analysis of Jesus' human subjectivity locates the decisive presence of God in him in terms of the primordial conditioning of his selfhood through the creator's formative proximity; the idea remains suggestive, however much it is vitiated by Schleiermacher's attempt to locate the exact point of this conditioning by means of his particular psychological theory of piety. Finally, there is Schleiermacher's insistence that the "local" existence of God within history need not involve a disruptive notion of miracle inimical to the world's causal continuity if it is conceived as the enhanced "reception" of human intentionality.

The retrieval of these promising elements of his Christology, however, requires thinking beyond the frame of reference in which Schleiermacher conceives the redeemer's status: an overall scheme of divine presence as a graduated intensity of the creator's intelligent causal efficiency. As was just noted, Schleiermacher proposed, first, the omnipresence of that efficiency as the source of all finite being; second, the heightened presence of that efficiency in the intentional receptivity of humanity, and particularly in the pious; and third, the supreme presence of it in the one human being whose God-consciousness was unconditioned by sin: Jesus. However, if it is true that this notion allows Schleiermacher to deflect Strauss' accusation that God's special presence in Jesus must rest on an anti-historicist miracle, its adequacy as a retrieval of ecclesial faith in incarnation is still open to question. Strauss did question it:

> This [graduated scheme] is nothing else than Spinoza's "eternal wisdom of God, which has manifested itself in all things, more especially in the human mind, and most of all in Christ Jesus." The escalation itself shows that here we are dealing with only relative entities and with something quite different from that which the church concept treats.[32]

As the term "escalation" (*Stufengang*) implies, Schleiermacher situates his model of the "local" presence of omnipotence in Jesus within a continuous three-step modulation of a single divine presence always "given"

32 Strauss, *Christus des Glaubens*, 28; *Christ of Faith*, 25.

in creation as a whole. Thus, Strauss concludes, whatever its functional uniqueness, Jesus' redemptive "divinity" for Schleiermacher differs ontologically from that of any creature not in kind, but only in degree.

It was one part of Strauss' case against Schleiermacher's that the latter's Christological categories deliver only an "ideal" Christ; this figure cannot be made actually historical in any way satisfying to modern consciousness. It can now be seen that the other part of his case was that Schleiermacher's Spinozist scheme of incarnation leaves his Christology unsatisfying to traditional ecclesial consciousness as well; the divine presence in him is reduced to a maximalization of merely creaturely possibility, a perfect actualization of human potential. Schleiermacher always insisted that he wished to have no part of the rational, speculative Christologies that appealed to the unification of divine and human natures as an eternal, philosophical principle. But the uncomfortable resemblance of his scheme of divine presence to Spinoza's threefold, even if Strauss' flat identification of the two is an oversimplification, suggests that Schleiermacher will continue to be haunted by his speculative "double" as long as he remains with this continuous and relatively undifferentiated account of God's grades of presence in the world.[33] If the possibilities embedded within his Christological categories are to be developed, a more satisfying account of "local" divine being will also be required. Schleiermacher's discussions of God's presence in the world and of Christology remarkably invoke, at several points, John of Damascus.[34] If even he found surprising potential in such an impeccably orthodox and classical thinker, it is not entirely unfitting if the next chapter modifies but preserves the most insightful aspects of his Christology by pushing his thought on God's relation to the world further in a classical direction.

33 Schleiermacher, "Über die Glaubenslehre," 348–49; *On the Glaubenslehre*, 62.
34 Schleiermacher, *Christliche Glaube*, 1:273, 275, 2:53, 61, 71, 76; *Christian Faith*, 208, 209, 394, 401, 409, 412.

6

Aquinas as Dogmatician of the *Religionsgeschichtliche Schule*

[God] begins to be there in a certain manner, in which previously he was not there.

Thomas Aquinas | *Summa Theologiae*

The ears of the spirit hear more slowly than the ears of the flesh.

Maurice Blondel | *History and Dogma*

I.

Strauss' triumph results in the ruthless exposure of the weakest elements in Schleiermacher's Christological approach, namely those points where it fails to deliver a genuinely historical incarnation. Schleiermacher's revenge lies in the way his deepest insights survive that test and become available for reshaping and reappropriation. Thomas Aquinas will here supply a more "classical" framework of assumptions about God and incarnation within which to develop those insights. But the greatest irony will be that this explicitly premodern framework will allow Schleiermacher's ideas, suitably adjusted, to succeed precisely where Strauss had shown them to fail: in the fullest engagement with authentic historicity.

Schleiermacher rightly perceived the absolute status of Jesus to lie in a primordial conditioning of his human subjectivity by a unique presence of God; but he could only conceive this anthropologically through a quasi-docetic removal of Jesus' *Innerlichkeit* from contamination by his own culture. Schleiermacher's notion of archetype rightly suggested a sort of quasi-formal causal relation to subsist between Jesus and the redeemed, but he could not combine this with the notion of a mediation of his effects solely through the immanent efficiency of history itself. Aquinas offers resources for developing both insights beyond their respective impasses, but before that the issue of the possible "local" presence in creation of creative omnipotence must be dealt with. Aquinas' insistence on the omnipresence of the creative causality at every place and moment was as exacting as one might wish, yet he was still able to speak to how God could "begin to be" in a place again, where he already had to be, yet in a new way. His way of effecting this inner-worldly "gradient" of divine being offers a most instructive contrast to the continuum envisioned by Schleiermacher, and rightly queried by Strauss.

Schleiermacher's scheme was faulted by the latter for explaining God's being in Christ along Spinozist lines, as in effect a mere intensification of the universal presentation of the creative intelligence in the world-order as a whole. Now, wittingly or not, Spinoza's threefold scheme cited by Strauss strikingly recalls Aquinas' tripartite arrangement of modes of divine presence in the world. Could Schleiermacher's fruitful Christological concepts still be preserved with this more classical scheme of divine presence, his overall approach would no longer be vulnerable to Strauss' verdict that his incarnation fails to meet the minimal demands of the ancient faith. Once this framing issue of God-in-the-world has been reconfigured, then the chapter can turn to examine the specific concepts needed to theorize Jesus' absolute status.

The threefold modality is clearly laid out in Aquinas' commentary on Lombard's *Sentences*.[1] "God is in all things through power, presence and essence; in the saints through grace; and in Christ through his being." The first of these modes is that of an omnipresence possible only to the creator of all things ex nihilo. This mode of presence is an intimate proximity to each and every individual thing: as the infinite causal force upholding the thing's actuality at every spatial point and at every moment ("through power"); as the unfathomably direct cognition or awareness providentially directing and connecting that thing in the web of interrelations and inter-

1 Thomas Aquinas, *In I Sent* d. 37 q. 1 a. 2. This scheme appears in later works as well, for example at *Summa Theologiae* I q. 8 a. 3.

actions that make up its history ("through presence"); and as the energy of unlimited being itself deficiently operative as the creature's finite act of existence ("through essence"). The second mode of divine presence is as the intentional object of those human beings enabled, through grace, to understand and love God in himself. The third mode is that of the hypostatic union: the personal identity of Jesus of Nazareth with the eternal Word, the second person of the Trinity.

The similarity of this model to Spinoza's leaps to the eye; they share three stages with the same contracting range (in all things, in some human beings, in Jesus). More significant for purposes of this essay is that Aquinas' scheme of the modalities of presence is arguably just as capable as that of Spinoza (or Schleiermacher) of providing an account of incarnation that does not rely on an anti-historicist rupture of worldly causality. But, and this is the crucial difference from Spinoza, it does so in a way that cannot be suspected of reducing that event to a continuous intensification of the creative omnipresence. The three modes are too distinct and their relations too differentiated to be smoothed into gradations within a single modality.

Look first at the way Aquinas relates the first mode, the omnipresence of the creative cause, to the second, the intentional presence of God in graced human subjects. God is present at every point within the created order as the absolutely conditioning cause of its actuality at that point. The world is the causal structure of every temporal event in relation to every other ("fate") as immediately grounded by an eternal and omnipotent intelligence ("providence").[2] Thus every worldly reality bears a relation to God. But Aquinas insists, repeatedly and emphatically, that what the graced person knows and loves is not God qua creator, that is, God insofar as he is the creative condition of the world.[3] Through the graciously infused virtues of faith and charity, God arrives in a radically new way in the world: as God in himself, not relatively, i.e., not simply in terms of his

2 Thomas Aquinas, *Summa Theologiae* I q. 116 aa. 1–2.

3 For example, Aquinas discusses at *ST* I/II q. 109 a. 3 the love of God as creator that would have been possible to unfallen humans using their natural powers, contrasting it (in answer to the first objection) with the love of God enabled by supernatural charity. For a brief but pregnant discussion of grace as immediate, intentional divine presence with numerous Aquinas references, see T. C. O'Brien, "Appendix 2: Faith and the Truth Who Is God," in Saint Thomas Aquinas, *Summa Theologiae*, vol. 31: *Faith (2a2ae. 1–7)*, ed. T. C. O'Brien (Cambridge: Cambridge University Press, 1974), 186–90.

creative relation to this world. To be sure, the fact that some human beings can actually understand and adore God simpliciter, for God's own sake and in himself, is itself a created fact enabled by a new quality ("created grace" in later parlance). If there are created events of this intentionality, then they, too, are caused by the providential, omnipresent creative power of God.[4] But what is *intended* in these created events is *not* God as the creator. How is this possible?

The problem is formally similar to the old Trinitarian conundrum revived in a typically incisive essay by Maurice Wiles.[5] If, as was classically affirmed, the creative act of God is a single, undifferentiated gesture in which the three intra-divine persons operate as one, indistinguishably, how could any of these persons come to be known in their distinctiveness by means of that act? The answer, Wiles asserts, is that they cannot; one must either adopt the unpalatable expedient of a direct supernatural disclosure in the form of divine "information," as a set of propositions so to speak, or else acknowledge that we have no knowledge of an inner divine constitution at all. (Incidentally, this echoes part of Schleiermacher's critique of classic Trinitarian doctrine: we can have no basis for asserting eternal differentiations within God on the basis of our immediate consciousness of God's creative causality.)

The lineaments of a traditional response to the kind of charge Wiles is making can be found in one of Augustine's sermons, and it will help to explain Aquinas' structurally similar position on God's presence in graced human beings.[6] Augustine took as his text Jesus' baptism and its Trinitarian phenomena: the proclamation of Jesus as Son of God, the heavenly voice of the Father making that announcement, and the Holy Spirit descending in the form of a dove to confirm it. How can the dictum that the acts of the Trinity are undivided be reconciled with the depiction of this event? Augustine answers in essence that the creative *activity* of God bringing about these occurrences is indeed single and unified; but the created *result* of this activity is differentiated in such a way as to reflect or

4 In the passage just cited from the Sentences commentary, Aquinas in his answer to the third objection notes the dependence of the two "higher" modes of divine presence upon the first mode.

5 Maurice Wiles, "Some Reflections on the Origins of the Doctrine of the Trinity" [1957], in *Working Papers in Doctrine* (London: SCM Press, 1976), 1–17.

6 Augustine, "Sermon 52," in *Sermons III (51–94): The Old Testament*, trans. Edmund Hill O. P., ed. John Rotelle O. S. A., *The Works of Saint Augustine: A New Translation for the 21st Century* (Hyde Park, N.Y.: New City Press, 2009), 50–65.

announce or portray within the world the distinct moments within the threefold identity of God. In other words, God's creativity can only be grasped in itself as the one, sheerly self-identical condition of all worldly being and activity. But there is nothing to prevent the appearance of one or another of the three divine persons, their distinct presentation among the effects of this unified cause. Or, to vary the metaphysical analogy, one might compare God's creative act itself as akin to an efficient cause, but one that replicates its multiform identity or formality within its effect, as operative instances of quasi-formal causality.[7]

In a similar way, Aquinas' position is that among those sanctified by divine grace, God acts creatively within their human faculties of intellectual knowledge and rational appetite (will); these capacities are bestowed with new habits or dispositions to operate beyond their innate human range. The result is the so-called supernatural virtues of faith, hope, and love (charity). Due to this gracious gift, the sanctified, in exercising their individual cognitive and affective capacities, achieve a grasp of divine identity, and an overall desiring orientation toward it, that would be naturally impossible, i.e., beyond the range of unaugmented cognitive and voluntary faculties. They are rendered capable of knowing and loving God in himself, that is, not simply as the first cause of all created being and activity. What they know and love is no longer an implicit extrapolation from the contingent world-order to its ultimate ground, but rather the very "selfhood" of God. Concepts associated with human interpersonal relations now become not just metaphors but literal truths.[8]

Another way of putting this would be to say that when God enters the world anew as the intentional object of graced faith and charity, there is

7 Karl Rahner famously employed the notion of quasi-formal causality to describe the role played by the divine being and act in the bestowal on humanity of supernatural grace; though my usage does not exactly coincide with his, there is a broad overlap. See Karl Rahner, "Some Implications of the Scholastic Concept of Uncreated Grace," in *Theological Investigations*, vol. 1: *God, Christ, Mary and Grace*, trans. Cornelius Ernst, 2nd ed. (London: Darton, Longman & Todd, 1965), 319–46.

8 This is the point of Aquinas' insistence that supernatural charity loves God in a higher way than any natural love of God could, since it involves "spiritual fellowship" with God (*societas spiritualis*), "friendship" with God (*amicitia*), with the latter implying mutuality (*communicatio*) or sharing in a common good (which is impossible unless God supernaturally donates himself, his own uncreated good, to the human being to be its good as well). See *ST* I/II q. 109 a. 3 ad1; *ST* I/II q. 65 a. 5; *ST* II/II q. 23 a. 1, etc.

a unification of object and subject via these acts that is no longer mediated by God's world-relation, but is rather a direct participation of God's self-relation. This eternal self-relation of God involves the processions and orientations of the divine essence, the intra-divine "persons." In faith and charity those being saved truly involve themselves in God's tri-unity, an issue which will be taken up later. The point for now is to mark the sharp distinction between Aquinas and Spinoza (and by implication Schleiermacher): the second mode of divine presence in the world is not simply the intensification through intentional replication of God's causal presence as creator; though causally effected by God's creative providence, in itself it is not the intelligent reception of that providence but an utterly distinct modality of God's presence, the formality of God's eternal identity.

Turning to the relation between the second and third modes of divine presence, the "step up" from the intentional presence of God in (some) humans to the unique indwelling of God in Jesus once again presents a superficial similarity between Spinoza and Aquinas that masks a deeper difference. Spinoza is willing to entertain the notion that Jesus is the highest instance of that "manifestation" of the "eternal wisdom" to be found in lower degrees in all other human beings, or at least in those who properly exercise their highest faculties. But note: Jesus' natural intellectual faculty, common to the species, would remain the essential ground of possibility even in this ultimate case. That means intensification along a continuum is once again the proper model for the relation of the second and third modes of divine presence: Jesus' particular unity with God merely touches the upper range of what is made possible in principle by his being human at all. The similarity to Schleiermacher is evident.

But Aquinas' scheme disallows any smooth transition between these stages. To be sure, the uniqueness of his Jesus, like Spinoza's, must not compromise his full humanity in any way. And Jesus' perfection for Aquinas is in the first instance the perfection precisely of a human being, not of God; not only is he completely free from any shadow of inherited or willed alienation from God (sin), but he supremely enacts those same supernatural virtues of faith, hope, and charity that connect all the sanctified with God himself as a personal counterpart. Jesus, then, is a saint, albeit the greatest of them; he is gifted with the highest degree of habitual grace possible to a human being.[9] But Aquinas' crucial difference becomes clear

9 Aquinas, *ST* III q. 7 a. 9.

at this point. Jesus' sharing in human nature is only a necessary but not sufficient condition of the possibility of his supreme degree of saintly perfection, for human nature in itself is completely incapable of actualizing it. This is partly because the fundamentally deficient and distorting social and personal relations that have taken hold in the human species (original sin) inevitably mar every nascent self and effectively impede the openness to God theoretically possible to human beings. But sin is only an accidental barrier; there is an essential one. As just mentioned, Jesus' highest graces (note the adjective "supernatural") represent an additional creative bestowal from God conjoined with, but in no way derivable from, the innate powers of even the most perfect exemplification of human nature as such. They flow from the unique appropriation of Jesus' humanity by the eternal Word.

Schleiermacher's Christology tends to picture the relation of the second to the third modes of divine worldly presence on the pattern of Spinoza. He argues, for example, that the advent of Jesus exemplifies the same mysterious fertility of human nature whereby the multiplying instances of the species periodically produce exemplars of human excellence or "genius."[10] But for Aquinas it is not the case that Jesus' personality can represent the highest mode of God's worldly presence merely in virtue of a full flowering of the powers inherent in human nature as such. In fact, the human perfection supremely instanced in Jesus is not in itself the new mode of divine presence in the world; it is rather the supreme instance of the second mode, that intentional presence of God by "habitual" grace present in all the saints. And if, as was seen, this grace cannot be a product of natural human variation, there must be a third mode of divine presence that makes possible this second mode, in Jesus and, derivatively from him, in all the other saints.

This third mode is the just mentioned personal union with the Word; it represents the full replication, under the temporal and limited conditions of a created human personality, of the eternal existence of a subsistent divine self-relation. This is what Aquinas calls the "grace of union," a "hypostatic" or personal union because the eternal "self" of God expresses or projects itself as (identical with) the personal history of an historical

10 Friedrich Schleiermacher, *Der christliche Glaube*, 2nd ed., ed. Martin Redeker (Berlin: Walter de Gruyter, 1960), 1:87–90, 2:44; English translation: *The Christian Faith*, ed. H. R. Macintosh and J. S. Stewart (Edinburgh: T&T Clark, 1928), 62–64, 386.

human being. For Aquinas, it is this unparalleled proximity of deity to Jesus' humanity, this new and unique mode of divine presence in the world, that enables the repletion of grace perfecting his humanity and overflowing beyond it into others.[11] Lacking this second "leap" disrupting the Spinozist continuum of "eternal wisdom," Schleiermacher's Christology cannot effectively answer Strauss' accusation of a secret betrayal of traditional faith in Christ's divinity. If Jesus were what he was as the highest instance of human nature, even as the providentially chosen outer boundary of the statistical range inherent in all instances, then his "divinity" is indistinguishable from consummate, archetypal humanity. Aquinas' scheme makes possible a definition of Jesus' divinity more appropriate to the traditional sense permeating worship, prayer, and theology, for on his account the third mode of divine presence in creation is the appropriation of Jesus' human person by the eternal divine person, such that they function as one person, one "I," one "who."

II.

Aquinas' threefold scheme of God's inner-worldly presence involves not just a gradation of intensity but a layering of distinct though related modes. It is the modal distinction which would allow Schleiermacher's "being of God in Jesus" to turn back Strauss' taunt that Jesus' divine status is a mere equivocation. But Aquinas' framework of divine creative engagement with the world also opens up the possibility of understanding God's incarnation in Jesus in a way compatible with an historicist sensibility, in effect attaining Schleiermacher's goal better than Schleiermacher himself was able to do. Aquinas' general assumptions concerning providence already suggest a "layered" approach to the divine presence in Jesus that is inherently fruitful, as will now be seen. Then, when the remainder of this section proceeds to the specific mechanism of incarnation, Aquinas' ideas will be seen to preserve what is positive in Schleiermacher's Christological categories without succumbing to Strauss' searching critique of them.

On the level of efficient causality, Aquinas grounds the events of sanctifying grace and of Jesus' humanity (the second and third modes) in the first mode, the single efficient act of God's omnipresent creative power. But those other two modes retain their superiority as higher grades due to their distinct quasi-formal status; they are not reduced to the role merely

11 Aquinas, *ST* III q. 7 a. 1.

of superior "expressions" of the wisdom of the universal world-cause. Yet the efficient omnicompetence of the general creative act relieves the other two modes from becoming ad hoc interruptions of the world's causal flow; this points toward a conception whereby even the supreme worldly advent of the deity demands no tear in the fabric of history. How so?

The total world-scheme of interconnected immanent causality is the product of the providential act of creation. This includes those particular arrangements of worldly events in which God's self-relations "arrive" as intentional objects for enhanced human faculties (saving grace), or in which one of God's self-relations (that of the Word, analogous to the self-presentation to the divine understanding) "arrives" as appropriately self-articulated through the human selfhood of Jesus (grace of union). In both cases, though these complex arrangements are actually divinized in terms of the truth they bear and the operations they enable, they remain, ontologically speaking, within the created realm. Hence these advents of God's more intimate presence are not to be construed as interventions that disrupt the regulated causal pattern of the created order. As logically prior ordinations shaping the creative act as a whole, they are the formal ends prepared by the dispositive efficiency of that act from the beginning. They arise from, or as, configurations of created events, unfolding from their natural causal antecedents; yet they are shaped so as to carry a transcendent meaning and efficacy.

Some of the analogical tools for grasping this "layered" causal approach were proposed in chapter 4. Remember the parable of audible transmission. Vocalization is a single act, the manipulation of vibrations in air in order to carry meaningful signs. It does not involve two different acts, as if the semantic act were causally separate yet on the same level with the physical act, and thus represented a kind of suspension of or interference with the rules governing oscillations in the atmosphere. Rather, the single act of vocalization involves both at once: shaping aerial waves in accord with a shared convention of signaling. The waves continue to follow exactly the same dynamic laws involved in meaningless audible events, like the crash of a boulder or the patter of rain. Indeed, the meaningful transmission depends upon those laws, else it could not reliably deploy the medium to convey specific, desired patterns.

So too the second and third modes of divine presence in Aquinas' scheme completely depend, in terms of efficient causality, upon the providential ordering of the created realm as a whole by God's one act of creation. True, in terms of their meaningful content they quite transcend the truths about the creative cause inscribed within every finite reality and abstracted or inferred from that reality by human intelligence (God's "power, presence, essence"). But this superimposition of meaning, analogous to a personal communication yet so perfect that it amounts to new immanent modalities of utterly transcendent presence, in no way interferes with or interrupts the network of worldly causality. As Augustine said, normally signs (*signa*) refer to things (*res*) distinct from them; only the creator of all things and of their patterns of relation is capable of rendering things themselves, the events of history, as communicative signs.[12]

So Aquinas' threefold scheme of divine presence is more faithful to traditional Christian notions of grace and incarnation than that of Spinoza (or that of Schleiermacher, to the degree the latter is reducible to Spinoza's). But it also honors the nondisruptive intent of Schleiermacher's scheme, as well as the latter's quite proper refusal to play local acts of God off against the universal act, a la Strauss. This scheme is not only an important conceptual tool for adjusting Schleiermacher's Christological approach in light of Strauss' critique. It issues in the instrumentality used by Aquinas to construe the specifics of God's incarnation as human. The rest of this section shows how they can guide the theologian beyond two other impasses in Schleiermacher previously identified by Strauss: God's forming of Jesus' person as a kind of transcendent psychology; and Jesus' archetypal redemptive formality propagated as an immanent historical influence.

In regard to the first issue, on Schleiermacher's model of incarnation, what he calls the special "being" of God in Jesus is a function of the latter's perfect God-consciousness. The creative act grounding all finite reality and thus expressed in the intricate order and beauty of that reality is, in him alone, perfectly received. It fundamentally shapes his personality and guarantees that his consciousness and activity at every point are perfectly permeated and governed by that reception. This does not mean the intellect of Jesus comprehended the creative act in its entire universal effect; the perfection here lies not in the scope or detail of cognition, but in the control of cognition by piety. The reception does not take place initially on

12 For an influential exploration of this theme, see Erich Auerbach, "Figura" [1944], in *Scenes from the Drama of European Literature* (Gloucester, Mass.: Peter Smith, 1973), 11–76, especially 28–49.

the cognitive level but on that of immediate self-consciousness or "feeling." The perfection in question is thus the completeness with which every moment of Jesus' experience from birth onward (including, derivatively, his knowledge) was decisively shaped by and suffused with awareness of God as the absolute ground of world and self. Unimpeded by the distorting repression Schleiermacher calls sin, the God-consciousness was free to express itself fully in his subjectivity and thus uniquely form his identity. However, as discussed above, the criticism of Strauss puts this psychological model of Jesus on the horns of a dilemma, both of which involve undesirable implications. Either the presence of God in his psyche is integrated with Jesus' personality, but then it cannot be kept free of the relativity and mutability of his specific ethnic and cultural consciousness; or else this presence does indeed reside as a timeless feature within Jesus, but then it is no way individuated in him but elevates only his empty, generic humanity.

An attempt to reshape Schleiermacher's conception of Jesus' absolute status along the Thomist lines indicated so far would commence from a different kind of criticism. One consequence of Schleiermacher's understanding of incarnation, ingenious as it is, is that Jesus' own self-understanding and its self-presentation in word and act can be attributed to God's special "being" in him, but they cannot, at least without crippling qualifications, be called acts appropriable to, or *self* disclosive of, God himself. The being of God in Christ, for Schleiermacher, is in a sense the perfect creaturely reception of the divine creative act; but it is not properly, in itself, the being of God acting in his own persona, so to speak. For Aquinas, as for anyone who understands the incarnation of God in Jesus to warrant the worship of Jesus, this will hardly be enough.[13] In Jesus' personal act one must encounter God's personal act, not just the perfection of humanity or even of creaturehood generally, as if the creator were present only in the form of his highest creative achievement. It must be possible to say, in some nonmetaphorical sense, that "who" Jesus is, is God.

This is possible on Aquinas' understanding because, although he too sees the incarnation to lie in the radically original conditioning of Jesus'

13 A sharp terminological distinction between worship strictly speaking and lesser but still exalted forms of veneration has not always been observed even in monotheistic contexts, but it seems that Schleiermacher, for his part, sought a theology of incarnation that would warrant divine worship being paid to Jesus. See Schleiermacher, *Christliche Glaube*, 2:88–89; *Christian Faith*, 423–24.

person by a special presence of God, he conceives the manner of conjunction quite differently from Schleiermacher, and in a way which leaves no room for the latter's transcendent psychology of untouched "inwardness." The divine presence is not, as with Schleiermacher, "inserted" into Jesus' founding self-consciousness as a force or influence predominating at each developmental moment; it instead eternally appropriates or "assumes" in a single act the entire course of his humanity. Talk of a "hypostatic union" means that the eternal identity of God (more properly, of God's self-relation as "Son") is formally operative within the efficient creative act in such a way that the humanity of Jesus exists and acts in the world as an exact reflection or "projection" of the intra-divine relational act. The eternal Word is spoken as a living human.

No particular isolated element or action, psychological or physical, of the human being Jesus is God; but his self or subjectivity as the dynamic shape enacted or narrated in his total history, coincides with the eternal shape of God's dynamic of selfhood.[14] One consequence of this different understanding is that Jesus' divinity is not equated with his personal receptivity-and-expression of God, as with Schleiermacher; this unique apprehension of deity is instead the result of the ontologically prior assumption by the eternal Word. The point is that Aquinas' notion of incarnation by assumption makes it possible to allow the entire psychic apparatus of Jesus, as such, to remain in the realm of immanent causality. The being of God in him is not a restricted zone within the structure of his subjectivity, but is the incorporation of the entirety of that structure in its historical actualization instrumentally within the personal self-relation of God.

It would unfortunately require a monograph of its own to set out in detail the different constructions of incarnation in Aquinas and Schleiermacher. An impressionistic series of contrasts is all that can be offered here. For the former the divine person assumes human nature; the Word subsists as a human being, adjoining a new, created mode of being to its divine mode. For the latter the terminology of assumption really refers to an insertion or implantation, in that the creator operates through human nature's inherent possibilities to co-produce a unique human personality. For Schleiermacher God decisively conditions an act of personal formation, recovering the full, unimpaired potential of human nature. But because the divine act must appropriate the natural person-forming mech-

14 Aquinas, *ST* III q. 2 aa. 1–8; q. 4 aa. 2, 3; q. 5. aa. 3, 4.

anism as a cooperative cause, it is limited by this instrument to a defined space within the personal organism. A split occurs within the person of Jesus between a triumphant "innermost" and everything else, such that his "real" self is not fully incarnated in his historical or cultural environment. Aquinas' scheme leaves open such a possibility, because for him, assumption need not mean the "working through" human nature to co-produce a newly pristine, "original" human; it could mean the appropriation of a "merely human," historically, and culturally formed person in its entirety. In short, on an understanding like that of Aquinas, the human personality of Jesus can be produced historically by a providentially guided process.[15]

On Aquinas' understanding, the elevation or divinization of the created humanity of Jesus happens as it is "used" instrumentally by God to bring about an effect beyond its inherent capacity, the effect being the presence and agency within the temporal order of the eternal Word. For Aquinas, unlike Schleiermacher, the instrument used by God is Jesus' humanity as such, not a natural person-forming process. Aquinas typically speaks of the "passing" of the primary causality "into" the instrument, not as a distinct component of the latter but only as a function of the total integrated process. It was seen that in Aquinas' Christology the grace of union overflows into the perfect habitual grace of Jesus' humanity. The hypostatic union with the humanity of Jesus (such that Jesus' personal identity becomes an extension of the eternal Son's personal identity), is God's use of his "mere" humanity instrumentally.[16] It is not his saintly human perfection but rather this event of utilization that constitutes the true divinity of Jesus, the "who" of God speaking and acting as a human person. The divine identity of a personal self-relation of God "passes into" and dwells in the humanity of Jesus. This presence is not temporary, as with most instrumental causality, only because the divine saving act of

15 It might be thought that this view is in tension with the doctrine of the supernatural, virginal conception of Jesus in Mary. Two things should be said. First, for Aquinas Jesus' birth of a virgin is not the introduction of divinity into him, but the removal of a negative barrier to the assumption of his nature. Second, even this particular manner of effecting that removal is not necessary for God. The hypostatic union, that is, is not dependent on the virginity of Jesus' mother as a concomitant cause or even a necessary condition, but makes use of this special conception as a fitting sign. See *ST* III q. 28 a. 1; q. 29 a. 1 ad2; q. 31 a. 1; q. 31 a. 4: "The Son of God could have taken [human] flesh from whatever matter he willed."

16 Aquinas, *ST* I/II q. 112 a. 1 and replies to first and second objections.

elevating human beings into communion with God through union with Jesus' humanity will continue as long as creation itself.[17]

Aquinas' scheme of incarnation as assumption not only avoids Strauss' proposed dilemma, it indicates a potential reconciliation of Jesus' divinity with his total causal integration into created history. For Aquinas, the creative act that establishes Jesus' humanity and its historical relationships is at no point suspended or interrupted by his divinity; rather that divinity is a particular, provident configuration of that creative act's intended effect, conjoining instrument and primary agent. Thus God, already present in Jesus as in every creature, comes to be present "again" in a new way. In the language of the New Testament, the Father sends the Son into the world. This new arrival of God himself, or more properly of a constituent self-relation of God, in the form of a created replication "operating" the divine actuality is therefore traditionally called a sending or mission. Thus in principle incarnation would not prevent Jesus' human consciousness, qua human, from being totally composed of ideas and imaginings drawn from the fund of cultural currency available to anyone in his time and place. That is, Aquinas' concept of the mission of the Son allows Schleiermacher's fruitful Christological notions (the local presence of omnipotence and its primal conditioning of Jesus' subjectivity) to be employed without falling into the trap of transcendent psychology. It is also the key to another critical appropriation of Schleiermacher, the final one to be discussed in this chapter: the move beyond immanent historical causality as the sole connection between redeemer and redeemed.

III.

It will be recalled that Strauss disputed the possibility that Jesus' archetypal status could effectively be combined with a truly historical account of his influence, in Schleiermacher's fashion. The latter hoped to construe the dissemination of Christ's perfect redemptive consciousness among

17 A full comparison between Aquinas and Schleiermacher on their respective notions of the relation of divinity and humanity in Jesus, the role of human nature in the assumption, the meaning of personal union, and the question of Jesus' proper divinity and worship would require a sizable study of its own. All that can be suggested here would be a review of Aquinas, *ST* III qq. 1–19, followed by a close reading of the Christological sections of Schleiermacher's dogmatics, of which the following passages might prove especially illuminating: *Christliche Glaube*, 2:35–37, 41–42, 47–48, 50–51, 53, 57–58, 60–64, 65–67, 71–75; *Christian Faith*, 378–80, 384, 388–89, 391, 393, 397–98, 399–403, 404–5, 409–12.

an ever-increasing number of the redeemed as a developmental process. Strauss sharply questioned the adequacy of this entire model, because it cannot be reconciled with the way historical development actually works. Its vulnerability shows itself at two points: causal and epistemic. On the first point, Strauss argues in effect that an historical development of humanity could never begin with the sudden and complete instantiation in some individual of a new quality or perfection, followed over time by a highly selective replication among others to a greatly varied and statistically unpredictable, but always inferior, degree. The rules of development in history envision an efficacy that is incremental and cumulative. On the second point, Schleiermacher presumed a living connection between redeemed human beings and their redeemer that both enabled and demanded their acknowledgement of a unique and absolute efficacy in the historical Jesus, to the point of necessarily determining actual aspects of his life and personality. But Strauss would reply that if Jesus' influence is genuinely historical, it cannot possibly supply the kind of epistemic privilege Schleiermacher grants to the redeemed. Historical development knows only the gradual accumulation of always partial and fallible insight into the past. Schleiermacher's scheme opens the door to what Strauss execrated: the purely dogmatic construction of historical facts.

The initial response from Schleiermacher's position would be, rightly, to invoke pneumatology to cover these deficits. He affirms the traditional position that the community of faithful persons who are being transformed by Jesus' redeeming power in fact enter into their own special union with God's being. This second conjunction of the creative essence with humanity, the Holy Spirit in the church, derives from Jesus' own union, but is different in kind because only progressively and partially formative of the identities of the redeemed, not (as with Jesus) absolutely formative. However, Schleiermacher critically weakens his pneumatology by conceiving this other new "being" of God in the world via the redeemed community to be explicable in terms of the social dynamics of human groupings in which an irreducible collective "persona" emerges with its own quasi-psychological identity and activity.[18] As with Jesus, the advent of divine being is once again "inserted" into an inner-worldly dynamic that provides a specific locus and function for that advent. Constrained within this immanent sociological framework, it is not clear that

18 Schleiermacher, *Christliche Glaube*, 2:262–68; *Christian Faith*, 572–77.

Schleiermacher's pneumatology can really overcome Strauss' accusation of an ahistorical process. On the one hand, the church as a perpetually produced collective "moral person" could convincingly be seen as a developmental mediation of Jesus' efficacy only on the highly doubtful historical conjecture that he himself caused (causes?) the church. On the other hand, it is not easy to see how the Spirit's formation of persons through the specified historical social mechanism would warrant in them any privileged cognition into Jesus' own historical being as the absolute fontal source of redemption.

Schleiermacher rightly perceived the necessary role of a second locus of divine presence in the world in order to account for the redeeming influence of Jesus, but its subordination to the dynamics of community formation, ironically enough, hindered its fuller absorption into history (in a way analogous to Schleiermacher's subordination of God's presence in Jesus to the dynamics of natural personal formation). By contrast the "stronger" pneumatological concept of Aquinas can once again point the way to a more genuine embrace of immanent historical causality than Schleiermacher. The Spirit in the world refers especially here to those operations of divine creative power providentially disposing history to the supernatural "arrival" of divine persons, whether the advent of the eternal Word in Jesus, or the advent of the eternal Love or Spirit itself, taking shape as the continual constitution of an historical community of those able to transformingly "hear" Jesus as the Word. A pneumatology strong enough to dispose the utterly enculturated humanity of Jesus for the Word's advent in him is also strong enough to dispose the utterly historical cultural processes that make up the Word's ongoing reception (redemptive and epistemic) in others.

Aquinas, like Schleiermacher, gives the paradigmatic and initiatory redemptive role to the graced humanity of Jesus, calling him the "author" of grace in others.[19] But for Aquinas the gifts of faith and charity, the divine enhancements to the capacities of the redeemed that form their subjectivities and enable their recognition of the divinity of Jesus, though ultimately divine bestowals via the instrumentality of Jesus' humanity, are not straightforwardly results of the historical influence of the savior. In fact, just as the personhood of Jesus replicates or expresses in a train of created events the eternal relation of God as Son to God as Father, so too

19 Aquinas, *ST* I q. 43 a. 7.

the reconfigured operations of human beings under the influence of saving grace predominately replicate or express as created realities the eternal relation of God as Spirit to God as Son and as Father. It is the dynamic orientation or impetus of their wills toward God in himself (charity) that shapes them as agents; implicated in this shaping is the empowerment of their cognitive faculties to rightly grasp the identity of God in the humanity of Jesus (faith). And just as the created expression of the eternal Son is in fact a real presence of divinity in the world, so, too, is the created expression of the eternal Spirit such a genuine presence.

In short, rather than Schleiermacher's two unions of God with humanity, of which the second is a derivative effect of the first, supposedly mediated by its historical influence, there is in Aquinas a double mission. He speaks of a "visible" mission in which the eternal Son appears as Jesus of Nazareth, and an "invisible" mission in which the eternal Spirit operates as the graciously bestowed ("supernatural") operations of the saints.[20] Note: the second mission is just as necessary to the redemptive event of Jesus, just as primal, as is the first, the assumption of his humanity or hypostatic union itself. Only the presence of God as eternal Spirit within persons initiates the transformative work that realizes charity in the will, energizing and coordinating all other capacities and thus pressing toward

20 For the two missions and their interrelations, see Aquinas, *ST* I q. 43. T. C. O'Brien gives a fine treatment of the Spirit and charity in "Appendix 1: Names Proper to the Divine Persons" and "Appendix 2: The Holy Spirit: Love," in Saint Thomas Aquinas, *Summa Theologiae*, vol. 7: *Father, Son and Holy Ghost (Ia. 33–43)*, ed. T. C. O'Brien (Cambridge: Cambridge University Press, 1976), 239–58. For the relation of charity and knowledge of Jesus, see Thomas Gilby, "Appendix 10: The Dialectic of Love in the *Summa*," in Saint Thomas Aquinas, *Summa Theologiae*, vol. 1: *Christian Theology (Ia. 1)*, ed. Thomas Gilby O.P. (Cambridge: Cambridge University Press, 1964), 124–32. Although helpfully schematic for the purposes of this chapter, the association in the text of the visible mission with Jesus and the invisible mission with the Spirit simplifies a more complex picture, as is clear from a reading of all of q. 43. There is for Aquinas an invisible mission of the eternal Son as well, and a visible mission of the eternal Spirit. The former is the grace-enabled knowledge of God through faith, which is tantamount to the presence anew of the Son (as perfectly reflecting the Father) in each believer, as for example assumed in much of Paul's language ("Christ in you," "growing up to the stature of Christ," etc.). The latter consists of those special phenomena that sensibly manifest the new epoch of the bestowal of the Spirit upon Jesus himself (the dove at his baptism, the cloud on the mount of transfiguration) and upon his earliest disciples (the breathing of Jesus upon the twelve, the tongues of fire at Pentecost). In spite of these complications, however, the larger role is played by the two missions discussed in the text: the incarnation is the primary visible mission, and the bestowal of charity is the primary invisible gift of grace.

a faithful recognition (in individual and collective humanity) of the presence of God in Jesus. In one sense the incarnate Jesus "sends" the Spirit, but in another deeper sense, Aquinas argues, the true eternal sender of the Spirit is not Jesus but the eternal Father and Son acting together.

Hence the priority of Jesus as author and fount of grace does not rob the Spirit of its own characteristic initiative, so to speak; the divine presence in Jesus reaches forward as redemption to the later faithful even as the Spirit in them reaches back as reception and recognition. The important thing to see is that the historical influence of Jesus is no longer required to shoulder the burden assigned to it by Schleiermacher, because it is only one aspect of the total event connecting redeemer and redeemed. And yet the lifting of this burden through the more transcendent, quasi-formal role of the missions is, as will now be emphasized, also what frees the course of history to maintain its causal integrity even as matter pneumatically appropriated and formed. The dogmatic picture of the two divine missions meeting and interlocking does not undermine, but is rather perfectly expressed by, the aggressively nontheological critical reconstruction of chapter 3, and the allegory of the guitar hero of chapter 4: the human life of Jesus and the pragmatic-interpretive receptions in the collectives faithful to him constitute a single "Christ-event."

To recall the path of the argument so far: the "comparative" or "history-of-religions" Jesus speculations of the Smiths were surveyed to experimentally isolate certain historical possibilities not typically salient within mainstream New Testament scholarship. The point was not to commend the adequacy of their accounts as a total picture, but, first, to suggest historically plausible resources that might play a role within reconstructions of Jesus and his early worship in a way that made sense of a genuine semantic continuity between Jesus himself and his later worshipers: a cultic recognition. Next, as part 2 turned from Strauss' historical-critical challenge to his historicist one, the same experimental history of cultic recognition served to hint at a model of incarnation as the historical utterance-and-reception of the divine Word, and remained in the background as an "extreme" historical test case for the theological viability of that model. An allegory was then developed to illustrate the functioning of the incarnation model; taking off from the picture of the Christ-event as cultic reception, it told the story of the inspired musician incarnating the aesthetic truth of music, of the necessary role of an ongoing, multiple, and imaginative (even partially creative) reception of his performance of that truth, and of the function in maintaining his performance of its projective transformation into new cultural media.

But the allegory had to prove itself: Could it be extended to cover the case where the human is the true incarnation of infinite deity itself, not just an avatar of the muse? Two questions in particular were urgent: Could a human individual really embody the infinite in this way yet remain, like all other individuals, constituted by merely parochial cultural transactions? And could such an embodiment still require an ongoing, communal process of constructive reception? This and the preceding chapter have intended to lay out, at least incipiently, positive answers to both questions. The highly illuminating comparison of Strauss and Schleiermacher on Christ and historicity guided the reading of Aquinas, helping to locate in the latter the conceptual tools that evolve the allegory of the rock-god into a theory of hypostatic union and double mission. The relative success of that evolution, in turn, largely determines the formal compatibility of Aquinas' understanding of incarnation and Pentecost with the "nontheological" history of the "Christ-event" as cultic recognition. That is, even that extreme historical scenario could serve as adequately disposed matter for the pneumatic shaping into the forms of divine persons.

As promised, Schleiermacher's insights have been critically appropriated by moving him further in a "classical" direction. Such a direction was, at times, not without appeal for him, though the proposals of this chapter would surely have taken him well beyond the bounds of what he could have accepted given his deeper commitments to a quasi-Spinozist monism of this world as a necessary expressionist emanation of God, and to a pietist scheme of redemption privileging victory over sin rather than supernatural elevation to union with God. At any rate, the focused discussion of Aquinas has opened up a new way of imagining the human Jesus, and his cultic unity with the faithful, that tries to do justice as much as possible to the heuristic ontology of historicism: the determination of the factual through its unruptured connection with the causal texture of finite events. The resulting picture of the "merely" cultural consciousness of Jesus and his continued constitution via cultic imagination naturally lie well beyond anything Aquinas himself could have countenanced. But the theoretical possibilities are there in his theology.

The two missions or descents of God, one historically completed in Jesus' life (hypostatic union), the other historically ongoing in the church (sanctifying grace plus further special charisms), are the two modes of divine presence beyond the grounding mode of creative omnipresence: gracious dispositions that, so to speak, rotate God's self-relation toward the world as an embrace, so that it touches the world at these two points. As Aquinas implies, any positive disposition of the creator, as such, to the world, involves the establishment of some reality within the created order.[21] In this case the double mission takes shape as the two factual complexes, Jesus of Nazareth and his receptions in communal faith. But the actual content of each mission, what is "sent," is God himself (not merely qua world-cause) in some subsistent quality of self-relation (either Son or Spirit). Yet it is the identical divine being or "self" that is equally expressed in each.

For that reason, the disclosive self-utterance in Jesus and its reception in the Spirit-filled communities constitute, in effect, a communication of God with himself, in which human beings come to be included. On the level of immanent historical causes, two event-complexes, on one side Jesus (with his "historical influence") and on the other the accumulation of collectives interpreting him, form a single occurrence of shared meaning; but this history is also the matter disposed for divine form, the completed circuit of transcendent communication just described. In themselves these events are "just" creatures, as in the case of the guitar hero, where performative achievement, projective media, and imaginative reception combine to render what is "just" vibrating air into the reality of musical beauty.

One could say that Jesus and his interpreters are, in a manner necessarily outside the horizon of historical perception, infinitely triangulated. That is, this symbolic agglomeration of first-century socio-religious facts becomes the incarnation as it is suspended or, as it were, "clamped" between the two temporal arrivals of deity itself, each such arrival (each mission) being an extension into the created order of the eternal self-relationality of God, one in a way more punctual and the other more processual or ongoing. What turns a particular tract of history into the Word, spoken as a human life and prolonged in its continually being partially and newly heard, is only this involvement of transcendence, from

21 Aquinas, *ST* I/II q. 110 a. 1.

what seems to historical consciousness an infinite distance. But if on this understanding one of the missions is still historically in process, then so is the history of the incarnation itself.

There are two sides to this unfinished aspect of the incarnation. First, although the true "signal" of God's own presence sent in Jesus has been and is being truly received, the "playback apparatus" which consists of Christians themselves with their efforts at individual and communal faithfulness, is continually varying the quality or fidelity of this reception. Individuals grow in virtue (but also falter), communities gradually attain freer unity and extension (but also harden and fracture), and over time this or that aspect of God in Christ is "heard" more or less clearly, though it is also possible to affirm a collective learning process, or accumulation of insights. Thus Jesus' characteristic marks come to be recognized more surely and deeply, but only with time. Second, however, it is vital to see that this progression in reception is not due simply to the contingent inadequacies of faith. It is, more importantly, a function of the infinity or inexhaustibility of humanly meaningful content located in Jesus due to God's self-expression in him. The reception of him by limited human persons is only conceivable as a piecemeal, collective, and endlessly extended enterprise, one involving many imaginative projections and cultural experiments, and issuing in many failures.

Strauss believed that he had discovered Hegel's Christological secret, hidden to the latter's "right-wing" followers but confirmed for Strauss by the results of historical criticism. "Hegel . . . understood the divine human character less as an objective shape situated in the life of Jesus in itself than as a meaning that the hearts of his followers deposited into that life out of their subjective warrants."[22] The quintessentially Neo-Protestant Christological move, openly announced by Strauss, is in just this way to oppose the objective (Jesus) to the subjective (faith). The next move might then be (as with the earlier Strauss himself) to celebrate the unconscious or symbolized truth in the subjective insight while abandoning its outmoded imaginative forms, including the notion of actual instantiation in an historical individual. Or perhaps it might be (as with Troeltsch and

22 David Friedrich Strauss, *Streitschriften zur Verteidigung meiner Schrift über das Leben Jesu und zur Charakteristik der gegenwärtigen Theologie*, vol. 3 (Tübingen: C. F. Osiander, 1837), 81; *In Defense of My Life of Jesus against the Hegelians*, ed. and trans. Marilyn Chapin Massey (Hamden, Conn.: Archon Books, 1983), 25.

many other "historical Jesus" theologies) to elevate the newly recovered objective Jesus over traditional subjective confessions. Or, finally, it might be some compromise between these extremes. But which is chosen ultimately makes little difference from the standpoint of the catholic confessions of faith; once the objective-subjective disjunct is assumed, the die is cast and the fruitless game is underway.

For Strauss, the necessity of the disjunct was obvious: any Jesus discernible to historical consciousness could not possibly be divine, so the subjective content of faith (divine-human unity) had to be "deposited" into the Jesus story since it could not be its "objective shape." The result of this chapter's selective exploration of Aquinas' Christology can be most succinctly described as the reversal of this equation: the subjective confessions about Christ do not gratuitously surpass the objective truth of Jesus; rather, the objective truth of Jesus surpasses (endlessly) the grasp of subjective confession. But even so there is no disjunction here; there is only the tension of an unfinished process of assimilation, whereby subjective recognition, centered within the history of the church itself, progressively approaches the objective reality of its founder.[23]

In concluding this second part of the essay, one must not be too glib about what has been accomplished here. True, the ideas seem to be in place that could make sense of the historical human individual Jesus as the temporal presence of the eternal divine Word and the unique source of graced existence before God for all, and do so in such a way as to avoid breaking with historical consciousness. However, it should be borne in mind that the essay's rapid sketch of these ideas no doubt skims over any number of hidden difficulties; only the systematic development and detailed elaboration of these ideas could begin to work these out. But even granting the limited ambitions of the essay, there is a more pressing issue. Strauss maintained that Schleiermacher's Christ failed to satisfy not only the modern mind, but the piety of Christians. What if the way that first failure has been overcome here has left the second still in place, or in fact made it worse?

23 Even apart from the unique circumstances of the incarnation, the relational and hermeneutic character of human lives makes it difficult to sustain too sharp a distinction between a person's "objective" acts and their "subjective" reception. At any rate, the interpretive reception or cultural presence of a personal history insures the transformation of its objectivity.

Strauss' second dilemma of historical consciousness, the incompatibility of Jesus as human "fact" and Jesus as divine "appearance," has been resolved, but only in principle. That is, the conceivability of an "absolute fact" has been maintained, and a compatibility disclosed between "mere" history and hypostatic union, without the need for apologetic adjustments (overt or hidden, conscious or not) to critical judgments. But in expanding Aquinas' theology of incarnation to cover this reconciliation, has it been stretched too far out of shape? Can these mechanisms (layered causality, assumption of Jesus' integral humanity, extended pneumatic reception) support the Jesus Christ of traditional belief? Otherwise put, even if the scheme outlined in the three chapters of this part issues in a "formally" orthodox Christ, can he be "materially" countenanced by faithful people, operative in their piety as the recognizable savior?

The historical possibilities left open by this scheme of incarnation seem disturbingly wide. Granted that such historical matter can still be disposed to assume divine form, could faith withstand a picture of the "real" historical Jesus that might be painfully distant from the Gospel portraits? Could faith accept its own creative role in recognizing Jesus ever anew? Can it tolerate the unfinished character of the incarnation, such that trying to fix and cling to Jesus' identity as if it were finished results only in a repellent caricature? The Thomist incarnational scheme sketched above would make the hypostatic union reconcilable with Strauss' magnificent critical deconstruction of the Gospels. Even those useful historical motifs drawn from the "history-of-religions" Jesus could be countenanced, enabling it to serve as a sort of "proof of concept" for the scheme. But such historical conditions seem unbearably harsh for the Christian's pious embrace of Jesus the savior; that is what makes the "extreme" possibilities useful as a test case. So the lagging epiphany of Jesus as God, even if technically orthodox, presents disturbing challenges to belief. But the final part of this essay will try to show how these challenges are not simply products of radical theological speculations, but are connected with the necessary and intrinsic demands of Christian faith in the divinity of Jesus. The struggle to assimilate modern historical consciousness does not create these difficulties; they were always implicit within the radical truth of incarnation, parts of its inherent scandal only lately come to light.

Part Three

CULT OF THE UNSPEAKABLE

From Aretalogy to Teratology

7

Perils of Recognition
Occluded *Claritas* and Surreal Testimony

[The Christians] claim that Jesus' body was just like the next man's, or was little, ugly and repugnant.
Celsus | *On the True Doctrine*

[In Scripture] the spiritual truth is often preserved in the material falsehood, so to speak.
Origen | *Commentary on John*

When man resolved to imitate walking, he invented the wheel, which does not look like a leg. In doing this, he was practicing surrealism without knowing it.
Guillaume Apollinaire | *Les Mamelles de Tirésias*

I.

The point of part 2 was to show how, employing Aquinas' understanding of incarnation, it becomes possible to render a twofold divine descent as the ultimate reality (the "truth") of the historical Christ-event, a quasi-formal reality that uses the integrated history of "fact" and "appearance" without disturbing its purely immanent, cultural dynamic. In this way the second opposition within the logic of Strauss' dis-integrating Christology can be overturned, but without biasing historical judgment in an apologetic direction or abandoning history's indispensable heuristic ontology, the continuous web of finite cause and effect. The human being Jesus according to Aquinas, embodying the Word's hypostasis in a life perfectly expressing faith, hope, and love, needed an historical shape that could be the cause historically, as nucleus and positive impetus, of his own cult. But when Aquinas' incarnational concepts are read as in the previous chapter, the history in which the perfection of divine grace in a human "appears" might well incorporate the cultural type of a "son of god," a "divine man," initiating followers into the mystery of his own intimacy with God, or some other of the elements discussed in chapter 3.[1] At this point it must give the theologian pause to consider that Aquinas' ideas could in this way be employed to appropriate for Christology an historical portrayal of Jesus that would have been as shocking to him as to every other premodern Christian (and even most modern Christians as well). In fact, anyone nourished upon the pious reception of the image of Jesus in the canonical Gospels will experience a similar disorientation.

It is the intention of the third and final part of the essay to address theologically this discomfort. The basic problem is this: the Christological tools developed with the help of Schleiermacher and Aquinas allow the "formal" appropriation by the divine persons of a "material" history of Jesus and his cult that is sharply at odds with the scriptural and traditional picture. Even if this incarnational mechanism is technically in accord with the conceptuality of Chalcedon, does it not present impassible obstacles to anything like traditional faith in Jesus' divinity? The present chapter will try to show that there are indeed stumbling blocks, but they do not present faith with a sheer impasse. They are structural aspects of incarnational faith, necessary ambiguities built into the notion of the God-as-human. They challenge faith in Christ, but they do not preclude it.

Using the causal language developed earlier, it can be said that these impasses result from the fact that, if God truly speaks the eternal Word into the flesh of history and culture, the divine presence as such (eternal, omnipotent, infinite) simply cannot be directly visible in any historical

1 The point, it bears repeating, is not to commend the specific critical reconstructions of Strauss or the Smiths, but to indicate how even some of their most troubling departures from traditional views, whatever their historical viability, need not be ruled out for theological reasons or even for orthodox belief. This should always be borne in mind when motifs from ch. 3 are recalled at various points in what follows.

phenomenon. The infinite triangulation of a particular stretch of historical material by the divine form can only be visible at the observational scale of the whole; no analysis of the historical microconstituents themselves will make it apparent. This is why ecclesial faith is necessary to confess Jesus' divinity, for it is the gift of joining this ongoing history via the Spirit, enabling partial and fragile views at the Spirit's level of the entire truth-event. But if recognizing Jesus entails the total self-venture of faith, it is a perilous undertaking always threatened by the distortion involved in the "direct" view.

This first section addresses the peril associated with "layered" causality: the divinity in Jesus cannot be read off anything phenomenally "extraordinary" about him, historically or religiously. The next section deals with the peril of Jesus' nontranscendent consciousness: how can his psychological constitution and cultural horizon be truly historical, truly human, if his "I" or "who" is also the "I" or "who" of God? The third section tackles a third peril resulting from the previous two. The Jesus traditions propagated in his cult, eventually inscribed in the Gospels, provided the symbolic transformation mediating the truth of Jesus' divinity. But what possible "rule of projection" could account for the faithfulness, the truth of this mediation? Jesus' eyewitnesses could not "see" his divinity, nor could he directly communicate it to them; no accumulation or selection of accurate historical information about Jesus could comprise Scripture's ability to delineate the truth of his divinity. What accounts for it?

Turning to the first stumbling block, can faith in his deity countenance the possibility that Jesus was not in any way an extraordinary phenomenon, historically or even religiously speaking? As an individual Jesus might have possessed no characteristics that rendered him (outside his initially marginal cult) a significant political or cultural influence upon local Palestinian or Syrian thought-forms and social arrangements, nor need he be understood to have brought about unprecedented "religious experiences" in those he encountered. This would, of course, accord well with the "comparative" Jesus of the Smiths. MS sees in Jesus' initial success a "flash in the pan," not different in kind from the impact of any number of successful magicians in his day and locale. JZS assumes that the eventual influence of Christianity is finally not due in any way to "Jesus," since the latter is more or less a construct of the religious imagination operative within the scattered groups of the nascent Christian movement. Whatever cultural, political, or religious impact may be attributed directly to Jesus as an individual human being during his lifetime, it notoriously left little discernible trace in the evidentiary record. But just how disturbed should faith be if Jesus turns out to be a negligible or all-too-typical figure? Bracketing his religious ordinariness for the moment, we begin with what should be easier to deal with: his marginality for "secular" history.

That Jesus could only have played a bit part in his contemporary public world is already suggested by his near total absence from contemporary chronicles. His memory, apart from a scatter of garbled rumors and polemical asides, was preserved only in the midst of his worshipers. This would hardly be surprising, if MS's reconstruction, for example, were even partially applicable; the magician is a disreputable outsider, invisible to the standard categories of historical influence, whether political power or high-cultural excellence. Only in the imaginations of his enthusiasts could the magician directly play a world-historical role, as with the fanciful and pretentious encounters with Titus, Vespasian, and Domitian that Philostratus attributes to his Pythagorean wonder-worker Apollonius.

Not that magic as such was historically marginal; though dishonorable, it was a widespread and familiar feature of ancient Greco-Roman culture. But, as the great classicist Ulrich von Wilamowitz-Moellendorff remarked in response to the discovery of the Greek magical papyri, this does not so much elevate (à la Philostratus) the magician in the historian's eyes as humble and humanize ancient culture.

> I once heard how a distinguished scholar lamented that these papyri were found, because they deprived antiquity of the noble gleam [*vornehmen Schimmer*] of classicism. That they do is indisputable, but I rejoice in it. For I do not wish to marvel at my Hellenes, but to understand them.[2]

One thinks of the analogous shock many experienced upon discovering that the mysterious elegance of classical statuary, with its idealized white surfaces and hauntingly blank eyes, was the fortuitous byproduct of time having worn away the original gaudy paint job.

But no more than the historian should the Christian believer be troubled by the insignificance of Jesus, even if he were reduced to the taw-

2 Hans Dieter Betz, ed., *The Greek Magical Papyri in Translation*, vol. 1, *Texts* (Chicago: University of Chicago Press, 1986), li, n. 31.

dry dimensions of a magician. In the New Testament, especially in Paul, Jesus is quite necessarily a marginal figure in the eyes of this world; he not only assumes the servile human form over against God, but even in comparatively human terms his entire life-course is described as an abasement (Phil 2:7-8). The mystery of his life, culminating in his humiliating execution, is precisely that divine irony which chooses "what is low and despised in the world" to annihilate the historical powers of the age (1 Cor 1:18-31). Had the *archons* of this *aion* understood this, "they would not have crucified the Lord of glory" (1 Cor 2:8). Jesus, in short, was not a "great man," and his worshipers will certainly not seek grounds for their conviction of his ultimate significance in a miserable last gasp of the "great man theory" of history.

For the political and intellectual historian, then, Jesus himself must remain an unremarkable specimen if not a sheer question mark. But if the noble shimmer of greatness was lacking to him, did he not "glow" in another way? This is the trickier issue, namely Jesus as a religious phenomenon. Surely the cultic communities that remembered him could only have originated from the ur-community of his immediate followers, and would the latter not have been precisely those dazzled by his power as a revelation of God? In other words, perhaps the secret to Jesus' direct influence lies, if not in world-historical terms, then in spiritual ones? Must not Christian theology, at least, see in Jesus the prime instance of that disclosive category beloved of the old tradition of religious phenomenology: the theophany? But if religion itself is a fully human and historical category, then the prohibition of any direct visibility of Jesus applies just as fully here. The theorization of religion as a cultural phenomenon in fact coincides well with the theological imperative; the supposed radiant phenomena of "religious experience" deliver no explanatory benefit for the historian or the theologian.

The problem lies initially in theophany as an historically unviable category. Quite apart from the proposals examined in chapter 3, the work of JZS is notable for its convincing deconstruction of the phenomenological appeal to theophany, especially as instanced in the influential studies of Mircea Eliade. The utility of that attack for this essay lies in its clarification of historical methodology, even if it rests on JZS's deeper philosophical commitments. These latter must at least be quickly canvassed in order to show they can be laid aside even while using his critique of religious experience.

JZS's philosophical dissatisfaction with historical appeals to categories like "theophany" or "the sacred" rests on what he sees as the conceptual incoherence of the implied notion of transcendence. He draws upon William P. Alston's critique of "pansymbolism," namely that it is epistemically self-defeating to assert a reality susceptible of symbolic description only, uncontrolled by at least some nonsymbolic claims, and upon Charles Hartshorne's complaint about the "monopolar prejudice" of traditional theism, i.e., that the classical account of God arbitrarily privileges single elements, like activity or stability, of the categorial pairs that constitute our experience, elevating them into divine attributes.[3] Only two things need to be said here. From the Thomist standpoint of this essay, there would be ready agreement with the refusal of pansymbolism: valid discourse concerning God must be capable of at least some literal or nonmetaphorical predications, even if their range of meaning cannot be fully specified. On the other hand, from that same standpoint one has to respond that the putative refutation of theistic monopolarity derives its force from a metaphysical analysis of God's relation to worldly process that is far from self-evident, and in fact highly debatable. In short, these considerations can be bracketed without diminishing the cogency of JZS's methodological critique of theophany.

Eliade was the prime target here. The influence of the latter upon JZS is evident in several ways, particularly in the privileged status both give to space and its imagined organization in their accounts of the functioning of the religious mentality. "It is by virtue of its view of its place that a society or an individual . . . takes place," i.e., concretely exists.[4] Human beings are those who situate themselves within a mentally constructed (but socially

3 Smith on more than one occasion signals his indebtedness to Hans H. Penner's "trenchant critique" of Eliade's phenomenology of the sacred on just these lines: Hans H. Penner, "Bedeutung und Probleme der religiösen Symbolik bei Tillich und Eliade," *Antaios* 9 (1967): 123–43. See Jonathan Z. Smith, "'Religion' and 'Religious Studies': No Difference at All" [1988], in J. Z. Smith, *On Teaching Religion*, ed. Christopher I. Lehrich (Oxford: Oxford University Press, 2013), 77–90 at 84. Cf. Jonathan Z. Smith, "The Wobbling Pivot" [1971], in *Map Is Not Territory: Studies in the History of Religions* (Leiden: Brill, 1978), 88–103 at 92, n. 27, and Jonathan Z. Smith, *Drudgery Divine: On the Comparison of Early Christianities and the Religions of Late Antiquity* (Chicago: University of Chicago Press, 1990), 54, n. 2.

4 Jonathan Z. Smith, "The Influence of Symbols on Social Change" [1973], in *Map Is Not Territory*, 129–46 at 143–44.

realized) cosmos, and both Eliade and JZS see as crucial to this process the founding or orienting locus, the sacred, which maps the cosmic space, distributing its valued and denigrated regions. But JZS strongly opposes two central features of Eliade's scheme. Eliade assumes, first, a prior apparition of the sacred to human beings; it must disclose itself, and only then can human beings arrange their space around it, seeking to preserve the power of its appearance through mythic and ritual repetition. Second, Eliade dualizes the relation of the sacred and the profane or worldly, such that the phenomenon of the sacred always implies an ontological breakthrough of the quotidian.[5]

Against the first of these positions, JZS insists that the historian or anthropologist must regard world-foundation not as an ontological but as an anthropological event, in fact an expression of human freedom. This means that the sacred object does not appear prior to the organization of space, but is rather a product of that organization. For JZS, following Mary Douglas, placement (an imaginative, cultural process) confers sacrality, not vice versa. This in turn leads JZS to reject Eliade's second position on "platonic" dualism; the profound title essay of *Map Is Not Territory* is an exploration and critique of this "ideology of manifestation" as an explanation of religion, offering a humanist alternative. "Religion is the quest, within the bounds of the human, historical condition, for the power to manipulate and negotiate one's 'situation' so as to have 'space' in which to meaningfully dwell."[6] This negotiation involves the cultural work of continually applying the available categories of general meaning to the contingencies of experience.

One of JZS's most characteristic and perceptive points is that, contra certain understandings which exaggerate the domination of our experiential horizon by given linguistic and symbolic structures, engagement in this work actually presupposes awareness of the recurring lack of fit between that experience and even our most encompassing interpretive patterns (frequently our religious ones). This recognition of incongruity (the map is *not* the territory), far from disrupting religious consciousness, is its motor. Myth, for example, is "a self-conscious category mistake"; it is the initial mismatch involved in its application that generates the truly

5 J. Z. Smith, "Wobbling Pivot," 92–93.
6 Jonathan Z. Smith, "Map Is Not Territory" [1974], in *Map Is Not Territory*, 289–309 at 291.

constructive work of religious consciousness.[7] Only the continued, experimental extension, combination, and reformulation of the categories of meaning in face of the seductive intractability (i.e., the mystery) of lived experience allows the periodic encounter with its invisible edges. Hence JZS can say that incongruity is the vehicle of religious experience.[8]

What happens when this account of sacred experience is used to specify the religious ordinariness of Jesus? First, there will be no call to theorize his impact, whatever it may have been, phenomenologically, in terms of some "glow" of the numinous playing about his person. Nor will the properly ontological category of the miraculous (the direct impingement upon history of otherworldly power) be confused with, or deployed to account for, the cultural actuality of his wondrous performances. (The theological question of miracle will be addressed at length in the following chapter.) Second, and this is the obverse of the first point, the religious significance Jesus had or came to have was not the spontaneous "appearance" of divinity in any form, but was a function of his self-interpretation through his actions, and of the interpretive work of those who encountered him or sustained his later tradition. The actualization within religious history of his hypostatic union with the eternal Word must therefore in the first instance (not ultimately) be rendered in cultural rather than ontological terms. Third, causally speaking, the phenomenon of the human being Jesus will remain fully integrated within the overall processes of history. In *Drudgery Divine*, his masterly critique of New Testament scholarship from the standpoint of religious studies, JZS forcefully exposes the crypto-apologetic bias whereby, repeatedly, a "mythic model" of Jesus' absolute significance "has been inappropriately projected into the historical realm."

> The centre, the fabled Pauline seizure by the "Christ-event" or some other construction of an originary moment, has been declared, *a priori*, to be unique, to be *sui generis*, and hence, by definition, incomparable.[9]

But the study of religion teaches us that if Jesus was a human being, he cannot be an "originary moment," inserted into history as if from outside: "In culture, there is no text, it is all commentary . . . there is no primor-

7 Jonathan Z. Smith, "Good News Is No News: Aretalogy and Gospel," in *Map Is Not Territory*, 190–207 at 206.
8 J. Z. Smith, "Map Is Not Territory," 301.
9 J. Z. Smith, *Drudgery Divine*, 143.

dium, it is all history."[10] Culture is an historical process where meaning, including religious meaning, issues from partial and fruitful failures of that ongoing experiment where the world is grasped in myth and ritual. It is not a repetition of eruptions of supposedly alien "power."

The use of the phenomenological category of theophany in some classics of comparative religion might seem to offer exegetes or theologians a tempting point of contact between the scholarly stance and the confession of faith in Jesus' divinity. But even an orthodox Christology that affirms Jesus' ultimacy should dispense with this ontological postulate of an absolutely original "religious experience" that seeks somehow to elevate Jesus above his fully mundane historical identity. Consider the suggestive claim of Aquinas:

> It was owing to a special dispensation in Christ that before the Passion the glory of His soul did not shine out in His body, in order that He might procure His bodily glory with greater honor, when He had merited it by His passion.[11]

When this logic is applied more extensively than Aquinas himself intended, the implications of JZS's non-numinous Jesus event begin to find their properly theological and confessional analogues. In this quote Aquinas has in mind a physically sensible *claritas* of the human body as glorified by a soul enjoying the vision of God. But the point can be generalized against the subtler view that the revealing power of Jesus' person and actions are explicable via an ontology of religious manifestation.

For historical interpreters of Jesus' transfiguration story, MS proposes the pertinent datum: "[H]e could not glow in the dark."[12] And though Aquinas would have granted the objectivity of the "vision" (*hórama*, Matt 17:9) of Jesus' glory on the mountain, MS's general principle, it can now be seen, is not totally foreign even to him. Still more telling, though, is the reason *why* Jesus did not "glow" for Aquinas. The glory of Jesus' personal union with divinity was fittingly expressed in the properly human work of historical existence, whereby the private mystery of his own boundless

10 Jonathan Z. Smith, "The Domestication of Sacrifice" [1983], in *Violent Origins: Walter Burkert, René Girard, and Jonathan Z. Smith on Ritual Killing and Cultural Formation*, ed. Robert G. Hamerton-Kelly (Stanford: Stanford University Press, 1987), 191–205 at 196.

11 Thomas Aquinas, *Summa Theologiae* III q. 49 a. 6, answer to third objection.

12 Morton Smith, *Jesus the Magician* (San Francisco: Hampton Roads, 2014), 207.

openness to God was publicly interpreted by him in the shape of his life and in a fidelity to his life-choices enduring even through the final brutalities of his execution. This again can be construed as a theological restatement of JZS's approach to cultural scholarship: the divinity of Jesus finds historical expression, not just among his followers but in his own individuality, via a cultural dynamic rather than a phenomenology of extraordinary manifestation, whether sensible or merely "religious."

Finally, Aquinas points out that this "blockage" of any luminous expression of Jesus' unity with God and its redirection, so to speak (its expression via the path of his mission of perfect humanity) is due to an arrangement of that divine providence which directs the entire flow of history. Hence the "hiddenness" of Jesus' divinity, in service to his obedience to the demand to be fully human, involves the unruptured causal continuity of his life with its historical human context and antecedents. Yet another aspect of Smith's model of religious experience, namely the rejection of any absolutely "originary moment" within history, hereby finds its Christological analogue. These reflections can fittingly conclude the section. A few considerations from theology as well as from cultural theory have been employed to make a basic point. The believer can fully acknowledge Jesus' divinity, yet need not assume that this divinity corresponded at any point to the categories of the historically extraordinary, whether that of human greatness, socio-cultural momentousness, or numinous efficacy.

II.

These considerations on the functioning of human culture are not just relevant to Jesus' outer extraordinariness, but inwardly too. Adapting Aquinas' incarnational ideas was supposed to have the advantage of leaving even the mind of Jesus, as divinely appropriated, just as human and historical as his embodied acts. No subtle, internalized miracle (Troeltsch) need be posited in his case; in regard to his human consciousness he did not arrive in the cultural world of first-century Palestine (to use Strauss' quip in regard to John's Jesus) "as if shot from a pistol."[13] To take advantage of another usage in Aquinas, Jesus was the incarnate Son of God but he was not, inwardly or outwardly, a "sacred thing." For Aquinas the sacraments of the new covenant instituted by Jesus are to be distinguished from

13 David Friedrich Strauss, *The Christ of Faith and the Jesus of History: A Critique of Schleiermacher's "The Life of Jesus,"* trans. Leander E. Keck (Philadelphia: Fortress, 1977), 62.

"sacred things" (which are instituted at the discretion of the community) because they bestow grace, and this power of the sacraments stems from their participation in Jesus' personal history.[14] The point is that the divine efficacy of Jesus happens through his embodied story itself; that is the medium or matter of the infinite Spirit.

It was argued in the previous chapter that the incarnation is not God's being slotted into a structural component of the human psyche. Even if it is possible to give a more sophisticated reading of "feeling" in Schleiermacher's consciousness-Christology than one that gives it a role uncomfortably reminiscent of Descartes' pineal gland, his approach will always remain vulnerable to a critique like that of Strauss. Aquinas points instead toward incarnation as an appropriation by God-the-Word of the full humanity of Jesus. And now, thanks to the reflections of JZS, the category of humanity can be expanded beyond an individually defined set of embodied capacities. Humanity more fully is the ongoing motion of the free use of those capacities in relation to the world and other humans. Humanity, in other words, is a process; humanity is history, the story of its social and interpretive relations with itself. This can only mean that when the Word is made flesh, that flesh is not just biological or even psychological but cultural flesh.

The Word could not be made human without being made cultural, since culture is the medium of the becoming-human of every person. Culture as used here points beyond any particular historical configuration of symbolic institutions ("a culture"), even that of first-century Palestine; it refers to a process or dynamic. This process should not be hastily reduced to that quasi-mechanical (super- or sub-personal) shifting of worldviews, mentalities, or epistemes beloved of structuralist and Foucauldian theorizing. It is a creative process, a process whose engine is the imaginative freedom of individuals to locally transcend their given symbolic materials by manipulating and augmenting them. As JZS argues, culture always incorporates its own subversion; it institutionalizes the "wink" that reveals to the most fervent participant of the tribe's rituals an awareness that it is, after all, just ritual.

This imaginative permeability of culture can readily be employed in thinking about the process of Jesus' cultic recognition by later worshipers. The complex process of the posthumous deification of Jesus could appeal

14 Aquinas, *ST* I/II q. 108 a. 2, answer to the second objection.

to JZS's structural comparison between joke-making and mythmaking, both involving a self-conscious play of applying thought-categories to experience only to (partially) revoke them again, in fruitful recognition of the incongruity. The process of the deification of Jesus (in the sense of pragmatic or doxological coalescence between Jesus and the transcendent creator God) likewise follows the mythic logic of the "self-conscious category mistake": for his worshipers, his deity in this strict sense only occurs (culturally, yet, for Christian faith ontologically as well, "in the Spirit") through the oscillation between affirmations and denials of his "divinity" (in the looser, Greek sense). The faith claim "Jesus is God" happens "between" variably repeated affirmations ("Jesus is a god") and denials ("Jesus is not a god, i.e., not one of the gods"). Otherwise expressed, without the "Spirit" work of communal reception (often symbolized as commencing with Mary's "Let it be . . ." in response to the annunciation), Jesus could not have been the incarnate Word. This collective interpretive labor should not be relegated to the strange workings of the "primitive mind." It involves just that tentative "extension of categories" in face of incongruity that JZS, in an arresting passage, detects at the root of both science and mythic thinking; the latter becomes "preeminently a rational and rationalizing enterprise, an instance of an experimental method."[15]

Culture includes the (only half-suppressed) consciousness of its own artificiality; only this allows the complex improvisation with it that characterizes the human as such. This is relevant not only to the question of Jesus' later reception, but also to the issue of concern in this section, his own psychological submersion in his cultural habitat. However deeply embedded human beings are within particular cultural configurations, they are never hermetically sealed within them, because culture itself is not an *integrum*.[16] Hence there is no need to follow Schleiermacher in trying to locate a zone of Jesus' psyche where he was free of ethnic or cultural limitations.[17] His divine transcendence takes place not in spite of but rather through the assumption of the "local" transcendence that humanity realizes in its interpretive history with itself. It is not only human freedom

15 J. Z. Smith, "Map Is Not Territory," 299–300; 307–8.

16 J. Z. Smith made this important point during the panel discussion of Walter Burkert's paper in *Violent Origins*, 185ff.

17 David Friedrich Strauss, *Das Leben Jesu, kritisch bearbeitet*, vol. 2 (Tübingen: C. F. Osiander, 1835–1836), 692–93; English translation of the 4th edition: trans. anon. [George Eliot] as *The Life of Jesus Critically Examined*, 3 vols. (London: Chapman Bros., 1846), ed. Peter Hodgson (Philadelphia: Fortress, 1972), 771.

that exploits the constitutive holes within culture; through them deity itself has "leaked into" the world not through gaps interrupting the causal fabric but simply as the assumed humanity of Jesus.

But the assumption of a first-century cultural mentality by the Word, even if technically possible, cannot but present a stumbling block to faith in Jesus. As MS's rhetorical question implies, if Jesus was truly human, and truly lived in the first century, then his self-understanding and view of the world had to share in the Hellenistic and Jewish mythic milieu in which he, like everyone else around him, was formed.[18] Yet can faith in Jesus as divine really tolerate this total immersion of his mentality, i.e., his worldview and self-consciousness, within the regnant cultural forms of his epoch? In particular, if Jesus really is the "who" appropriated to the eternal Word, must he not have shared God's perfect self- and world-knowledge? As the created intellect fully elevated by grace, must he not have enjoyed the bliss of beatific vision at every moment? This is an old theological conundrum: As God he had, somehow, to "know everything"; but how could he live anything like a human life if he did? Fortunately, theology provides some conceptual resources which can be drawn upon to head off any irremediable conflict between Jesus' divinity and non-transcendent psychology, i.e., his possession of an historically, culturally, and otherwise humanly limited psyche. This section can make do with a brief outline sufficient to show that the problem is not insoluble.

For some time the real issue has not been that of any crudely understood omniscience of Jesus. It has been accepted by many Protestant theologians since the nineteenth century, and by many Catholic theologians since the middle of the twentieth, that the incarnation of the eternal Word in Jesus need not involve Jesus' actually possessing the creator's total cognition of all created reality. But a serious obstacle remains. There is a long-standing theological consensus within the Catholic tradition that insists that the human being Jesus throughout his earthly life enjoyed the full apprehension of God's essence (the so-called "beatific vision" of the angels and saints in heaven). The two problems this raises are, first, how can a perfect grasp of God's essence be compatible with Jesus' first-century mythological worldview; and, second, how can such a cognitive union with God not overwhelm Jesus' consciousness to the exclusion of all doubt, temptation, or suffering (i.e., to the exclusion of a genuinely

18 M. Smith, *Jesus the Magician*, 5.

human existence)? A better understanding of this vision of God helps to moderate these concerns (without removing the necessary tension they introduce for faith in the incarnation).

Although what follows goes well beyond anything Aquinas could have accepted, his insights provide the crucial starting point.[19] First of all, for Aquinas Jesus' unique epistemic state is an aspect of the total perfection of his human person through the special influx of God's grace. But this perfection, as was seen above, is strictly pursuant to the function of Jesus' humanity as a salvific instrument of God. The perfection, in other words, is just that perfection that enables Jesus to live a completely human life, yet free of that alienation from God called sin. This is the perfection of a particular individual in his particular history; it is not the actualization of every possibility, cognitive or otherwise, of the human nature or essence as such. The point is that "in Aquinas the principle of perfection as the basis of Christ's special knowledge was not proposed in an abstract essentialist way but was open to being qualified existentially by the demands of Christ's mission."[20]

Second, for Aquinas Jesus was cognizant of all within the created order that was directly relevant to him and his divine mission; but he had this knowledge only in and through his perfect vision of the creator's essence. This means that his perfect grasp of himself and his worldly situation was only implicit; it was not present to his consciousness as an infinite array of facts, but was rather implicated within the single, global cognitive act of knowing God.[21] Finally, for any human being the vision of God is a supernatural operation, beyond her or his immanent capacities. Aquinas takes this to mean, however, that "the beatific vision is so out of proportion to our ordinary faculties of knowledge, imagination and expression that in no way does it cut across the usual activities of these powers."[22]

Karl Rahner has been credited with helping establish in the 1950s a new paradigm for dealing with the question of Jesus' knowledge, one that enabled Catholic theology to break with the standard scholastic approach.[23] Even so, it is clear as well that in seeking a more plausibly

19 For the following compressed treatment, I gladly rely upon the illuminating survey and proposals of Raymond Moloney, S.J., *The Knowledge of Christ* (London: Continuum, 1999).

20 Moloney, *Knowledge*, 61.

21 Moloney, *Knowledge*, 60.

22 Moloney, *Knowledge*, 62.

23 Moloney, *Knowledge*, 88.

human mode of cognition for Jesus, Rahner was exploiting in a new way some of these promising avenues opened by Aquinas. Rahner himself begins from existential anthropology; the human self is essentially unbounded, with all its particular acts of will and cognition representing concretizations of a prior, pre-thematic apprehension of itself as constitutively open to the limitless horizon of being, of "what is." This is a kind of primordial experience of the self, but as oriented to the infinite act of being; hence, it is in principle also a nonconceptual grasp of God (who is the infinite act of being). Hence Rahner can argue that Jesus is the human being "who, precisely by being man in the fullest sense . . . is God's existence in the world."[24] By thus casting Jesus' unique vision of God in terms of an unequalled openness to the horizon that defines every act of human existence, Rahner adapts Aquinas' key insight that this vision is a function of Jesus' mission of perfect humanity.

Moreover, Rahner's distinction between pre-thematic experience of the self's constitutive horizon and concrete acts of cognition takes up Aquinas' understanding of implicit worldly knowledge as eminently contained within the global vision of deity. This in turn leads to the third point about the fully human modes of functioning of Jesus' cognitive faculties; they are elicited over the course of Jesus' temporal existence even as they represent concretizations of Jesus' "eternal" or "divine" but pre-thematic orientation to God. Crucially, this means Jesus' fundamental awareness of God had to be progressively translated into conceptual knowledge. This allows the affirmation both of a normal development of cognitive capacities and of growth in knowledge in Jesus, and of the inevitable expression of all Jesus' conscious awareness in terms of the cultural milieu in which he developed.[25]

Bernard Lonergan, another key contributor to this question, likewise developed insights of Aquinas into Christological positions broadly similar to those of Rahner, but improved upon the latter in certain respects. The differences between the two positions are complex, but some brief indications will suffice here.[26] Lonergan locates the primordial element

24 Moloney, *Knowledge*, 72. The wording is reminiscent of Schleiermacher; the approach is similar in some ways and different in others, as will become clear.

25 Moloney, *Knowledge*, 87.

26 The comparison is undertaken in greater detail in Raymond Moloney, S.J., "The Mind of Christ in Transcendental Theology: Rahner, Lonergan and Crowe," *Heythrop Journal* 25 (1984): 288–300.

in Jesus' subjectivity not in a pre-thematic experience of the self's infinite orientation but rather in the pre-reflective and preconceptual moment in every act of cognition. By thereby making Jesus' immediate vision of God a matter of cognition or intellection (rather than immediate self-consciousness), Lonergan shifts the intentional term of this vision. Rahner "locates Christ's immediate vision of God within his self-awareness" where, "as a function of his self-consciousness, it becomes focused on the Word of God rather than on the Father."[27] Lonergan, though, by making the vision of God a matter of intellection or understanding (which "grasps things from the point of view of their unity"), sees in that vision not Jesus' implicit awareness of his own identity with the eternal Word but rather "a mysterious and inarticulate grasp of the unity of all things in God."[28]

This has two advantages over Rahner's approach. First, the "ego" of Jesus was in fact identical with the "ego" or "I" of the divine person of the Word, but the fact of this identity does not comprise an immediate knowledge of this identity. This identity that Jesus was concretely existing, he had to "learn" through existing it (cf. Heb 5:8), complementing the immediate vision of God with a progressive judgment as to its factuality. Second, the divine term of Jesus' vision no longer becomes the Word but, more in harmony with New Testament assumptions, the Father (i.e., Jesus is the Word, but is such as perfectly knowing the Father). This makes more readily understandable how his immediate cognitive union with God could take human shape not as an awareness of being God but rather in the form of believing in God and obeying God.

The point of this very hasty overview is simply to note the availability of theological means for affirming Jesus' unique identification with God without positing a transcendent psychology. Granted the "local" transcendence of culture at the disposal of every human, there was in Jesus no sector of his consciousness detached from the cultural conditioning of his age. His self-awareness need not be located somewhere behind or above the symbolic world of his epoch, as if using it to accommodate himself to human limitations, all the while ironically enjoying a divine perspective. But if this is so, it cannot be ruled out of hand that even MS's speculated magician could have been the church's Son of God with his beatified consciousness. The possibility is only slightly more paradoxical

27 Moloney, *Knowledge*, 100.
28 Moloney, *Knowledge*, 96–97.

than the underlying assumption that he tasted the heavenly vision even as he remained a wayfarer in the world: *simul viator et comprehensor*, in Aquinas' formulation.[29]

It might seem such an extreme possibility must be ruled out since the dubious culture of magical vocation and practice could only have been fraudulently embraced by Jesus. In fact, the opposite is the case: only if Jesus truly possessed the mythological self-consciousness universal in his day could he have avoided being a charlatan. His hypostatic union with God had to assume in his consciousness contemporarily available cultural forms. There is nothing theologically that prevents the historian or exegete postulating one of these forms to involve sharing with others his own proximity to the God of heaven through the manipulation of spirits and theurgic spells. Only conscious deceit in these practices would imply a sinfulness conflicting with the ecclesial confession of his divinity. It was seen earlier that Aquinas argued for a providential dispensation of the creator allowing for the full integration of Jesus into human interactions, preventing the light of divinity from saturating his visible semblance. A similar arrangement is envisioned here, upholding in Jesus' psyche the human actualities of terror and anguish even in face of the almost preconscious enjoyment of a real but unthematized subjective immediacy to God.

> [B]y the power of the Godhead of Christ the beatitude was economically kept in the soul, so as not to overflow into the body, lest His passibility and mortality should be taken away; and for the same reason the delight of contemplation was so kept in the mind as not to overflow into the sensitive powers, lest sensible pain should thereby be prevented.[30]

III.

The last section of this chapter must deal with a third stumbling block, and perhaps the most imposing one. Christian worship of Jesus as the Son of God has from the beginning nourished itself on a sense of quasi-personal acquaintance and engagement with him as a real human being. His identifiability as a distinct individual or personality has always centered on sanctioned narrative depictions of him. His healing encounters, his wise

29 Aquinas, *ST* III q. 15 a. 10.
30 Aquinas, *ST* III q. 15 a. 5, answer to the third objection.

or startling utterances, his emotional reactions to events, all of these have been putatively conveyed to believers, first in the form of oral anecdotes and liturgical recitations, then assembled into written catenae and eventually fashioned into larger quasi-biographical confessions (gospels).

Yet the model of incarnation developed in part 2 has been structured to allow maximal openness to historical judgments about Jesus and the early church unconstrained by the traditional records. Even granting the limited but real utility of these Gospels as data for reconstructing the real Jesus, there are plausible historical grounds for accepting, and even expecting, critical results that sharply and multiply diverge from the Gospel accounts. The details are a matter of ongoing debate among exegetical scholars, but the theological question here is this: If the likely life and actions of Jesus are factually incompatible with much, or even most, of the gospel portrayal, is it possible to claim that Christian faith can identify him, and even become acquainted with him, by means of the canonical portraits? And if it is possible, how so? The upshot of the two previous sections would seem to be that the Word's appropriation of Jesus could not have been conveyed by historical reports concerning him, no matter how accurate, and that Jesus himself might well not have been in a position to bear conscious and direct witness to it either. And yet the truth of the incarnation can only and ever be available in and through the rendering of a portrait of that man that bears some kind of truth.

In what sense, in other words, can the true personal identity of Jesus, human and divine at once, be accessible through multiple, often divergent narratives, mostly devoid of eyewitness information and assembled according to mythic and aretalogical principles rather than historical ones? Entry into the question will be provided by a characteristic (and very well-informed) historical-critical judgment of the ancient materials followed by the retort of a traditionally minded literary scholar. In this memorable passage, C. S. Lewis responds to Rudolf Bultmann.

> Bultmann: "The personality of Jesus has no importance for the kerygma either of Paul or of John. . . . Indeed the tradition of the earliest Church did not even unconsciously preserve a picture of his personality. Every attempt to reconstruct one remains a play of subjective imagination." So [Lewis replies] there is no personality of Our Lord presented in the New Testament. Through what strange process has this learned German gone in order to make himself blind

> to what all men except him see? . . . If anything whatever is common to all believers, and even to many unbelievers, it is the sense that in the gospels they have met a personality. There are characters whom we know to be historical but of whom we do not feel that we have any personal knowledge—knowledge by acquaintance; such as Alexander, Attila, or William of Orange. There are others who make no claim to historical reality but whom, none the less, we know as we know real people: Falstaff, Uncle Toby, Mr. Pickwick. But there are only three characters who, claiming the first sort of reality, also actually have the second. And surely everyone knows who they are: Plato's Socrates, the Jesus of the Gospels, and Boswell's Johnson.[31]

Lewis goes on to assert that the "flavor of the personality" of Jesus in the canonical Gospels, with its mix of "peasant shrewdness, intolerable severity, and irresistible tenderness," is so distinctive that those familiar with it can reliably discern the wrongness of so much attributed to Jesus by the authors of apocryphal gospels.

What is to be made of this confrontation? Many considerations suggest themselves, but all that can be done in the remainder of this chapter is to show how the pneumatological scenario proposed in part 2 makes it possible to see beyond the apparent incompatibility of the positions of Bultmann and Lewis. First, as to Bultmann, it is hard to disagree with his assessment of the historical situation. The sort of biographical and psychological interests that motivate an evocation of "personality" as we understand it today do indeed seem absent from the culture within which circulated the anecdotes of Jesus' miracles and *logia*, eventually coalescing in the Gospels. That genuine reminiscences here and there were preserved need not be denied, but form-criticism has argued that their details and original contexts might quickly have been reshaped in the process of communal oral transmission. Besides, whatever literary skills we might wish to attribute to the final redactors of the canonical Gospels (and there are surely some grounds for admiration on that score), they do not show the kind of mastery of delicate psychological delineation possessed by some authors even in the ancient world, to say nothing of what became possible in the age of novelistic realism. In short, those who find Jesus' personality

31 C. S. Lewis, "Modern Theology and Biblical Criticism" [1959], in *Christian Reflections*, ed. Walter Hooper (Grand Rapids: Eerdmans, 1967), 156. Lewis is citing Rudolf Bultmann, *Theology of the New Testament*, trans. Kendrick Grobel, vol. 1 (London: SCM Press, 1952), 35.

portrayed in the Gospels must reckon with the fact that these documents sprang from a milieu that lacked the motive, the evidence, and the technique for that kind of composition.[32]

Yet on the other hand, there is a force in Lewis' claims that somehow remains, even in light of these historical difficulties. To be sure, not much weight can be put on the judgments of taste that reject the apocryphal Jesus stories as inappropriate. Those judgments can be readily accounted for by the overwhelming familiarity of the canonical portrait; so steeped are believers and many others in the usages of the New Testament in private devotion and public worship (and even in the mass media) that the Jesus presented there takes on a contrived naturalness. We have largely lost any sense for what is implausible or bizarre in the canonical Jesus, but are all the more readily struck by it in the unfamiliar extrabiblical accounts.[33] Christians lack the ability to encounter the Jesus of the four Gospels straight on, so to speak; every reading takes place within a long-established context of worshipful assimilation. But this integral, personal connection of readers with the material provides an initial clue for justifying Lewis' instinctive insistence that in these readings we have "met a personality."

The argument in previous chapters was that the total process of incarnation involves formative appropriation of the historic "Christ-event" by dual divine missions, one in the individual Jesus himself and another in the communities worshiping him. Jesus "rises," historically speaking, as the cultic presence of the original wonder-worker is received and processed through the imaginative labor of cultic recognition. Theologically speaking, it is the providentially arranged double-arrival of the eternal

32 Lewis knows perfectly well that the art of modern realistic narrative was lacking to the gospel "authors." How else, then (he concludes), can we account for their "realism" than by conceding that the Gospels are "reportage" based on direct contact with Jesus? See Lewis, "Modern Theology," 155. But this depends upon the prior literary judgment that these narratives are indeed "realistic." Is this a sound judgment, or is it inevitably informed by the devotional familiarity of these texts, which has (rightly) drawn from believers a rich, imaginative investment that continually "fills out" stories in which incident and character are barely indicated?

33 Cf. William Wrede's comment, cited in Morton Smith, *Clement of Alexandria and a Secret Gospel of Mark* (Cambridge, Mass.: Harvard University Press, 1973), 200: "Schleiermacher has already remarked that [the Gospel of Mark] approximates the characteristics of the apocryphal ones. . . . [O]ne thing seems to me certain: If this Gospel came to light today, for the first time, in some grave, Schleiermacher's judgement would be approved by more than a few."

Word and the eternal Spirit in the respective complexes of facts inhabiting the two sides of this transaction that fuses them into a single communication of divine truth, where God in Jesus is truly (which also means transformatively) heard, and the incarnation itself continues to occur. But according to the allegory of the guitar hero, the original formation and the continuing religious reception of the Gospels is itself an integral part of this entire process; it is a crucial part of the system of projection that makes Jesus' characteristic humanity posthumously living and available for later generations. The point is that the ongoing possibility of recognizing Jesus as a distinctive individual in and through the Gospels cannot reside exclusively in the biographical accuracy or literary skill of those documents, a weight they could not bear; it must also be grounded in the theologically postulated ontology underlying the very particular reading communities in which they are interpreted, making up the church. Only through the special involvement of God both in Jesus and in a divinely determined segment of his worshipers can the Gospels connecting them be literally nonfactual to a large degree, and yet in effect true.

To apprehend this possibility in more detail, start with a prior question: how does a human personality "happen"? Embodiment (with its equipment of innate impulses and biases) is initially trained through socialization; the organism acquires an expanding repertoire of meaningful gestures, words, and actions, as elicited and shaped by institutions and personal engagements. Over a span of time, "character" is built up as these gestures congeal into habitual patterns; both in routine performances and in spontaneous reactions to unforeseen events, the range of human attributes becomes uniquely configured, expressing an elusive but recognizable human center: the universal mystery of personhood takes form as an individual. In the case of Jesus, however, superimposed upon that general human mystery and expressing itself through it is the even deeper mystery of the divine self-relation, the eternal Word. As was said, this does not actualize in Jesus the totality of human possibility and meaning; however, as unified with the infinite significance of deity he nonetheless enjoys an unfathomable surplus of humanity, as it were.[34] This surplus extends far

34 Cf. on this point Cornelius Ernst, "Theological Methodology" [1970], in *Multiple Echo*, ed. Fergus Kerr O.P. and Timothy Radcliffe O.P. (London: Darton, Longman & Todd, 1979), 76–86 at 84–86; and the comments of Rowan Williams, "The Finality of Christ," in *On Christian Theology* (Oxford: Blackwell, 2000), 93–106 at 93–94.

beyond what Jesus himself could have presented even in a longer span of biological life. Besides, such a span in others typically leads only to further concentration of their own basic personal qualities, slowly hardening as new characteristic gestures give way to mere repetition. The personality of Jesus, however, did not become exhausted in this way; it was a kind of reservoir waiting to enter into catalytic engagements with ever-new human situations. But how could this happen after his death?

Most Christians believe (and this is perhaps the most basic, and basically scandalous of all their beliefs) that Jesus, though he really died, is not now dead but alive. He exists as a new body, a part (in fact, the axis) of the new aeon, the world as it is to be transformed by God. But in this form Jesus is not directly accessible under the conditions of the old aeon; he no longer enacts his personality in this world through a body whose physicality is compatible with our own. That is where the Jesus-communities play their part, embodying the second mission of God, the sending of the Spirit. The Spirit is, like the Word, God's own self-relation. This means that the same human personality expressing the hypostatic union with the Word comes to find thousands of new shapes, new embodiments, in the communities whose worshipful interpretations of Jesus are possessed and directed by the divine Spirit which is the selfsame "Spirit of Jesus." Providential guidance shapes their individual and collective cultural transactions into an ongoing temporal arrival of the eternal Spirit. Which brings us back to the point of concern in this section: one product of this process is multiple new imaginings of Jesus' humanity. Possessing only fragmentary lore concerning his real history, worshipers from the beginning have elaborated upon and recombined these fragments and unconsciously united them with what seem fitting characterizing moments gathered from their own experiences of personhood, as lived day by day in the community of the redeemed. The result is a kind of imaginative mosaic that nonetheless supports a continually renewed sense of what Jesus "must have been like," and therefore who he continues to be.

But how can this composite persona, cobbled together from select pieces of later and different lifeworlds, be the form in which believers become genuinely acquainted with Jesus, especially given that his historical (i.e., past) persona is now inaccessible? This would demand, first, that the "surplus" of humanity in Jesus is truly being shared out among the human beings falling within the field of his instrumental use by God.

The particular human possibility resulting from the Word's union with an individual self, definitively yet only partially expressed in Jesus' lifetime, enters via God's providential shaping of historical causality into catalyzing connections with the particular possibilities of other human beings and groups and hence comes to fuller human expression. These elements are "borrowed" from the reservoir of human personhood implicit within Jesus; as catalyzed by him, he has mysteriously anticipated these moments in his own earthly life, though they could not have attained their later forms within the limits of his original story.

But for these variant repetitions of Jesus' humanity to enable an acquaintance with his original persona, there is needed, second, the work of the Spirit. The Spirit shaping the communities of his followers was his Spirit as well, and after his resurrection continues to be the "breath" which enlivens his new, absent body as well as the body of believers still living under the old aeon. In other words, because both the Word (in Jesus) and the Spirit (in the communities of faith) are self-relations of the selfsame God, a single respiration organically unites with Jesus' new body the communal body that continues to represent Jesus as a sign in the old world. The continuing cultural process of faithful interpretation and assimilation in Christian lives, as formed by the eternal missions, constitutes Jesus' "sign-body"; it is not really detached but a kind of living appendage pneumatically directed by the risen embodied Jesus as its "head." Under the force of this providentially engineered organic arrangement, when members of the community, as members of his body, continually project back upon his earthly life their imagined instances of his humanity, some of these fragments of meaning are marshalled into events of partial but genuine recognition. That is, aspects of this composite imagined persona are, again and again, selectively verified as identifications of him. This can happen because the assembled units of later "redeemed" human meaning are catalyzed by and appropriated from his personal surplus, and thus are expansions, transpositions, or transfigurations of the human personality actually expressed in his original life.

The oral and literary prehistory and eventual composition of many "gospels" concerning Jesus are special instances within this general series of events, but the communal selection of the four canonical examples is, for believers, an especially privileged moment, guided by God and decisive for all later recognition of Jesus. The result can be likened to the familiar biographical phenomenon of the incorrect but nonetheless "true" anecdote. The recounting of some statement or gesture has come to partially define our image of some well-known figure, though research reveals it to be falsely attributed. Yet those who are deeply familiar with the person, either personally or archivally, reply that the witty saying (for example), though not literally factual, is nonetheless utterly true to her character and manner, genuinely revealing her personality: she may not have said it, but she certainly could have, or should have. In the divinely guided relationship between Jesus of Nazareth and the cultural processes active among his later worshipers, something like this arises in the gospel phenomenon, only on a much larger scale. The miracle stories, memorable quips, polemical exchanges, discourses, passion accounts, and resurrection appearances that make up the canonical Gospels are not just incompatible with each other at numerous points, as Strauss expertly showed. They are not even for the most part factual reportage, or have been decontextualized and resituated to such a degree that their original reference has been forgotten. And yet in the properly disposed mind of the readers seeking to encounter Jesus, they do coalesce into an imaginative portrait that genuinely discloses the narrative shape of his personal identity, and even, perhaps, conveys the flavor of his personality.

The many details of what is being proposed in this section would require extensive development. The major point to be emphasized is that even the most thorough historical skepticism about the literal truth of the Gospels cannot exclude the theological possibility that they function as a genuine medium of personal recognition. The interaction of Christians in prayer and worship with the living Jesus, though inevitably steeped in their contemporary imaginative forms, is still an ever-new encounter with his first-century personality as mediated by the rough but generatively authentic diagram of that persona obliquely rendered and fixed within the Gospels. The current imaginings, inserted into the framing depiction of the Gospels, fill out his recognizable persona with ever-new details (though this supplementation is typically spontaneous and unconscious). The critic might be compelled to judge the Gospels as they stand to be largely a tissue of historical fabrications, and yet the believer is not mistaken: the true face of Jesus of Nazareth, his modes of encounter with others, his personal presence, his "style," are, still and always, to be found there. The interpretive route is neither straightforward nor without risks, but in these writings the faithful can come to know not a principle or idea, but the one whom they follow, petition, and worship.

So then Bultmann's protest stands, yet Lewis wins his point as well. To be sure, though, the latter's adduced parallels obscure what is unique in the case of the writings about Jesus. Boswell's biography was informed by a longtime intimate friendship with his subject, to say nothing of a rare skill in realistically depicting character in words. Plato's early dialogues likewise spring from a personal familiarity with Socrates, and many passages strike us as masterful evocations of an unmistakable voice; notably, though, Plato's passionate "interest" in that voice as an oracle of truth progressively drains the life out of his Socrates, eventuating in the pallid spokesman of the later dialogues. By contrast, the transmitters and redactors of the gospel Jesus somehow render a real personality though lacking any direct familiarity with him. And unlike Plato's dialogues, in the Gospels, communal products arising from the continuing process of the incarnation, the "interest" of later religious passion does not overwhelm the past persona, but more energetically evokes it. In the end, Bultmann's "play of subjective imagination" and Lewis' "knowledge by acquaintance" are, by means of the Spirit's communal operations, one and the same.[35]

The Gospels therefore present an array of partial recollections transformed and supplemented by a much larger accretion of material filtered through the community's mythic and confessional consciousness. This disparate mass is fused into an authentic rendering of Jesus' divine humanity not by artistic genius but by the energy of Spirit, what might be called the spiritual "heat" emitted in Jesus' resurrection. This is not to say the Gospel writers wrote without genre exemplars or literary technique; it is not easy, however, to identify the kind of literary skill or artifice at work in the Gospels. Though Hans Frei argued for the utility of "realistic narrative" in understanding how these writings convey the personal identity of Jesus, the circumstances of their production as envisioned in this chapter limit the applicability of that stylistic category.[36] For his part, Paul Tillich suggestively compared the New Testament portraits of Jesus to expressionist art; this certainly captures their fantastic or nonrealistic

35 Lewis, "Modern Theology," 156.

36 Hans W. Frei, *The Identity of Jesus Christ: The Hermeneutical Bases of Dogmatic Theology* (Philadelphia: Fortress, 1975).

component, but from the present perspective it misplaces the emphasis.[37] Seeing in them a recognizably real figuration whose exaggerations and distortions bespeak the personal and evaluative stance of the chroniclers is instructive but does not take us very far.

For the accuracy of the Gospels lies not in their subjective authenticity, but in an almost eerie kind of objectivity. Yet neither does their "realism" spring from reliance upon an evidentiary record provided to their creators but from a pneumatic automatism; divinely inspired, the Christians collectively and spontaneously produced their Jesus. This is not at all to revive the crude picture of the biblical writers as mechanical "scribes" of the Spirit; here as always providence works through human freedom, not contrary to it. Rather, they simply wrote what was in them, and in so doing wrote truly. In bringing together the most diverse imaginative elements, and in default of factual support that an historian would regard as reliable, they somehow "found" his persona. For actual stylistic models the later Gospels had Mark, and Mark perhaps had aretalogical precedents; but to account for their mysterious verity-without-verisimilitude there is no real technique to be isolated, only the following loose analogy.

The French poet Pierre Reverdy located a special revelatory power in "a juxtaposition of two more or less distant realities": "The more the relationship between the two juxtaposed realities is distant and true, the stronger the image will be—the greater its . . . poetic reality." André Breton gave a key role to this insight in his 1924 Surrealist Manifesto.[38] Perhaps the Gospels are best understood as surrealist artifacts avant la lettre. These spontaneous narrative transcriptions of faith in Jesus are extravagantly nonfactual, and yet not false; their personal accuracy is poetic, a product not of descriptive fidelity or critical judgment but of uncannily juxtaposed sayings and stories and the repeated clash of realistic and fantastic narrative registers. How else to express the truth of an ordinary history in the grip of transcendence?

Something of what is in mind here is evoked by Hannah Arendt's reflections on Walter Benjamin's compositional strategy of obsessively stockpiling quotations and excerpts for redeployment in his own texts. "The main work consisted in tearing fragments out of their context and

37 Paul Tillich, *Systematic Theology*, vol. 2, *Existence and the Christ* (Chicago: University of Chicago Press, 1957), 115–16, 151.

38 André Breton, *Manifestoes of Surrealism*, trans. Richard Seaver and Helen R. Lane (Ann Arbor: University of Michigan Press, 1969), 20.

arranging them afresh in such a way that they illustrated one another and were able to prove their *raison d'être* in a free-floating state, as it were. It definitely was a sort of surrealistic montage."[39] The communal production and/or reproduction of the Gospels suggest a similar process at work, though no doubt driven less by a self-conscious strategy than an implicit sense of fittingness. The very rationale of the reverse-aretalogy presses toward a surrealist mosaic that disrupts the archaic contexts of religious veneration to liberate fragments naming the newly elusive presence of deity. Even the motivation here is similar to that of Benjamin: the past has become radically questionable in light of "eschatologized" transcendence, its truth no longer retrievable via the solid authority of tradition but only through subversive bricolage. The Gospel portraits, in short, are perhaps best thought of as super-real, delivering in language an individual self-presentation that really is that of Jesus, though it does not (literally) reproduce what his personality "looked like."

To conclude, this chapter has identified three kinds of danger associated with the sort of processes of imaginative recognition of Jesus' deity demanded by the model of incarnation developed in part 2. The thoroughly ordinary historical and religious efficaciousness of Jesus; his complete psychic submersion in the symbolic systems common to his location; and the unreal yet unerring transmission of his divinized truth via oral and literary media: these have been shown to be authentic possibilities, theologically speaking. However, even if faith in the Savior can, and in some sense must reconcile itself to these possibilities, there is no denying the keen challenges they will continually present to that faith. They cannot be intellectually dissolved or dismissed; they must be painfully worked through, again and again, by the faith that seeks understanding. Each of the three are rooted in the paradox arising from the basic idea of the incarnation as an infinite deposit within the human world of meaning: Jesus as God's perfect sign in history can only be read as such as the sign itself disappears from direct view.

Jesus and his "original" deity had to get out of the way, so to speak, in order for his divine humanity to be repeatedly and variously "discovered" again by his communities. Thus it was good for him to leave, good *for us* as the evangelist has him say (John 16:7). The necessary conjunction between the bodily absence of Jesus and the collective, "spiritual" (i.e., at once cultural/linguistic

39 Hannah Arendt, introduction to *Illuminations: Essays and Reflections*, by Walter Benjamin (New York: Schocken Books, 1968), 47.

and divinely inspired) modalities of his posthumous power and presence have been explored in complementary ways by Eberhard Jüngel and Michel de Certeau. For Jüngel, "Jesus' effectiveness consists in his *death*, in his *withdrawal*, which faith in his resurrection does not reverse but rather confirm.... [T]he *absence* of Jesus gave rise to the *New Testament* as a testimony to his presence."[40] And Certeau concludes that "Christianity was founded upon *the loss of a body*—the loss of the body of Jesus Christ, compounded with the loss of the 'body' of Israel, of a 'nation' and its genealogy."[41]

These observations on Jesus' generative absence are usefully elaborated upon in Certeau's brilliant reflections regarding Christian faith as an historical phenomenon. The fundamental approach of this chapter, indeed of the entire essay, is deliberately continuous with Certeau's position, the spirit of which is well summarized in the following:

> The process of the death (the absence) and the survival (the presence) of Jesus continues in each Christian experience: What the event makes possible is different each time.... There is a relation of kenosis to glory, of disappearance to manifestation. . . . The "empty tomb" is the condition of possibility for a spiritual knowledge, i.e., for a "verification" which expresses itself and extends into the era of the word and the Spirit. . . . Thus, the initial event becomes an *inter-locution*: something *said-between*, implied by all the Christian languages but given by no one of them.... [T]he founder disappears; he is impossible to grasp and "hold," to the extent that he is incorporated and takes on meaning in a plurality of "Christian" experiences, operations, discoveries, and inventions. . . . *[T]he "kenosis" of presence gives rise to a plural, communitarian language.*[42]

40 Eberhard Jüngel, "Die Wirksamkeit des Entzogenen: Zum Vorgang geschichtlichen Verstehens als Einführung in die Christologie," in *Gnosis: Festschrift für Hans Jonas*, ed. Barbara Aland (Göttingen: Vandenhoeck und Ruprecht, 1978), 15–32 at 32; English edition: "The Effectiveness of Christ Withdrawn," in *Theological Essays*, trans. John B. Webster (Edinburgh: T&T Clark, 1989), 214–31 at 231 (emphasis in original).

41 Michel de Certeau, *La Fable Mystique: XVIe—XVIIe Siècle* (Paris: Gallimard, 1982), 109; English edition: *The Mystic Fable*, vol. 1, *The Sixteenth and Seventeenth Centuries*, trans. Michael B. Smith (Chicago: University of Chicago Press, 1992), 81 (emphasis in original).

42 Michel de Certeau, "La rupture instauratrice" [1971], in *La Faiblesse de Croire*, ed. Luce Giard (Paris: Éditions du Seuil, 1997), 183–226 at 213–14; English edition: "The Inaugurating Rupture, or: How Is Christianity Thinkable Today?" *Theology Digest* 19 (1971): 334–45 at 337–38 (emphasis in original).

If there is a submerged connection between this theological insight and JZS's humanist critique of the phenomenology of epiphany, it is because both are guided by an analysis of culture as the open-ended exchange and communication of meaning.

To make the connection explicit, if the Word inhabits the cultural flesh of history, then the incarnation will bear some of the marks of human semiosis. This includes the three perils of recognition discussed in this chapter, all of which turn on the unavailability, the absence of Jesus' own historical body. There is a fundamental semiotic truth here.

> The structuredness of the sign system presupposes time, for it is time, as Hegel already demonstrated quite nicely, that by letting a sound sink into the past (and thus fade out) first allows the following sound to articulate itself in its differentness from the previous one. . . . [T]he disappearance of the body of the word, by making room for a second one . . . simultaneously allows the internal element—the significance of the sign—to appear.[43]

The implication is that the stumbling blocks to belief in the incarnation are not accidental byproducts due to secularity, inhospitable philosophies, or other supposed manifestations of our age's faithlessness. They are rather necessary and inherent in the incarnational faith itself; they mean that faith's natural urge to grasp for a direct visibility of Jesus within history is to be resisted as a temptation. That is, they are conceptual explications of that enigmatic provocation that seems to emanate from Jesus' person in the Gospel narratives.

The "inaugurating rupture" in the webs of human speech of which Certeau writes is not "epiphanic" if that is supposed to mean a punctual event where meaning is simply given to the observer. Here as everywhere in human semiosis, there is no provision of meaning apart from the constitutive human act of interpretation. The Word, like every word, must be heard, and hearing is always in part determined by the hearer; as Aquinas insists in many places, "The thing known is in the knower according to the mode of the knower."[44] To put it semiotically, the sign is not a radiance, and if Jesus is indeed the Word made flesh, his epiphany is not like a

43 Manfred Frank, *What Is Neostructuralism?* trans. Sabine Wilke and Richard Gray, Theory and History of Literature 45 (Minneapolis: University of Minnesota Press, 1989), 354.

44 For example, *ST* I q. 14 a. 1 ad 3.

beacon, centered and powerful at its point of origin, illuminating passive viewers. It must rather suffer the detours and delays of belief's repeated acts of interpretation. This lagging epiphany is again not unfamiliar from certain discussions of linguistic meaning; the quote from Frank finds its complement in one of the epigraphs opening this book: "There is thus no phenomenality reducing the sign or the representer so that the thing signified may be allowed to glow finally in the luminosity of its presence."[45] This delay of epiphany is a key to understanding the dimension of possible Christological offense built into the faith; the final two chapters now turn more explicitly to explore this dimension, including its particular manifestations under the impact of historical consciousness, and the corresponding ways faith must endure the challenge.

45 Jacques Derrida, *Of Grammatology*, 40th anniversary ed., trans. Gayatri Chakravorty Spivak (Baltimore: Johns Hopkins University Press, 2016), 54.

8

The Sign of Offense
Miracle as Fact and as Trial

> The external . . . sign is always known both as a real fact, interwoven with the entire fabric of human experience, and . . . as constituting part of another world, [for] inner grace does not present us with new objects of knowledge. . . . The apostle Thomas "saw the man and believed in the God," as the Fathers quite aptly put it. But the God and the man were the same Christ Jesus.
>
> **Pierre Rousselot | "The Eyes of Faith"**

> Signs are taken for wonders.
>
> **T. S. Eliot | "Gerontion"**

I.

Jesus, though he was the absolute fact (*because* he was the absolute fact), was historically unexceptional, ordinary through and through. Though he was the eternal Word incarnate (*because* he was the eternal Word incarnate), the consciousness in which he experienced his world and himself was saturated by the cultural currents of his time. The Gospels, though they truly testify of the absolute fact (*because* they truly testify of the absolute fact), are filled with mythic fictions and contrafactual claims. The previous chapter has examined these stumbling blocks merely objectively, that is to say, as qualities inherent in Jesus or the New Testament that are defensible in terms of the logic of incarnation. The task in the final two chapters of the essay will be to turn toward pondering some of the subjective impact of the overall picture suggested by these paradoxes. Faith as a mode of existence in history can never acquire a fully unambiguous perception of Jesus' divinity. How does it avoid succumbing to the lure of claiming, or attempting to realize, its direct visibility?

In particular, our concern here will focus on two manifestations of that constitutive possibility of offense that faith in Jesus must confront, both springing from the utter historicity and quasi-semiotic character of God's full appearance in time (what we have called lagging epiphany). The first, dealt with in this chapter, is the invincible ambiguity of the superhuman performances attributed to Jesus by which faith has traditionally been assured of his absolute or divine status; the second, reserved for chapter 9, is the disorienting lack for faith of any secure personal and imaginative grasp of Jesus' unified and final human identity or personhood. The goal in each chapter will be to indicate all too briefly how these possibilities must inevitably haunt faith, how both have been exacerbated by modern historical consciousness, and what, in response, is the narrow path that faith, guided by theological reflection, must tread.

The accounts of Jesus' deeds of power are treated here from a quite specific (and specifically theological) point of view, namely as a salient aspect of the offense faced by faith in the incarnation. Our particular concern must be disentangled from other connected issues; the question of interest is neither historical nor metaphysical. Not historical: the question is not whether Jesus claimed to perform extraordinary acts of power, or was credited with such performances during his lifetime. That is a question for exegetes and historians. One could imagine MS and Strauss standing at different poles on a question like this. The former hypothesizes that wondrous performances were central to Jesus' public career; the latter is more or less free to attribute most or all of these accounts to the mythic and legendary imagination of the later generations of Jesus enthusiasts who eventually produced the New Testament. Not metaphysical: the question is not whether an omnipotent creator could cause, in or through Jesus, various acts which were scientifically inexplicable or which suspended or violated natural law. If omnipotence is taken in the classical sense, as Aquinas does, for example, such acts would certainly not be impossible.

The question of concern is not these, but is properly theological: Is it necessary for faith in Jesus as the incarnate Word to believe or assert that he performed miraculous deeds? Must one grant not just that he regularly performed extraordinary or inexplicable actions, but that these actions were in fact direct interventions of divine power, objectively disrupting natural regularities?[1] The question, as Lessing saw long ago, is one of religious testimony and religious faith's role in assessing that testimony.[2] It is a matter of theologically weighing the claims of tradition and Scripture that Jesus actually performed this or that miracle. But though the issue is now situated firmly within the theological sphere, it is still not precise enough; even granting faith in Jesus as God incarnate, there are different possible grounds for theologically (in service to religious belief) asserting that Jesus performed miracles in the strict sense.

Theology might adduce historical grounds for asserting Jesus' miracles, indirect faith grounds, or direct faith grounds. However, from the standpoint developed in this essay, the first two kinds of argument carry no weight. The first occurs when faith itself wants to appeal to evidence and historical judgment to maintain that something strictly miraculous must have occurred; a transcendent cause beyond history is said to be the only satisfactory way of accounting for what happened. But invoking a nonhistorical cause cannot serve as an historical explanation for any event. The entire logic of historical method makes it pointless to propose suspensions of natural regularity in an explanatory way; to do so tends to dissolve historical judgment as such, substituting arbitrariness and special pleading. Historical consciousness need not proclaim the global impossibility of miracles, which would be beyond its competence anyway. It simply needs to point out the vanishingly small probability in any given case that one has occurred. Prejudice or misunderstanding in the particular source testifying to a miracle is always bound to appear historically more likely. The second sort of argument mentioned, indirect faith grounds, refers to the general erosion of credibility potentially suffered by tradition

1 The appeal, frequent in these discussions, to the prescientific worldview of the scriptural authors is not pertinent; they understood perfectly well that multiplying food, exorcising demons, or walking on water were impossible in regard to natural human abilities and required transcendent intervention.

2 Gotthold Ephraim Lessing, "On the Proof of the Spirit and of Power" [1777], in *Philosophical and Theological Writings*, ed. and trans. H. B. Nisbet, Cambridge Texts in the History of Philosophy (Cambridge: Cambridge University Press, 2005), 83–88.

or Scripture generally should the miracle accounts prove historically unreliable (a major concern for Schleiermacher, for example). Clearly the discussions earlier in the essay concerning the kind of historical truth attributable to the Gospels rob this argument of force.

The foregoing comments, hardly adequate as an analysis of the highly ramified problem of the miraculous, are meant only to specify the question of concern here: What dogmatic stake does faith have in asserting positively that Jesus performed miracles, formally defined? Now the answer can be proffered: none at all. There is no inevitable and essential connection between belief in the hypostatic union and the claim that Jesus repeatedly performed acts that transcended the regular course of nature. The historical surmises introduced in chapter 3 invite us to accept wondrous performances as playing a big role in Jesus' activity, bigger, perhaps, than many exegetes might be comfortable with, but the theological model of incarnation developed in part 2 removes any compelling reason for insisting that these performances must have been miraculous, and therefore that the reports about them must be fundamentally distinguished from the infinite number of similar reports from other religious and cultural contexts.

The situation is this. There can be no solid historical evidence for miracles as such, and no good historical reason for asserting them. For that very reason, their apologetic value, once held to be so important, must be radically questioned. Then again, understanding and believing the Gospel witness to Jesus' divinity is in no way dependent upon accepting his performances as miracles, even when their factuality is not in doubt (and a comparative cultural study of the way religious veneration commonly shapes narratives might provide plenty of reasons to question that factuality). Finally, these performances themselves play no systematic role in actualizing the union of the eternal Word and the human being Jesus. They could never be ruled out, of course, granted any full-blooded doctrine of God's creative transcendence. But historically speaking either contemporary magical practices (MS) or the fictions of mythic imagination (Strauss) or some combination of the two will be sufficient to account for the miracle stories of Jesus. As for faith, the believer can never *know* what they were.

In other words, Jesus' deeds of power must remain ambiguous for faith. Their essential role as testimony is thereby undisturbed; they are textually indispensable, along with other key semantic tokens woven into the evangelical narratives witnessing to Jesus' true divine identity. But they share in the sign-character of the Word made flesh. Neither historically nor theologically can their ambiguous ontological status as actual events be resolved, i.e., made theoretically decidable. They might have been Jesus' masterly human exploitation of an available structure of cultural expectations (in fact, if they occurred they were certainly at least that); they might also have been extraordinary omnipotent interventions. But Christological orthodoxy can have no theological interest in compelling the latter view. As wonders they prove nothing; as signs they indicate the truth, but they must be interpreted aright, within the entire web of believing consciousness. Their potential to scandalize faith cannot be removed, but this ambiguity is part and parcel of incarnational belief itself; it is not a byproduct of modern considerations, though they undoubtedly render it more arresting and more urgent.

The ambiguity in question is already presumed in the Gospel accounts themselves, and accords well with the reverse aretalogical style of hypertranscendence. Most of the observing crowd, and even the disciples themselves at their least perceptive, see and believe in the "miraculous" status of Jesus' deeds, yet fail to discern their meaning as markers of his real nature. Hence "flesh and blood" cannot reveal this nature (Matt 16:17); it must be revealed from above. This traditional form of unreadability might be called "epistemological ambiguity," because the presupposition is that Jesus' deeds really were miracles in the strictest sense, but they were empirically indistinguishable from magical or demonic operations. The model of layered causality employed in this essay, however, where immanent history is informed by transcendent appropriation without interrupting its strict causal rhythms, invites a deeper unreadability of Jesus' deeds, an "ontological ambiguity."

On this account, theology should begin from the assumption that his acts are humanly explicable as such, at every point, scientifically, psychologically, culturally. Belief, however, is challenged to read them as historical ingredients taken up by a strong pneumatology (a providential, incarnational shaping of the temporal order from within); they are part of the array of signals surrounding the temporal presence of the eternal Word. In other words, not even the mighty deeds of Jesus represent the Word's breakthrough to direct visibility. This theological picture dovetails with a critical historical assessment of the Gospels and other Jesus traditions that can convincingly trace the utterly typical and culturally stereotyped character of these wonder-stories. The recognition of that character thanks to modern historical consciousness in no sense inaugurates a brand-new situation. Ontological ambiguity is not a terrible novelty faith must bear, but an aggravation of the burden that has always been present. It keeps open the dangerous possibility that Jesus' acts might be, instead of the self-presentation of the Word, *no more than* fully human acts, because it maintains that they were always *at least* fully human acts.

II.

This question of ambiguity requires further theological exploration which can only be initiated here. First, it should be noted that the focus is on discrete actions attributed to Jesus' own agency. Strauss, following Herder, had recognized an additional sort of gospel miracle: those "three luminous points in the life of Jesus which attest his heavenly mission," namely the phenomena attending his baptism, his transfiguration, and his resurrection. Analogously, this discussion will bracket special cases where the narrative "relates to a miracle which took place *in* Jesus instead of a miracle performed *by* him."[3] Two such cases in particular should not be regarded as spatiotemporally isolable happenings but rather as grand configurations of events, observable as such only on the level of the "whole" incarnational reality. These two cases do not correspond to any particular identifiable historical occurrence, and faith cannot grant the possibility of their merely human reduction without collapsing.

One such "miracle which took place *in* Jesus" might symbolically be termed his "transfiguration," but this would not refer to the narrated luminous episode on Mt. Tabor when Jesus' face and clothing "*metemorphōthe*" (Mark 9:2). It would rather designate the entire metamorphic event that historically includes the cultural processes of his posthumous apotheosis, and that theologically signifies the ongoing unfolding of his actual identity in his communities. There is here no isolated fact but an entire pattern of events. The other bracketed case would be the resurrection, that "sign of

3 David Friedrich Strauss, *Das Leben Jesu, kritisch bearbeitet*, vol. 2 (Tübingen: C. F. Osiander, 1835–1836), 238; English translation of the 4th edition: trans. anon. [George Eliot] as *The Life of Jesus Critically Examined*, 3 vols. (London: Chapman Bros., 1846), ed. Peter Hodgson (Philadelphia: Fortress, 1972), 535 (emphasis in original).

Jonah" that even some of the Gospels have Jesus put in a special category.[4] The standpoint of this essay, as should by now be clear, shares the assumption of traditional Christian faith that Jesus is really, bodily alive and not dead; his reality cannot be subsumed into the believing attitudes of his followers. Instead, the faith is compelled in regard to the postmortem existence of Jesus to speak in an unusual sense of "the king's two bodies," i.e., Jesus' sign-body effective in history (the church) but also his hidden life even now clothed in the new flesh of the coming kingdom. In this case, too, historically speaking there is no positive fact at issue in the raising of Jesus, but rather a mysterious kind of absence or empty space in the texture of the temporal world-order. These two provisos still leave, of course, the great bulk of Jesus' marvelous deeds to be dealt with.

Whatever the metaphysical intelligibility or plausibility of possible divine suspensions of natural law, historical judgment gives no ground to assert them, and an orthodox Christological confession in no way demands them, as explanations of Jesus' recorded actions. Jesus is the formal and operative self-presence in the world of God the eternal Word, but this is not an operation in isolation; in this sense too the patristic dictum holds true: *opera trinitatis ad extra indivisa sunt*. The incarnation involves the double mission, where the Word formed as Jesus is communally heard by the Spirit formed as the church; both presuppose the Father's providential disposition of the efficient patterns of historical causality. Jesus' humanity can operate as the Word because it is a created instrument of non-created power, but as human it is not thereby detached from the created order; in the production of worldly effects, it is still integrated with or mediated by the regulated providential flow of the cosmos as a whole.

Whatever discrete deeds Jesus performed, they were human deeds, finding their significance and effectiveness where his own self-understanding expressing itself through them entered the field of public, already-given symbolic meanings in which all such acts occur. Their function as signs of his deity relies upon, in fact is part of, the same act of divine appropriation that defined the pattern of his personhood as a whole; it relies as well upon the Spirit at work shaping their reception. Hence, there is no direct Christological need to be met by taking "signs," the recorded performances of Jesus, for "wonders" (*miracula* in Latin) in the strict sense. Positing them as miracles, divine interruptions of worldly process, is a way of neutralizing,

4 Strauss, *Leben Jesu*, 2:318–20; *Life of Jesus*, 579–80.

on the level of theory, that crucial ambiguity, that always present possibility of misrecognition or offense, that makes recognition of his authentic divinity a dangerous venture of interpretation (i.e., faith).

This ambiguity has always hovered around the reports of Jesus' marvelous actions, but here, again, modernity has intensified its existential recalcitrance by a twofold intellectual legacy: a more rigorous insight into the regularity of natural processes, and (the main issue of interest here) heightened awareness of Jesus' miracle stories as quite typical instances of a widely diffused cultural motif. The Christological position sketched in this essay does not in itself forbid the miraculous possibility; it simply cannot make anything essential of it. Nor is this a new insight. Dietrich Bonhoeffer, for example, saw well the structurally necessary connection between faith and the scarcely bearable "incognito" of God's hiddenness in Jesus.

> How then are we to understand the fact that Jesus does in fact do miracles? Are they not a breaking of the incognito? . . . [Or s]hould we go along with liberal theology and see the miracles as superstitions of the time? . . . The miracles do not break the incognito. The world of the ancient religions was full of miracle workers and saviours. In that, Jesus does not stand alone. The miracles may well rise above the everyday happenings, but they are only one step up within the created world. The concept associated with miracle is not that of God, but of magic. Magic remains within this world. When Jesus does miracles, he thus preserves his incognito within the magical picture of the world. It is not because of miracles that he is accepted as the Son of God in the New Testament. On the contrary, his power is declared to be demonic.[5]

The only addition we would make to this excellent statement is to point out that his power need not merely have been *declared* to be demonic (i.e., by his enemies). For all practical purposes (as suggested, say, by the extreme scenarios outlined in chapter 3), it *could well have been* demonic, even, it may well be, in the self-understanding of Jesus. Not, of course, in the sense that Jesus served a Satanic agenda, but in that the cultural "script" within

5 Dietrich Bonhoeffer, *Berlin 1932–1933*, ed. Carsten Nicolaisen and Ernst-Albert Scharfennorth, vol. 12 of *Dietrich Bonhoeffer Werke*, ed. Eberhard Bethge et al. (Gütersloh: Christian Kaiser Verlag, 1997), 346. Translation cited from Dietrich Bonhoeffer, *Christ the Center: A New Translation*, trans. Edwin H. Robertson (New York: Harper & Row, 1978), 111.

which he interpreted himself cast him as a thaumaturge privileged by the high God to initiate others into the heavenly realm, triumphant over all spiritual impediments through his mastery of the daemonic sphere. Not even such a seemingly outlandish possibility would have prevented his deeds of power being also signs of his hypostatic unity with the eternal Word, of his direct vision of God, or of his flawless expression of that unity and vision in the course of his human life of loving service. But even if exegetical reconstructions do not go that far, history will again and again present faith not simply with a generically human "incognito," but with a figure empirically indistinguishable from a fanatic or a mountebank.

Besides the telltale usage of "incognito," Bonhoeffer's Christology lectures provide other clues of close attention to Søren Kierkegaard. In fact, it is Kierkegaard who has furnished the deepest analysis of the disturbing Christological terrain being reconnoitered in this essay. He was emphatic on the point: if Jesus really was God, in the monotheistic and not the pagan sense, he could not for that very reason appear as such. A perusal of Kierkegaard's *Philosophical Fragments* would make plain any number of points at which the current project only tries to adapt and extend his essential reasoning. Jesus' assumption of humanity was not a kind of mimicry, as with those bugs whose bodies have evolved a protective likeness to some other species. That is, the temporal tissue of historical causality is not a "parastatic body" for the Word, but rather totally constitutes its worldly life.[6] Jesus does not stand ironically above the religious and mythical culture in which he is born; even in the case of his innermost consciousness, "The news of the day is the swaddling clothes of the eternal, is indeed its actual form."[7] Although in their "performing the Scriptures" (Nicholas Lash), believers can truly come to know more of Jesus' human person than the bare confession that God was a human who lived and died (the minimal "*dass*" celebrated by Bultmann, another student of Kierkegaard), the point is that the possibility of a decisive encounter with him does not rise or fall with the historical attainment of more or fewer critically verifiable facts about him.[8] Even eyewitnesses to his life were in

6 Søren Kierkegaard, *Philosophical Fragments / Johannes Climacus*, trans. and ed. Howard V. Hong and Edna H. Hong (Princeton: Princeton University Press, 1985), 55.

7 Kierkegaard, *Philosophical Fragments*, 58.

8 Kierkegaard, *Philosophical Fragments*, 103–4. Bultmann's indebtedness to the Christology of the *Fragments* is well-documented. Particularly relevant here is the way in which Bultmann's historical judgment that Jesus was not conscious

no way contemporary with his actual person, for that peculiar proximity is not distributed by the accidents of chronology, but by a constellation of decision.

On the miracle question in particular, Kierkegaard's key point is that miracles fall under a general principle: the divine-human Jesus necessarily called a certain sort of attention to himself, but not one in any way unavailable in principle to other human beings.[9] This in-principle availability brings Kierkegaard's position on miracles into proximity with that of Strauss and Hegel, but with a crucial difference. For the latter two, Jesus' miraculous performances are part of his "appearance" for empirical consciousness only; as part of his givenness to immediate experience, these "shining phenomena" must finally be detached from Spirit's grasp of his true meaning as God-man.[10] Kierkegaard, rather than locating the miracles of Jesus on one side of a dialectical opposition as Hegel and Strauss do, stresses simultaneously their invincible ambiguity and their integral role within the total presentation of his person and life to faith. They are indeed signs of his divinity, but legible only by faith. For Kierkegaard, the tired naturalism of modern Protestant belief was only another way of neutralizing the savior's offense; he will have nothing to do with it. But it is just as important that he sees an equal threat to faith presented by the comfortable, apologetic objectification of Jesus' miracles. Faith can disentangle itself from these mutually opposed evasions only when it exposes itself to the threatening ambiguity of the God in time, integrating the wondrous records of Jesus into the mystery of his person as a whole.

> The miracle can make aware—now you are in the tension, and it depends upon what you choose, offense or faith, it is your heart

---

of his Messianic status leads to a theological insistence that faith in him cannot be divorced from faith in the church's witness to him. Although the arguments of this essay construe the eschatological (absolute, time-transcendent) agency of Jesus by means of a Thomist ontology of mission and providence rather than a Heideggerian ontology of existence, they clearly resonate both with Bultmann's critical historiography of the Jesus event and with his stress on the necessary mediation of the community's fidelity. For a brief treatment of Bultmann's debt to Kierkegaard, with useful citations, see Heiko Schulz, "A Modest Head Start: The German Reception of Kierkegaard," in *Kierkegaard's International Reception*, tome 1, *Northern and Western Europe*, ed. Jon Stewart (Farnham: Ashgate, 2009), 307–420 at 338–41.

9 Kierkegaard, *Philosophical Fragments*, 56–57.

10 David Friedrich Strauss, *In Defense of My Life of Jesus against the Hegelians*, ed. and trans. Marilyn Chapin Massey (Hamden, Conn.: Archon Books, 1983), 34.

> that must be disclosed. . . . [I]n Christendom [i.e., false, objectified "cultural" Christianity] one has only a fantasy picture of Christ, a fantasy God-figure, directly related to performing miracles. But this is an untruth; Christ never looked like that. The Christianity of Christendom is fantasy in both respects—with respect to miracles and with respect to Christ. In the situation of contemporaneity you are placed between this inexplicable thing (but from that it still does not follow that it is a miracle) and then an individual human being who looks like others—and it is he who does it. The possibility of offense is not to be avoided. You must go through it.[11]

For Kierkegaard, in short, Jesus' incognito is too good; not even his deeds of power ruffle it. In Greek myth, when the gods take on a human disguise they are betrayed by small hints: an almost too-perfect beauty; glittering eyes that do not blink; the awful weight that overburdens boat or chariot when they board it.[12] Closer to home, even the Christian God's camouflage fails in Chesterton's dazzling allegory *The Man Who Was Thursday*, given away by the impossible facial expanse of the President of the Anarchist Council: "The face was so big, that one couldn't focus on it or make it a face at all. The eye was so far away from the nose, that it wasn't an eye."[13] As the final chapter of this essay will suggest, Jesus is similarly an unrecognizably extended sort of life-form. But in his case, there is no "tell" that objectively betrays the god in human form.

Indeed, from the standpoint adopted here, Kierkegaard's position, like that of Bonhoeffer, might even be pushed further from an epistemic toward an ontological ambiguity. To be signs, Jesus' deeds of power could not have been fraudulent (intentionally deceptive), but they did not have to be miracles at all: given his cultural context, wizardry might have been good enough. In the same way, his genuine deity had to express itself cultically in the borrowed forms of Hellenistic or Semitic divinity. Kierkegaard opposed to Christian incarnation the false Greek divinization of the human.

11 Søren Kierkegaard, *Practice in Christianity*, trans. and ed. Howard V. Hong and Edna H. Hong (Princeton: Princeton University Press, 1991), 97–98; cf. 41–42, 126.

12 M. L. West, *Indo-European Poetry and Myth* (Oxford: Oxford University Press, 2007), 133.

13 G. K. Chesterton, *The Man Who Was Thursday and Related Pieces*, ed. Stephen Medcalf (Oxford: Oxford University Press, 1996), 148.

> Since paganism as a whole and Greek religion in particular are lacking the decisive "distinguishing mark" between the divine and the human . . . a confusion between the two realms is the inevitable consequence: mankind as such—or at least mankind in its most striking individual manifestations (magicians, emperors, heros, and so on)—is erroneously mixed up with the divine through the "fantastical fabrication" of elevating or exalting the former to the latter.[14]

But precisely recognizing the monotheistic mark of the infinite creator-deity makes possible an assumption of worldly, historical, and cultural flesh that undercuts just this opposition. For the conceptual tools developed in part 2, layered causality or the "formal" appropriation of purely historical "matter" mean that God's becoming a human being in Jesus attains its historical actuality not instead of, but by means of, that human being's Greek "fabrication" into a god. The speculations around the "history of religions" Jesus indicate the way available cultural elements might have been pneumatically drawn into such a fabrication.

This variant of Kierkegaard's position on Jesus' marvelous performances, which in effect extends their ambiguity from the phenomenal to the ontological plane, can be connected back to some broader theological reflections of Bonhoeffer by way of a surprising maneuver once employed by JZS. One important implication for faith, due for discussion in the following section, emerges from the considerations above: the historical incognito of the Word means that theology, as it investigates its founding texts and traditions, can have no interest in blurring the sharp intellectual boundary between mythical and historical or scientific discourses. This falls in nicely with JZS's humanist, scholarly suspicion of Tillich's correlational attempt to posit a "religion" (or "revelation") sufficiently distinctive over against "culture" as to confront the latter with "answers" to its aporias. JZS's retort to this approach insightfully if unexpectedly invoked Bonhoeffer: this supposed function, relying on a dichotomous privileging of "religion" over "culture," cannot be "the role of Christianity in a 'world come of age.'"[15] He presumably had in mind Bonhoeffer's complaint that theology has "allowed God to function only as deus ex machina in the so-

14 Heiko Schulz, "Rosenkranz: Traces of Hegelian Psychology and Theology in Kierkegaard," in *Kierkegaard and His German Contemporaries*, tome 2, *Theology*, ed. Jon Stewart (Aldershot: Ashgate, 2007), 161–96 at 173–74.

15 Jonathan Z. Smith, "Tillich['s] Remains . . . ," *Journal of the American Academy of Religion* 78 (2010): 1139–70 at 1159.

called ultimate questions, that is, God becomes the answer to life's questions, a solution to life's needs and conflicts."[16]

Bonhoeffer's alternative vision has become famous, but the argument of this section can place the emphasis where JZS could not: that the world has "come of age" has a specifically Christological rationale.

> The same God who makes us to live in the world without the working hypothesis of God is the God before whom we stand continually. Before God, and with God, we live without God. God consents to be pushed out of the world and onto the cross.[17]

The spatial image makes evident a paradox: a God who is more present to the world precisely in lacking a special defined zone of presence, i.e., lacking a manifestation or revelation ontologically distinct from the human cultural actuality. But the paradox is only apparent, because the space God takes up in the world is not the world's space.

> It is intrinsic to God's revelation in Jesus Christ that it occupied space in the world. It would, however, be fundamentally wrong simply to explain this space empirically. When God in Jesus Christ claims space in the world—even space in a stable because "there was no other place in the inn"—God embraces the whole reality of the world in this narrow space and reveals its ultimate foundation.[18]

The Christological proposals of this essay are in the identical spirit: in the utterly human life and death of Jesus, the integrity of the human order is not breached but divinely affirmed. Because God is edged out of the world, because his "space" in the world disappears as a definite

16 Dietrich Bonhoeffer, *Widerstand und Ergebung*, ed. Christian Gremmels et al., vol. 8 of *Dietrich Bonhoeffer Werke*, ed. Eberhard Bethge et al. (Gütersloh: Christian Kaiser Verlag, 1998), 503; English translation of this version: *Letters and Papers from Prison*, trans. John W. DeGruchy, vol. 8 of *Dietrich Bonhoeffer Works*, ed. Victoria J. Barnett and Barbara Wojhoski (Minneapolis: Fortress, 2010), 450.

17 Bonhoeffer, *Widerstand*, 533–34; *Letters and Papers*, 479.

18 Dietrich Bonhoeffer, *Ethik*, ed. Ilse Tödt et al., vol. 6 of *Dietrich Bonhoeffer Werke*, ed. Eberhard Bethge et al. (Gütersloh: Christian Kaiser Verlag, 1998), 48–49; English translation of this version: *Ethics*, ed. Clifford J. Green, vol. 6 of *Dietrich Bonhoeffer Works*, ed. Wayne Whitson Floyd Jr. (Minneapolis: Fortress, 2005), 63. The concentration of the space of worldly actuality within the narrow breadth of an individual life is reminiscent of Walter Benjamin's "*Abbreviatur*," referred to in ch. 9 below.

zone (even from the Savior's *Innerlichkeit*), he can now be at the center of all human life-situations. Jesus could not have "been" God, in the sense of defining a divine space within the world. Personal identity, divine or human, takes up no natural space; a human person is the only creature that could be divine without taking up divine space. This is why, for Aquinas as for Schleiermacher, only human intentionality could have served as the temporal vehicle for the eternal. But, beyond Schleiermacher, only the immense God conceived as the creator from nothing could be fully incarnate in the way assumed by Bonhoeffer's imagery. Only transcendence is capable of this immanence. In various medieval writings there pops up the geometric definition of God as an infinite sphere, whose circumference is nowhere and whose center is everywhere. Bonhoeffer presents a Christological variant of this: God in Christ can have his center everywhere in the world *because* his circumference is nowhere, defining or enclosing no space against the world.

III.

The question of Jesus' miracles foregrounds both the understanding of the incarnation pursued to this point, as well as the related insistence that fictional narratives must play a central role in the true testimony of the canonical Gospels to the incarnation. If the Christian believer finds these theological proposals acceptable or even unavoidable, she will have to accept the different but complementary roles of history and myth in the scriptural witness; she will not try to elide the distinction, or attempt to finesse some kind of return to precritical naivete. The most promising response under contemporary conditions will neither be a rationalist attempt to salvage miraculous factuality, nor a hoped-for return to premodern consciousness supposedly enabled by "postmodern" complications. There will instead be a simultaneous embrace of D. F. Strauss and Origen, that is to say, a forthright acknowledgement of the fictive and mythic elements that at the deepest levels constitute the past's witness to Jesus, combined with a realization that discerning the deeper truth in the falsity of that witness is part of faith's interpretive work in the present. Only such an ever-repeated work of faith, energized and guided by the Spirit, enables the continual overcoming of offense at the incarnation of the Word. More needs to be said about this difficult combination.

The overlapping outlines in the Gospels of different traditions and narrative conventions, smoothed into a coherent picture by centuries of reverent usage, have become discernible again, and for many impossible to ignore. The premodern mind, excepting a nascent critical skepticism occasionally evident among some intellectuals, quite comfortably assimilated the mythical elements of the Gospels to the other narrative features bearing some historical verisimilitude.[19] It does not seem possible today, at least for those whose critical faculties have been aroused, to ignore this suturing together of radically distinct discourses. To put it bluntly, much of the Gospel account of Jesus is cast in fabulous terms. At this point, however, no one will be surprised if it is affirmed with equal vigor that Christian faith can and must claim complete truth for this integral fabricated dimension of the Gospels. The entire trend of discussion leading up to this point invites the reader to recognize the possibility and necessity of the role of fictive truth in Christology. But how?

The presence of divine "persons" in history, dealt with above as the theology of mission, involves no puncture in the world's causal surface; instead, the embodied but elusive patterns of human personality (in Jesus and in his communities) assume shapes (respectively, either perfectly or partially and gradually) resonant with God's self-relations. This resonance is effected providentially, reducible to an infinitesimal torque in the network of innumerable causally interconnected microevents that enter as variables into the constitution of those patterns. The crucial point is that the causal chains of history remain unbroken. This position invites the faithful reader of the Gospels to recognize, at least prima facie, the physically impossible and hence legendary character of a large portion of the narrative. Otherwise put, even if Jesus' cultural apotheosis (the immanent expression of the transcendent unity of Son and Spirit within God) involves, as has been repeatedly argued, a weaving together of multiple historical and mythic or fantastic symbolic elements into the single truth of Jesus Christ, a noninvasive ontology of mission will nonetheless give no warrant to assume that the discursive distinctions involved between fact and fiction have been suspended or should be ignored. Indeed, perhaps something akin to the logic of metaphor has always been at work in

19 For a fascinating discussion of modes of premodern critique, especially as instanced by Pausanias, see Paul Veyne, *Did the Greeks Believe in Their Myths? An Essay on the Constitutive Imagination*, trans. Paula Wissing (Chicago: University of Chicago Press, 1988).

the Christ-event: the semantic force of metaphor, and hence metaphorical truth, turns on the implicit denial of literal truth. A similar dialectic is at work in the anxious mergers of surrealist imagery. Modernity eventually brings explicit awareness of this constitutive poise: even the truth of the incarnation itself is not a matter of supernatural "facts" but only of the stylized patterning of natural facts in tensely calibrated arrangements.

Though its application to the scriptural and ecclesial traditions of Jesus may be discomfiting, there is nothing so radical in the notion that fiction may well be in some cases a necessary component in the truthful apprehension of certain realities. Under modern conditions, such apprehension, even for religious belief, will involve explicit awareness of the fictional element and its demarcation from claims to literal reference.[20] Indeed, the imperative to distinguish history and myth is more than just a modern innovation, and looking again at the reflections of JZS might even suggest that it elaborates upon a more basic and universal dynamic operative within human culture generally. As was seen above, JZS's retort to Tillichian "correlation" was in effect that there can be no noncultural (i.e., purely "religious" or "revealed") answer to a cultural question. The discussions throughout this essay have tried to honor this insight by rendering the human being Jesus as God's incarnation not simply in terms of physical or even psychological embodiment, but more fundamentally in terms of a cultural event, culture being the symbolic extension of embodiment that recursively operates to humanize the individual body and its acts. The (divine) Word, in short, could not become flesh if (human) flesh could not become word.[21]

But the point under discussion here approaches the issue of culture from another side: there can be no cultural meaning, no humanly relevant "answer" to human problems, where no question has been put (i.e., culturally or from within culture). Now, this essay assumes the metaphysical actuality of transcendence and its involvement in human history. However, and this is the crucial point, it concurs with JZS's denial that transcendence could gain any purchase on human life if it is conceived as an

20 For thought-provoking methodological reflections relevant to this point, see Nicholas Lash, "Ideology, Metaphor and Analogy," in *Theology on the Way to Emmaus* (London: SCM Press, 1986), 95–119.

21 The point generalizes the frequently noted insight of Maurice de la Taille that Jesus at the Last Supper inaugurates a semiotic operation with his own body: "He placed himself in the order of signs." Maurice de la Taille, S.J., *The Mystery of Faith and Human Opinion* (London: Sheed & Ward, 1930), 212.

interruption or displacement of the human cultural imagination (i.e., as a demarcated epiphanic moment, a pure givenness). The thrust of this entire essay has been that if transcendence cannot occur in spite of culture, then it must occur as providential configurations of the cultural dynamic itself. To see the harmony with JZS's approach to culture, consider an illuminating example of that approach.

In his meticulous study of J. G. Frazer's *Golden Bough*, JZS concludes that the work is a failure not because its colossal heap of facts fails to give correct answers to its two central questions (Is the inviolable tree-branch of the sanctuary of Nemi to be identified with Aeneas' golden bough? Does it belong to the same mythic motif as the mistletoe with which the Norse god Balder is killed?), but rather because these very questions, as Frazer himself eventually discloses, are merely opportunities to "set up" the marshaling of the material, such that nothing important rides upon their respective answers. But for JZS the mass of cultural fragments collected by Frazer has no utility whatever, illuminates nothing, unless it is argumentatively structured as the solution to a definable problem. Thus Frazer "deliberately fails," he "chose to make his central work a joke," perhaps (JZS hints) to model and disclose the massive labor of human culture as nothing but a futile and absurd gesture of resistance to the meaninglessness of death. Yet the value of Frazer's work for JZS lies precisely in demonstrating the pivotal humanist tenet that no cultural complex delivers humanly relevant meaning without its being configured within a pattern of human inquiry: no question guarantees no answer.[22]

The point, then, is that any disclosure of truth through culture depends upon the use of culture, the imaginative and (to some degree) self-aware manipulation and application of cultural elements. And yet meaning, new truth and illumination, does indeed occur; culture, that is, is not closed in upon itself, but is ceaselessly generative. This is the insight behind JZS's claim about culture being constitutively self-disintegrating. Religious studies, above all, shows that culture is not about "responding" to self-positing "manifestations" of the ultimate: the study of religion as a human phenomenon affords "the realization that, in culture, there is no text, it is all commentary; that there is no primordium, it is all history;

22 Jonathan Z. Smith, "When the Bough Breaks" [1973], in *Map Is Not Territory: Studies in the History of Religions* (Leiden: Brill, 1978), 208–39 at 238–39.

that all is application."[23] If, roughly speaking, the Jesus-dimension of the present essay responds to the first-mentioned point that only culture can answer itself, then the Spirit-dimension responds to this latter insight, that answers can only respond to questions. Jesus' deity only "occurs" as received within the demanding, inquiring body of his later worshipers. There is no transcendence in spite of culture, but there is transcendence in and through culture, made possible by the fact that culture itself is a never-ending process of subverting and surpassing itself. This in turn requires that all cultural users must (as "individuals") always partially transcend their cultural material, a requirement extensively explored, in the wake of Schleiermacher's hermeneutic theory, by Manfred Frank.[24]

Which brings the discussion back to the discernment of discourses: the cultural "moment of truth" demands the gesture whereby fiction is posited as such. It is the moment when Frazer confesses that Balder, like the Priest of Nemi, is "merely a puppet, and it is time to unmask him"; it is the moment "[w]hen you have the unmasking of the actors after the ceremony," an "act of criticism of collective representation"; it is the moment when the map is divulged as *not* the territory.[25] This basic and universal cultural impulse, then, is played out once again in the modern, humanist form of a necessary critical suspicion; many of the deepest truths can only be articulated using fictional modes, so fiction can indeed be true, but with modern historical consciousness, it can no longer function as truth unless its pretensions to nonfictive status have been exposed.[26]

23 Jonathan Z. Smith, "The Domestication of Sacrifice" [1983], in *Violent Origins: Walter Burkert, René Girard, and Jonathan Z. Smith on Ritual Killing and Cultural Formation*, ed. Robert G. Hamerton-Kelly (Stanford: Stanford University Press, 1987), 196.

24 See, for example, Manfred Frank, *What Is Neostructuralism?* trans. Sabine Wilke and Richard Gray, Theory and History of Literature 45 (Minneapolis: University of Minnesota Press, 1989), 359–66.

25 J. Z. Smith, "When the Bough Breaks," 238; *Violent Origins*, 185.

26 The present performance, too, requires its moment of unmasking. The Latin "excerpt" contained in the appendix, credited to John Selden, is actually my own concoction, with a couple of McGuffins thrown in from H. P. Lovecraft ("The Dunwich Horror") and C. S. Lewis (*That Hideous Strength* [1945], ch. 1). For that matter, the book that inspired the title of this essay (see fn. 2 of the introduction above) is hard to obtain because nonexistent; it is an invention of the great pulp writer Robert E. Howard ("The Black Stone" [1931]). Religious scholarship occasionally intersects in strange ways with popular fictions. As MS inquired of Gershom Scholem: "Are you familiar with *Vathek*?" See *Morton Smith and Gershom Scholem, Correspondence 1945–1982*, ed. Guy G. Stroumsa (Leiden: Brill, 2008), 2.

In short, there is no theological justification for disregarding or blurring the boundary between history and myth. Their integrity as discourses must be maintained not just out of intellectual honesty, but in the interest of theological viability. A deep convergence of interest here unites incarnational belief and the humanistic study of religion. Much of the overall argument so far can in fact be read as suggesting a theological rationale for some of JZS's most characteristic theoretical (decidedly nontheological) insights. He is theologically quite correct, that is, in protesting the immediate junction of mythic and historical discourses.[27] The argument here has been that indeed these should not be directly fused, either theoretically or experientially, but rather can only be mediated through a theology of provident transcendence. He is likewise correct that nothing is sacred in itself, but only through relation to something else.[28] The argument here has been that Jesus and the church manifest divinity not as "theophanies" but only via the infinite relations so to speak "behind" their historical appearance.

The position of this essay on the historical incarnation of the Word can be formulated thus: enchanted history without enchanted facts. It is a theoretical outworking of the classical Christological creedal definitions, by means of broadly Thomistic conceptual tools. As just now seen, with the theory in place, the confession of Chalcedon can also be promulgated into a theological charter for the purely humanistic theoretical analysis of religion that JZS has argued for and expertly practiced (though of course the humanist as such needs no such charter). For if theology can take up the stance recommended in this essay, it will see that historical explanation can never go "too far" or "too deep" or be "too exhaustive" for faith. The scheme of layered causality functions to license the unlimited application of historical consciousness in a manner analogous to the way the Ideas in Kant establish the open field of empirical science: in each case, experience is constituted in such a way that it can never arrive at its own bound.[29]

27 Jonathan. Z. Smith, *Drudgery Divine: On the Comparison of Early Christianities and the Religions of Late Antiquity* (Chicago: University of Chicago Press, 1990), 39.

28 Jonathan Z. Smith, "The Bare Facts of Ritual" [1980], in *Imagining Religion: From Babylon to Jonestown* (Chicago: University of Chicago Press, 1982), 53–65 at 55–56.

29 Immanuel Kant, "Prolegomena to Any Future Metaphysics That Will Be Able to Come Forward as Science," trans. Gary Hatfield, in *Theoretical Philosophy after 1781*, Cambridge Edition of the Works of Immanuel Kant (Cambridge: Cambridge University Press, 2002), 140–53.

But quite apart from this methodological harmonization of theological history and history of religions, the main point is the one already discerned by Rousselot. The "external sign" which is Jesus' divine humanity is always at one and the same time a "real fact, interwoven with the entire fabric of human experience" and "part of another world." For the task of faith is not the disclosure and vindication of a new set of supernatural facts, but the interpretive penetration of already given facts as matter for the supernatural form. Reading Rousselot through the lens of Kierkegaard, a "pagan" divinization of the human comes to be seen as the matter of the Word's incarnation in Jesus, and the latter's "wonders" as the stuff of his Hellenistic/Semitic environment divinely appropriated as signs of his true status.

One final word on faith's contemporary situation should be added. A theology of incarnation viewed along the lines of this essay provides a certain rationale for the indispensable theological role of historical-critical exegesis of Scripture. It is undeniable that historical judgment, once it seeks to disencumber itself of any implicit or explicit theological "interest" in the historicity of biblical narrative, finds itself shaping a picture of the past in countless ways incompatible with the scriptural "saga" of Israel, Jesus, and the early church. This is because truth is indeed, as MS says, *necessarily* stranger than history; historical reasoning must adhere to its proper canons of judgment, appealing to the regular and analogous character of factuality.[30] Lacking direct evidence, it must opt for the more probable. Those who confess the strange truth of God in Christ have good reason to keep historical discourse uninfected by that strangeness, even if this leaves constructions of past history increasingly looking like funhouse-mirror distortions of the comfortably familiar "salvation history" of the Old and New Testaments. These texts surely have a claim upon the professing Christian, but so, too, does the actual past in its otherness, its resistance to our desires.

To put the case more positively, there is an irreplaceable value for the theologian and, indeed, for many believers as such, of a kind of hard-edged historical framework within which they are compelled to build their theological positions. There are negative or indirect benefits from a purely intellectual perspective. Openness to skeptical conclusions avoids

30 Morton Smith, *The Secret Gospel* (1973; repr., Middletown, Calif.: Dawn Horse Press, 2005), 138.

diluting the criteria for our judgments about the past with nonhistorical considerations. Moreover, by defamiliarizing our sense of the past, "hard" history exposes the often-hidden apologetic bent that keeps nudging the theologian's picture of Israel, or of Jesus, back into maximal conformity with the time-honored biblical narrative, contrary to what a candid and culturally comparative approach to the evidence would suggest.

But there are more positive theological payoffs as well. First, embracing critical or skeptical judgments about the past rather than forever fighting rearguard defenses of the accuracy of this or that biblical report is the equivalent in historical argumentation of Aquinas' noble rejection of apologetic overreach in philosophical theology.[31] Second, frankly acknowledging the limits of what can be historically supported is one step on the path of theology's reclaiming citizen's rights within the republic of intellectual inquiry. Third, and of direct concern to belief itself, only the uncomfortably sharp edges of an historical counternarrative to the Bible help us discern the actual contours of witness in the New Testament, the precise nature of its implicit and explicit claims. This was far less important in premodern centuries, where the cultural consciousness did not sharply dissociate mythical and historical discourses; the established "saga" of salvation history did not then appear a forced construction, and hence did not interfere with the communal reception of what God was disclosing in Scripture. Now, however, in a radically different context only a more aggressive assessment of factuality will allow the believer to see where the sacred texts are departing from it; discerning their reshaping of the past is a precious clue to the decipherment of the meaning of the first witnesses. For the reflective believer, this kind of history begins to restore the true "pastness" of the Scriptures, helping to recover the clarity of their testimony by making the reflective believer aware of the thousands of unconscious accommodations which make up the customary "religious" patterns of reading.

To be sure, not all or perhaps even most Christians will be ready for the full force of this reorientation. For them, faith will continue to mean, quite naturally, inhabiting (at least fitfully) the semi-mythical world projected in the Bible, practically accommodated by all kinds of subliminal adjustments to their everyday world, ruled as it is by structures of power and scientific technique. Theologians, however, should consider carefully whether they

31 Thomas Aquinas, *Summa Theologica* I q. 32 a. 1.

can afford this luxury. And they might conclude that it is better in the long run to make the reorientation possible for all others who need it, if it will enable them to remain worshipers of the divine incarnation in Jesus.

There is even something exhilarating, as it seems Bultmann found, in the adventure of a strong faith in Christ that remains fully open to the verdicts of history. Something of this comes across as well in Strauss' important letter to his friend Märklin, laying out his envisioned book on the life of Jesus and indicating the necessity of finally acknowledging the valid insights of the most radical rationalists, skeptics, and deists. His reading for the critical part of the book "begins with writings from old Celsus and continues through the English and French authors (for which I perceive a true yearning, just as one will play gladly with a wild animal when he knows that it cannot do him any harm)."[32] To be sure, the expression of invulnerability here is perhaps a bit overdone. Strauss (as in a different way Bultmann) relies on a systematically neat separation (even a dialectical opposition) of faith and history that this essay has consistently eschewed. The alternative Christological scheme it has developed assumes their unavoidable entanglement, yet tries even so to render the relations of orthodox faith to historical evidence flexible enough to engender, if not Strauss' certainty of safety, at least constantly renewable grounds for confidence.

But such confidence is only won in the face of the possibility of offense, which can never be eliminated. The susceptibility of the theologian or exegete to historical bias is not contingent but structural; it springs especially (though not exclusively) from the special dual burden under which she typically labors. Each of her decisions about the past will explicitly seek its warrants in the accepted scholarly canons of historical judgment, but will also (at least implicitly and in many cases) seek to maintain the contemporary possibility of religious belief within her tradition. Kierkegaard already grasped this duality as the suspect quality distinguishing theological history within the wider world of scholarly approaches to the past.

> One occasionally hears uneducated or half-educated individuals or pompous geniuses scoff at critical work with ancient writings. They belittle the learned researcher's scrupulousness about the most insignificant detail, which is precisely to his credit, that scientifically

32 Horton Harris, *David Friedrich Strauss and His Theology* (Cambridge: Cambridge University Press, 1973), 34–35.

> he does not consider anything to be insignificant. No, philological scholarship is wholly legitimate, and the present author certainly has respect, second to none, for that which scholarship consecrates. On the other hand, one gets no unalloyed impression of critical theological scholarship. Its entire effort suffers from a certain conscious or unconscious duplexity. It always looks as if something for faith, something pertaining to faith, should suddenly result from this criticism. Therein lies the dubiousness.[33]

The mental agility that might avoid this dilemma by combining orthodox faith with an (at times) anti-theological historical "scrupulousness" will be called for again and again. To show how it might be possible has been one goal of this essay.

33 Søren Kierkegaard, *Concluding Unscientific Postscript to "Philosophical Fragments,"* ed. Howard V. Hong and Edna H. Hong (Princeton: Princeton University Press, 1992), 25.

9

Campus Crusade for Cthulhu
Modernity and Monstrosity

Well! This is not very reassuring.
Jacques Lacan | *Seminar XI*

Every object whose end is unknown to
us is provisionally monstrous.
Jorge Luis Borges | **"A Defense of the Kabbalah"**

It was everywhere—a gelatin—a slime yet it had shapes, a
thousand shapes. . . . Carter, it was the unnameable!
H. P. Lovecraft | **"The Unnameable"**

I.

The invincible ambiguity of the wondrous acts of Jesus means that theology must always reckon with their principled explicability in purely human and historical terms; this, in turn, entails a willing acknowledgement of mythical and counterfactual elements in the authoritative Jesus-tradition. The chapter just concluded dealt with this as one way that incarnational theology refuses to grasp after the direct visibility of Jesus' divinity; the present chapter will now discuss another instance of this principle. This essay has worked with a picture in which two historical event-complexes, that of Jesus (completed) and that of the church (ongoing), are unified or made a single sign or event of meaning as they are "triangulated" by God's transcendent arrivals as Word and Spirit, making them jointly participant in God's communicative self-relation. The man confessed and worshiped as "Jesus Christ" is therefore the past Jesus *as organically unified with* the sign-event of the church (the penumbra of later witnesses); this one living thing results from the new but hidden body of Jesus even now extending itself into history as a cultural body, his "sign-body." However, this understanding is tantamount to the claim that the "complete" Jesus, the fullness of his human presence and profile, is never available for faith. Why not?

That this single historical event is "organic," like a living body, is not as such observable or even conceivable in purely historical terms. It is only graspable by one who is, by faith, part of that organism, a cell within its historical metabolism. This was earlier expressed by reversing Strauss' formula and maintaining that the objective truth of Jesus continually surpasses its subjective reception, not vice versa. But because the Word must be heard, this surpassing is what supports and drives the ongoing existence of that subjective reception, the enduring history of the sign-body. This results in a *process* of recognizing Jesus, a process begun before the Gospels were finalized, and, though henceforth decisively molded by the canonical portraits, continuing into the present. As long as the "sign-body" of witnesses remains both an integral part of Jesus' fullness of humanity and yet itself still in process, still under way, then the Word's incarnation is still unfinished. To put it differently, Jesus' excess of humanity means that the church in history is forever seeking to catch up to him, to construct a truly adequate body of human meaning for him.

As will be proposed in this chapter, the community of faith will more fully recognize Jesus only as it more fully recognizes itself, or rather realizes itself in the world. But short of the eschatological consummation of all human history, the full humanity of Jesus is to be found neither in his original historical earthly life, ambiguous and truncated, nor in the transfiguration of that life by a communal testimony that is as fragmentary and insufficient as the community itself. Though they diminish in no way the actual advent in history of the eternal Word, these accompanying defects (unavoidable just because of the deforming of finite history under the weight of that infinite arrival) make their presence felt in a kind of disfigurement of Jesus. Theology must insist that the savior's visage, though still as compassionate and exalted as in the old traditional depictions, also bears from certain angles a rather alienating and even repellent aspect. According to the Gospel of Mark (6:50, NRSV), the disciples "all saw him and were terrified. But immediately he spoke to them and said, 'Take heart, it is I; do not be afraid.'" When belief sees its Savior, one might ask, what is there to be afraid of? More than is commonly acknowledged. Like the disciples who thought they were seeing a ghost when Jesus walked on water, believers at all times can never completely be sure, when they view Jesus, what they are looking at. Once again, this is a necessary aspect of incarnational faith, albeit one that the modern sense of history has made more obtrusive and intractable.

An initial feel for the necessity of this unavailability of the total Jesus, and the consequent distortion of any picture, might be provided by an analogy from psychoanalysis. Illustrating the nature of "libido" in his Seminar XI, the drive of "indestructible life" that precedes and evades all incorporation within the individual ego and its symbolic structures, Jacques Lacan memorably depicted the "hommelette" or "lamella." This quasi-membrane "flies off" as the human ovum is ruptured by the emergent foetus (i.e., it is the symbolically unassimilable byproduct of sexual differentiation); it is "something extra-flat, which moves like the amoeba"; and because "it can run around," perhaps it sometimes "comes and envelopes your face while you are quietly asleep."[1] The point of this alarming little fable is that life is a force detached, as it were, from the living themselves, confronting them as a blind nightmarish compulsion, a mindless drive to repeat the fixed gestures of animation even if it kills the living being. In the end, the impulse to survive is identical with the death-drive. Indeed, it is another figure of the primordial Real in its terrifying transcendence of all articulate human meaning, "the primordial abyss which swallows everything, dissolving all identities."[2]

Is there not something here strangely familiar to the incarnational theologian? Jesus is not just alive, he claims to be "the Life." He is, as has been seen, the surplus of humanity that enters into other human lives, the breath of a Spirit that "takes over" other persons from within. This intrusion of Jesus' enormous vitality Paul likened to a replication within his own daily experience of Jesus' tortuous execution, such that he himself was dead, with room left in him only for the life of Jesus (Gal 2:20). As in

1 Jacques Lacan, *The Four Fundamental Concepts of Psycho-Analysis*, ed. Jacques-Alain Miller, trans. Alan Sheridan (New York: W. W. Norton, 1978), 197–98.

2 Slavoj Žižek, *How to Read Lacan* (New York: W. W. Norton, 2006), 64.

Lacan, the invasive, compulsive life of Jesus is what confronts believers with the Real that is God; for God is the sheerly actual, what inescapably grounds us yet endlessly refuses to be securely situated within the collective symbolic framework of our meanings and ends. Jesus, then, is a kind of monster of Life; as the one who humanizes others from within, he is yet more than human.

So for faith Jesus is in some ways, i.e., in his inexhaustible humanity and threatening intractability, a kind of monster. Lacan's psychoanalytic creature is close kin to the theological truth about incarnation that has been stressed in this essay, namely, that believers in Jesus are colonized by the divine that is resident in his humanity, yet they find it impossible to directly grasp that presence. The nature and implications of this dangerous feature of incarnational thinking will be helpfully specified by contrasting this theological monstrosity with a superficially similar but ultimately opposed one. Language of the "monstrosity of Christ" will, for some readers, especially call to mind the work of that title where Slavoj Žižek confronts John Milbank, but care is needed at just this point. Žižek's account of Jesus' monstrosity follows Hegel, who referred it to the conceptually repellent composition of divinity and humanity affirmed in the ancient creeds. In our presentation, too, Jesus' monstrosity springs from a kind of composite life, but the terms and conditions of this theological composition are quite different from those of Hegel's philosophical one.

In some of his earliest writings on Christianity, Hegel had perceived how the spirit of that particular religion works itself out in the necessary yet appalling *worship* of Jesus, risen ideal and material historical particularity collapsed into a single object: "It is this monstrous combination over which millions of god-hungry souls, for so many centuries, have tortured and fought themselves to exhaustion."[3] Already, from his own quite different perspective, Hegel had touched the crux of this essay: monotheistic worship of a human being. Though by the time of his religion lectures Hegel's developed philosophy allowed him to situate and assess the phenomenon differently, the fact remains unchanged: the essential Christian "idea" of the "God-man" is a monstrosity for the understanding.[4] Strauss

3 "Diese ungeheure Verbindung ist es, über welche seit so vielen Jahrhunderten Millionen gottsuchender Seelen sich abgekämpft und gemartert haben," in G. W. F. Hegel, *Hegels theologische Jugendschriften*, ed. Herman Nohl (1907; repr., Frankfurt/Main: Minerva, 1966), 335.

4 G. W. F. Hegel, *Lectures on the Philosophy of Religion*, ed. and trans. Peter C. Hodgson, vol. 3 (Berkeley: University of California Press, 1984), 315.

in his turn characterizes the drastic juxtaposition in Christ of the most elevated and the lowliest categories as a "monstrosity [*Monstrosität*]."[5]

According to the mature Hegel, followed by Strauss in his Hegelian period, faith's traditional confession of Christ, operating in the religious medium of sensual picture-thinking, had to force together conceptually incompatible quantities (the Absolute and an individual human being). Only philosophy eventually provided thought with the tools to decipher the truth hidden within this grotesque but necessary coincidence; reason, following the movement of the dialectic, understands finite spirit as a moment within the eternal logic of infinite spirit. This unity of finite and infinite must "appear" in a temporal, individual form only that (beginning from the crucifixion) it may be sublated into the Spirit as the communal truth of humanity.

In our own time, Žižek has pushed this conception in an even more "left-wing" direction than Strauss, straight toward atheism. The human, mortal Jesus is the exhaustive, (literally) kenotic self-revelation of God; Jesus' death is thus God's death, signaling the final loss of any "reserve" of eternal divine substance. Jesus opens up the possibility of Spirit in humanity, but no transcendent almighty Father remains; "God" has fallen totally into the world.[6] God is "real" only as the historically immanent mechanism of objective spirit, that dynamic dimension of the "more than human" that enables individual finite subjectivity yet remains constitutively prior to any enclosure within the ego.[7] Christ, for Žižek, is an "anamorphosis of God," what God "looks like" from the distorting, external perspective as "over against" humanity.[8] Only assuming the proper perspective, realizing that there is no "Big Other" up there controlling things (that the Father really has forsaken the dying Jesus), corrects the apparent deformation of God's appearance in Christ.

5 David Friedrich Strauss, *Die christliche Glaubenslehre in ihrer geschichtlichen Entwicklung und im Kampfe mit der modernen Wissenschaft dargestellt*, vol. 2 (Tübingen: C. F. Osiander, 1841), 143.

6 Slavoj Žižek, *The Puppet and the Dwarf: The Perverse Core of Christianity* (Cambridge, Mass.: MIT Press, 2003), 125–37. Cf. Slavoj Žižek and John Milbank, *The Monstrosity of Christ: Paradox or Dialectic?* ed. Creston Davis (Cambridge, Mass.: MIT Press, 2009), 40.

7 Žižek and Milbank, *Monstrosity of Christ*, 240. Christ is precisely the "name" or historical appearance of this "inhuman excess" constituting the human. See Žižek and Milbank, *Puppet and the Dwarf*, 143.

8 Žižek and Milbank, *Monstrosity of Christ*, 81–82.

For Hegel the monstrosity of Christ is the reaction of the understanding (*Verstand*) to the conceptually grotesque combination of the absolute and the particular; only reason (*Vernunft*) grasps the dialectical movement of the concepts that defuses this static oxymoron and unveils its truth. Similarly, for Žižek the monstrosity of Christ springs from the distortion consequent upon the "impossible" identity of a particular human sign and the divine excess transcending every sign, the "short circuit" between positive singularity and divine event.[9] Each thinker roots the monstrosity in the impossibility of a "direct" grasp of this unity, but each resolves the problem on the level of philosophy, through rational dialectic or psychoanalytic materialism.

But whatever the surface similarity, the monstrosity being proposed in this essay is completely different; what is grotesque in Jesus as envisaged here is not defined by this structural and "vertical" superimposition of deity upon humanity, but by a processual and "horizontal" composition, an historical formation. His "wrongness" is not a matter of anamorphic but of metamorphic distortion; his human shape is temporally prolonged, an image "smeared" across centuries. There is something unsettling about any composite lifeform, that is, a single organic entity, which somehow involves or incorporates into itself more than one bodily structure. This is true even in the radical biological development among certain lower animals, where clashing morphologies succeed one another within the organism's lifespan. Some insects, in particular, are known for "holometabolism" or complete metamorphosis; here the development of the individual involves larval, pupal, and adult ("imago") stages with startlingly different bodily formations and patterns of behavior. Direct comparison of the adult configuration with its larval stage produces a kind of shock: How can this elegantly structured and highly differentiated insect possibly develop from a blindly groping worm that does nothing but gorge itself?

Žižek is quite correct that the true grasp of the significance of Jesus must acknowledge its traumatic aspect, that side of his truth that wounds us in our illusions and that we would gladly suppress. But here we are defining the nature of that trauma in a new, non-Hegelian way. Jesus truly is the God-man, the divine identity of a fully human existence, but he is not yet manifested in accord with this final truth. He must be recognized from his initial appearance, and yet the very humanity asserted even in

9 Žižek and Milbank, *Monstrosity of Christ*, 258.

the Gospels will always grind against faith's divinizing sensibility. That the believer might stumble, taking offense at him, is an ever-present possibility. The scandal for belief in Jesus Christ is precisely Jesus of Nazareth, the "larval" form of the total event of Christ. This trauma of faith confronting the humanity of Jesus is the key to his monstrosity.

The ongoing wound of faith is the lack of a fixed and final image which it can embrace and rest in. Jesus, once recognized in the Gospels and in worship, must still continually be reidentified in new forms, much as a target must be "reacquired"; belief oscillates between his initial larval form and the local phases of its current metamorphosis, an identity under unending construction (as long as history lasts). The biblical figure in its particularity somehow contains *in nuce* this entire later development, but repels any direct attempt to perceive its unity with his elusive presence now, much less with his completed future "imago." For Hegel and Žižek the church's Jesus (the "God-man") was "this . . . monstrous compound [*diese ungeheure Zusammensetzung*], which directly contradicts both representation and understanding."[10] In our counterproposal the original humanity of Jesus is metaphysically much closer kin to Walter Benjamin's "[n]ow-time, which, as a model of messianic time, concentrates [*zusammenfasst*] the history of all humanity in a monstrous abbreviation [*eine ungeheuren Abbreviatur*]."[11] The monstrous Jesus is not the *ungeheure Zusammensetzung* of God and a human individual, but rather the *ungeheure Zusammenfassung* of the billion human histories catalyzed by his divinity, an "abbreviation" whose patient unravelling in time is faith's painful work in a process it can never arrest.

Hegel correctly identified the scandal of the composite Christ as the challenge inherent from the beginning in monotheist worship of a human being. But from the standpoint of this essay, he misidentified the nature of the composition: Christian monstrosity is not the vertical superimposition of divinity upon a mere human being, but the way the assuming Word horizontally dilates that human being, so to speak, in an unending history of reception that extends and expresses him. To

10 Hegel, *Lectures on the Philosophy of Religion*, 3:315.

11 "*Die Jetztzeit, die als Modell der messianischen in einer ungeheueren Abbreviatur die Geschichte der ganzen Menschheit zusammenfasst, fällt haarscharf mit der Figur zusammen, die die Geschichte der Menschheit im Universum macht.*" Walter Benjamin, "Über den Begriff der Geschichte" [1940], in *Gesammelte Schriften*, vol. 1, part 2, ed. Rolf Tiedemann and Hermann Schweppenhäuser (Frankfurt am Main: Suhrkamp Verlag, 1974), 691–704 at 703.

keep recognizing the original human identity of Jesus in the continually new forms of its temporally exploding human presence, both within the church (i.e., the communities of those dedicated to such recognition) and outside it, has ever been and will ever be a labor of faith. The believing community over time must keep imagining for itself an unending procession of Jesus-figures that join together in new ways the Spirit's witness to his active presence here and now on one side, and the scriptural portrait of his initial human life on the other. But unlike Hegel, the Christian has no rational or dialectical way to resolve the difficulty of seeing Jesus now in the Jesus of the Gospels. Origen already suggested that Jesus had been a shape-shifter, even in his life prior to cross and resurrection appearing differently to different viewers.[12] But the composition of the posthumously present Jesus, assuming far more extravagantly different shapes as history goes on, with the Jesus inscribed in the New Testament, has never been easy. Indeed, Scripture already represents the initial, classic attempts at this composition; the monstrous combination of humanity and divinity in these stories has always supplied a possible offense to faith that no philosophy could eliminate.

What has made this task harder today is the historical-critical handling of the Gospels that has unmasked Jesus even here, from the beginning, as a composite, in fact a partially mythical construct. The visible glow of divinity has been lifted away from history, leaving only the humanity; and even the humanity might have taken offensive form (e.g., that of a Palestinian magician, if MS is right). The Gospel accounts have imaginatively put together their Jesus out of disparate materials and traditions. Mark's Gospel thus typifies the kind of bricolage at work in the cultural construction of Jesus' divinity. Burton Mack can even argue (another "extreme" historical possibility that neither history nor faith can eliminate) that Mark mingles elements drawn from "movements in Palestine and southern Syria that cultivated the memory of Jesus as a founder-teacher" with quite distinct matter originating in "congregations in northern Syria, Asia Minor and Greece wherein the death and resurrection of the Christ were

12 For an overview of this theme, see John A. McGuckin, "The Changing Forms of Jesus," in *Origeniana Quarta: Die Referate des 4 Internationalen Origeneskongresses, Innsbruck, 2–6 September, 1985*, ed. Lothar Lies (Innsbruck: Tyrolia Verlag, 1987), 215–22.

regarded as the founding events."[13] But where disparate and often extravagant elements are superimposed in this way, with their original elements fused together but nonetheless retaining their differentiated, not quite compatible forms, the result (as in a photographic double exposure) cannot help but enhance the monstrosity of the original Jesus.

It was argued in the previous chapter that faith should not take signs for wonders. This is a theological fulfillment of the cultural logic of reverse-aretalogy. Jesus' words already cited in chapter 3 (John 6:26) chide those hearers (and those Gospel readers) who see in the miraculous deed an "impossible" event rather than an identifying signal, fixating on deed rather than doer. This cultural lesson had its theological counterpart in chapter 8, and is taken up again in a new way here. The space of encounter in which Jesus can truly appear is defined by only two possible states: worship or offense. Hence, to read correctly the "signs" presented by Jesus' recorded feats requires the proper stance toward his divinized humanity as a whole; that in turn means reading correctly the encounter with his composite life. Premodern consciousness can more readily fuse the historical and the marvelous in his story to correctly read his original appearance. But modern critical awareness inevitably sharpens their distinct outlines and heightens their mutual tension. On one side there is the historical Jesus as "larva" (in Latin, the ghost or mask): a man who, placed in the landscape of the past, must appear at once all too typical (i.e., boring) and "divine" (i.e., grotesque). On the other side there is the interpretive clutter of his posthumously "raised" cultural body: the Christ-event put together from the religious legends at hand, a fabric of truths and fictions.

The gap of the centuries heightens the potential offense. The cultural terms which conveyed Jesus' peculiar excellence for his era, the "divine" marks that effected his deity in his contemporary world, are largely inscrutable to all save specialist historians. The symbolic systems which were the inevitable substance of his humanity and within which his deity was realized are for the most part foreign to the values that modern people might cherish. Thus, when historical investigation attempts to make contact with Jesus yet simply sets aside the categories which framed the cult of his deity,

13 Burton Mack, *A Myth of Innocence: Mark and Christian Origins* (Philadelphia: Fortress, 1988), 11. Cited at Jonathan Z. Smith, *Drudgery Divine: On the Comparison of Early Christianities and the Religions of Late Antiquity* (Chicago: University of Chicago Press, 1990), 138.

the purely human remainder that is exhibited will all too likely show up as at once blandly familiar in his own context, bizarre in ours. There will certainly be no ground to expect some perennial, recognizable "greatness."

The potential offense to faith is obvious. Yet even historical Jesus scholarship is tempted to work into its reconstructions a patchwork of what seem from a contemporary point of view the promising elements carefully sifted from the Gospels and rounded out with some comparative material, proffering it to believers as the "real" historical basis of the Christian faith. One unfortunate result of these forays has been a series of "inspiring" Jesuses, remarkable individuals worthy of our collective esteem. Worse, critical judgment can be subtly and unconsciously warped by this pressing need to nudge the "historical" Jesus into some religiously or ethically satisfying shape: the consummate Israelite, the proto-Nietzschean sage, the crypto-feminist, the guerilla destabilizer of the social order, etc. Even Schleiermacher long ago complained of the formally similar attempt of "Enlightened" dogmatics to present the "wise man of Nazareth" or the "simple country rabbi" as the true object of Christian belief.[14] It is a misunderstanding of the meaning of incarnation to assume that Jesus looked like any of these heartening exemplars.

The New Testament itself, on the other hand, displays a proper anxiety before the constitutive ambiguity of Jesus. "Signs and wonders" are the distinguishing mark both of God's "holy servant Jesus" (Acts 4:30) and of "false Christs and false prophets" (Mark 13:22, RSV). The Greek word for "wonder" is also the word for "monster."[15] This happy lexicographical possibility specifies what faith is forever to be confronted with in Jesus: ambiguous miracles and a never-ending series of imagined variations grafted upon an historical "larva." *Semeia kai terata*, signs and monsters.

14 Friedrich Schleiermacher, "Über die Glaubenslehre. Zwei Sendschreiben an Lücke," in *Kritische Gesamtausgabe, Erste Abteilung*, vol. 10, *Theologisch-dogmatische Abhandlungen und Gelegenheitsschriften*, ed. Hans-Friedrich Traulsen (Berlin: Walter de Gruyter, 1990), 347; English translation: *On the Glaubenslehre: Two Letters to Dr. Lücke*, trans. James Duke and Francis Fiorenza (Atlanta: Scholars Press, 1981), 62. The English translation is misleading at one point: the idiom "*sich etwas gefallen lassen*" is misrendered as "dispense with" rather than "stand" or "put up with" or "tolerate."

15 On the ambiguity of the phrase, see Leo O'Reilly, *Word and Sign in the Acts of the Apostles: A Study in Lucan Theology* (Rome: Editrice Pontificia Università Gregoriana, 1987), 161.

II.

The association in the quote from Mark of signs with prophecy indicates a necessary connection: every correct reading of Jesus as divine involves an indirect perception or vision that is divinely (or otherwise) inspired. This is most obviously the case in regard to the past; in fact, the entire essay up to now has been about the impossibility of a direct inspection of the incarnation and the need for an imaginative and interpretive process to construe it properly. To believe that Jesus is God means to enter the community of those who share his embodied humanity, and that means in turn to take a certain existential stance toward a series of past events. These events are factual, part of the flow of history, and yet they also enter into a configuration that cannot be captured by the ideally neutral instruments of historical judgment. A kind of discernment, superimposed upon but not altering or determining the historian's reconstructions, is necessary to see the past facts enter into the requisite pattern; it is a reading of signs, an interpretation that requires both the disposition of belief and the agency of God's Spirit. To continually purify and renew this vision of the past is what has here been called the "cultic recognition" of Jesus.

This has never been possible without risk of offense, where faith is challenged by a vision of Jesus' divinity that is repellent or "wrong"; the elements giving rise to this risk are structural, part of the incarnation itself, but have become variously sharpened with the arrival of modern thinking. The original, historical Jesus was already "wrong" to his contemporaries; in this initial, "larval" form the supposedly divine human being was stubbornly ambiguous, always threatening to appear a fanatic or impostor. Hence the need for the symbolic operations transacted in his cult over time, to which the protracted emergence of the Gospels bears witness. The emergent canonical portrait, though definitive for the community, was from the beginning always susceptible to misreading, generating many "wrong" (heretical) Jesuses. But these perennial threats to communal cultic recognition have all been made worse in modernity, due to three factors.

First, the merging of realistic and fantastic elements by which the Gospels truly rendered Jesus becomes more defamiliarized and alienating as historical awareness grows of the radical differences between these discursive formations. Second, as Bultmann constantly emphasized, the fantastic or mythic elements in themselves no longer speak immediately to the modern reader. Having lost the receptive instincts of mythological consciousness, the contemporary interpreter either balks at, or, alternatively, inappropriately literalizes the accounts. The Gospels become a semi-legendary tale of a demigod named "Jesus" who walks on water, passes untouched through a murderous crowd, or transfers a throng of demons into a herd of swine.

The third complication of the believer's vision of the past by historical consciousness has to do with the way the community of interpretation itself is now understood. The communal dimension is our entry into the real concern of this final section. The churches, the Jesus groups throughout history, are the spaces in which the vision of Jesus' divinity is always (in principle) granted; only now the common justification for this hermeneutic privilege, the church as the direct historic extension of Jesus' activity and intentions, has become far more problematic.

Even when the traditional notion of Jesus consciously and quasi-officially "founding" the church has been abandoned, history has long recognized the difficulty of including later communities in a clear causal chain reaching all the way back to Jesus. Alfred Loisy rightly stressed the processual unfolding of Christian truth in history, against what might be called Harnack's "big bang" theory, i.e., the totality of Christian truth as a timeless "kernel" fully recoverable from the teaching of the historical Jesus.[16] But he still saw the church historically as a natural, organic outgrowth from Jesus; the limits of that metaphor were exposed in the masterful work of Walter Bauer.[17] It was his insight that this process of unfolding was more essentially contested, historically contingent, and multiply constructed than Loisy's model of a continuous, living growth would suggest.

Following his lines, the assumption has become more common that there was no original unique community carrying or transmitting the pure influence of Jesus; orthodoxy emerged later, out of a sea of gnostic and retrospectively "heretical" communities. This cacophony was no aberration but simply *was* Christianity. In fact, at first there were only "heresies," competing groupuscules, with (maybe) Pauline

16 See Alfred Loisy, *The Gospel and the Church* [1904], trans. Christopher Home (New York: Charles Scribner's Sons, 1912).

17 See Walter Bauer, *Orthodoxy and Heresy in Earliest Christianity* [1934], ed. Robert A. Kraft and Gerhard Krodel (Philadelphia: Fortress, 1971).

or Johannine cells just part of the mix, their differences bewildering to outsiders (when noticeable at all).[18] Some of these scattered cliques, the ones articulating what Christians now claim to be authentic "recognitions" of Jesus, were probably driven by their struggle against the much weightier cultural presence of alternative Christianities to develop an extensive epistolary activity; the cross-network of appeals to similarly minded communities across geographic regions became the distinguishing mark of nascent "orthodoxy."[19]

Thus the exercise of faithful discernment of the past that has always been incumbent upon Christians in order to recognize God in Christ is troubled for modern believers by the inescapable knowledge of their own conflicted past as a group. The faithful today must discern how the work of the Spirit shared or communicated between Father and Son gradually came to shape out of the confusing mass of modalities of Jesus-veneration that select body of communities for whom the prime mark of fidelity to him was community (*koinonia*) itself, both internal (*agape*) and external (translocal coordination). But with this emphasis on the communal and processual dimension of discernment another note emerges: to rightly read Jesus as God, retrospect is not enough. The believing community, like any cultural unit, understands itself not just from its past but equally from its anticipated future.

The discussion up to this point has emphasized the possible offense, the forms of Jesus' "wrongness," that always endangers the church's backward search for the correct view of its Lord. But the hazard of incarnational monstrosity has another aspect, just as perennial and just as susceptible to modern intensification. The Word's reception in history suffers a double defect, or, to put it differently, the believers always find their vision of Jesus Christ threatened by a twofold lack. They are suspended between the incompleteness of Jesus in his original "larval" form (what could be called the infinite yet still unexpressed surplus of his meaning) and the unfinished character of his communal expression. Every faith construal of Jesus

18 Bauer, *Orthodoxy and Heresy*, 236, provocatively invites the reader to consider Paulinism as the original heresy and Paul as "the only heresiarch known to the apostolic age."

19 Bauer, *Orthodoxy and Heresy*, 93–94; cf. 231. Rowan Williams develops these insights of Bauer in a fascinating article, "Does It Make Sense to Speak of Pre-Nicene Orthodoxy?" in *The Making of Orthodoxy: Essays in Honor of Henry Chadwick*, ed. Rowan Williams (Cambridge: Cambridge University Press, 1989), 1–23.

as the humanly, culturally incarnate Word, at least every such construal that seeks to be adequate to its present, will involve cultic recognition; that means Jesus envisioned from the stance of the worshiping community, incorporating as much as possible of the collective past insight of that community (scripturally formed with, for Catholic and Orthodox, further creedal and liturgical definition). But every construal will also involve a kind of anticipatory vision or prophecy.

This is an adaptation of one of Troeltsch's insights; he insisted that the essence of Christianity as an historical phenomenon could not be historically grasped unless the interpreter projected it into the future as an ongoing, living, and creative force.[20] Here the emphasis is Christological, however. If Jesus is indeed the incarnation in human history of the infinite Word, his very humanity can only bear and transmit this burden of meaning as it extends itself into the unfolding of the history of humanity itself. This is not unlike the claim of the early Strauss, for whom the divine truth could only be expressed in humanity as a whole; the crucial difference is that Christian faith demands the originating plenitude of that truth in the human individual Jesus, the divine utterance of the Word as "inaugurating rupture" (Certeau), followed by the extended hearing of that utterance in the form of the church, and the church's ongoing engagement in the construction of a communal human totality only to be completed at the eschaton, the end of history. Fully discerning the Jesus of the past as God means discerning his human significance in its eventual complete flowering, but that significance for now is truncated and distorted by the sin of the church. Thus every prophecy of who Jesus is labors under its own threat of wrongness or monstrosity.

To illustrate the connection of anticipatory prophecy and wrongness, consider the following curious example of fictional prophecy. The third chapter of this essay joined together the work of MS and of JZS, first to bring to light some marginalized elements from the history of religions for critically interpreting the Jesus of the past, and second to suggest the unification of Jesus and his cult into a single, cultural "Christ-event" which could then serve as historical "matter" for a causally layered model of

20 Ernst Troeltsch, "Was heisst 'Wesen des Christentums'?" in *Gesammelte Schriften*, vol. 2 (Tübingen: J. C. B. Mohr, 1913), 423–32; English translation: "What Does 'Essence of Christianity' Mean?" in *Writings on Theology and Religion*, trans. and ed. Robert Morgan and Michael Pye (Louisville: Westminster John Knox, 1977), 156–63.

incarnation. This close pairing of MS and JZS as part of a research project was without precedent in the scholarly literature known to me, but there did come to my attention an older work in which a British interviewer yoked them together even more closely than has been attempted here.

In particular, two memorable passages from that work, one associated with MS, the other with JZS, turn out to be surprisingly relevant to this essay. The first nicely captures the thrust and anticipated import of MS's then still unpublished research on Jesus the magician. Gesturing toward "my *magnum opus*—the pile of papers on the side table," the interviewee confesses with arch solemnity that "[i]t is my analysis of the documents found in the Coptic monasteries of Syria and Egypt, a work which will cut deep at the very foundations of revealed religion." The second passage is an amusingly vivid description that will be instantly recognizable to those familiar with JZS's striking physical presence, visible year after year in the halls between sessions at the American Academy of Religion: "[A] gaunt, aquiline face . . . with piercing dark eyes, which lurked in deep hollows under overhung and tufted brows. His hair and beard were white, save that the latter was curiously stained with yellow around his mouth. A cigarette glowed amid the tangle of white hair, and the air of the room was fetid with stale tobacco-smoke."

Now to the point. Unexpected as it was to find such telling evocations of both MS and JZS together in a single publication, a much bigger surprise was the identity of the interviewer: Sherlock Holmes. The two quotations are drawn from one of Arthur Conan Doyle's detective stories, published in 1904, and though in the story both the "magnum opus" boast and the facial features belong in fact to a single character, their latter-day application to our two scholars is unmistakable.[21] In other words, not just the coming of the Smiths, but their conjunction in a single purpose, was here anticipated in a striking vision of the future. Doyle prophesied the present essay. His words unerringly referred to the future, though they remain perfectly situated within Doyle's fictional past. The prophetic imagination has poetically but not unfittingly fused together the coming figures: in the oracle, MS and JZS compose a single living character, the mysterious "Professor Coram." If the logic of prophetic vision mimics that of dreams, then we have here a case of what Freud called "condensation," a merging

21 Arthur Conan Doyle, "The Adventure of the Golden Pince-Nez," in *The Complete Sherlock Holmes*, vol. 2 (New York: Barnes & Noble Classics, 2003), 165–66.

of figures that foreshadows their community of concern (not to mention their identity of surnames). This, of course, is a key element within surrealist strategy and, it was argued here, a modality of the Gospel compositions as well: yet another anticipation of the present project.

This strange interlude has a point, similar to the one made by Troeltsch: the mutual involvement, for good and ill, of reading the past and anticipating the future. What is true, and consequently what is wrong, in a prophecy can only be determined by looking back from the fulfilled future events originally envisioned. To the extent those events are still only partially completed, assessment of the accuracy of the forecast, and even of its meaning, will be hampered. Doyle correctly foresaw the functional union of the Smiths, but, perhaps confused by the shared surname, incorrectly (and, from the present perspective, grotesquely) fused them into a single individual. But this assessment, and in fact the proper apprehension of the nature of Doyle's short story *as* a prophecy, had both to bide their time, awaiting the completed project of this essay.

In a similar way, the proper apprehension of Jesus as the Word incarnate, as well as the ability to see past the "wrongness" to the truth of the fusion of fact and myth in the Gospels, both depend upon participation in the unfolding ecclesial event of Jesus' pneumatic future. Here is the difference, however. The only perspective from which Jesus can be seen as God, the only place from which the Spirit's point of view can be adopted, lies in the unfinished process of ecclesial witness. This means that the failure to grasp the true shape of the past Jesus as the Christ of the present is always a function of the church's failure to be the Kingdom, the fulfilled human body of meaning fit to express the infinite Word originally uttered as a human life.

All recognitions of Jesus are embedded within the larger, unfinished process of faith living in history. The second divine mission, the personal arrival of the Spirit spread among the multitude of believers, sets up a field of force operative among the discrete facts of history. This field fills the space, opened up by Jesus' ascension, between his physically absent new body and his sign-body continuing its pilgrimage through time. This force bends the facts into figures of God's filial self-relation, but without breaking their natural causal linkage. This Spirit-force is thus released by Jesus' resurrection, and it provides the "heat," as has been said, that fuses the diverse cultural elements into the single living being of the Christ-event;

even the fictional elements become integral parts of his true identity, part of his historical carapace, as it were. It is the same force that converts material objects and gestures into sacraments. It is the energy enabling the discursive "capture" of local spans of history for the master pattern of human belonging together under God (the "Kingdom"). Finally, it is the motor of Christian prophecy, enabling the ongoing imaginative grasp of who Jesus is now, pivoting between the biblical remembrance of his past and the partial apprehension of his future fullness.

The process of fully recognizing Jesus, and the community-shaping and inspiring work of the second personal mission of God that enables it, is an ongoing affair, unfinished until the fulfillment of the present order. This means that every vision of who Jesus really "was" is, at the same time, an anticipation or prediction of his full eschatological identity in his people. It is, then, the inherent incompleteness of the Christian community, its still needing in so many ways to grow up to the full stature of Christ, that is retarding that presence and generating new prophetic attempts to "name" him in the space between past and future. It is important to remember this dimension of ecclesiality. The church is said to have been built on the foundation of apostles *and* prophets, but there is a tendency to elevate the former, which signifies the element of ordered traditioning, into the exclusive mark of fidelity. The other foundation, the unruly imaginative improvisations of prophecy, must receive its equally due honor, lest the unbalanced emphasis on apostolicity pervert the justifiable hierarchical functions of the church into tools of domination and static integralism. This risk has always been present; it is a perennial aspect of the risk of offense proper to the future anticipation of Jesus' fullness of meaning.

However, this irremovable forward-looking or prophetic dimension of the recognition of Jesus as God becomes especially salient within modernity, often painfully so, for two reasons. First, the progressive discovery by historical investigation of the role of communal tradition and imaginative construction in determining the shape of the Gospel portraits has cast a glaring light on the imaginative and constructive role of the community in rightly hearing the Word in Jesus. Just this awkward but inevitable bond between Jesus as object of worship and the constructions of the communal subject aggravates the risk of Jesus' monstrosity, for it reveals his scriptural portrait, not as a full and sufficient image calling only for the gaze of reverence, but as the prophetic outline of his fullness, awaiting varied and creative expression in the history of his community. The Gospels were never the completion of Jesus' identity construction but only its initiation. They are like those ultrahigh shutter speed photographs of an atomic explosion in its first fractions of a second. The terrible flash of the Christ-event in its initial moments is in them fixed forever, our only light in the murk of the first century; but though the Gospels are the church's indispensable orientation for all future efforts at further identification, each is nonetheless only a snapshot of what is after all a kinetic reality. They are products, that is, of the same process of ecclesial (prophetic) recognition that is also happening now and will continue, both in true and in failed presentations of the savior.

The second way modern consciousness aggravates the potential offense of prophecy is that it holds up a pitiless mirror to the Christian community; history cannot ignore the church's repeated failures of witness, its performative perversions of its own truth. If the identity of Jesus for faith today is elusive and, at times, grotesque, it is partly because his body continues its vital development in history and cannot be arrested for inspection. But if the evolving aspect of that body is identical with the community of those who seek to know whom they worship, and who seek in that knowing the perfection of their own communion with each other, then its motion is a sign not only of its continued growth, but also of its need for growth, that is, of its own persistent failure to complete itself as a community of love.

In his marvelous essay on the ideological function of horror fiction in capitalism, literary critic Franco Moretti has argued that in the figure of the monster bourgeois civilization simultaneously registers awareness of its own failure as a society (i.e., as an inclusive, cohesive community), and represses that consciousness by expressing it in mystified form.

> The literature of terror is studded with passages where the protagonists brush against the awareness—described by Freud—that the perturbing element is *within them*: that it is they themselves who produce the monsters they fear. . . . [But t]he lesson these books wish to impart is that . . . one need not fear one's own repressions. . . . No, one should be afraid of the *monster*, of something *material*, something *external*.[22]

22 Franco Moretti, "Dialectic of Fear" [1978], in *Signs Taken for Wonders: Essays in the Sociology of Literary Forms*, rev. ed., trans. Susan Fischer et al. (London: Verso, 1988), 102 (emphasis in original).

> The monster, then, serves to displace the antagonisms and horrors evidenced *within* society *outside* society itself. . . . The monster, the utterly unknown, serves to reconstruct a universality, a social cohesion which—in itself—would no longer carry conviction.[23]

This insight is readily adaptable to understanding the disfigured visage of Jesus in the church's failed recognitions as the threatening aspect of the church's judge. Once it has been grasped that the progressive recognition of Jesus is a human, interpretive, and cultural process of the believing community in the world, the community's prophetic vision of Jesus cannot evade the disturbed realization that the persistent distortions and indefiniteness in its sense of his identity is a product of its own failure to be true and faithful.

Faith today is frightfully aware that the scanty and imperfect objective outlines of Jesus' person can only be made alive by the creative subjectivity of the believer. It is always tempted to reject this agonizing tentativeness of prophecy for an illusively solid Jesus, historical or doctrinal. But when it tries to set up an objective Jesus as something simply "out there," over against the community, it will always be faced with a monstrous torso that mirrors its own broken communion. The suppressed possibility of offense has simply returned in yet another form. Instead, the true Jesus will always be an objective-subjective hybrid, and hence a projection of the community's own unfinishedness, the defect that constitutes it as a living, growing entity in time but that is also "wrong," what should not be. It must accept this monstrosity, and its own complicity with it, in order to surpass it in faith. The unfinished nature of the community that is not yet the Kingdom means that it cannot yet adequately speak the Word it hears through its worship.

"Thanks be to God for his unspeakable gift!" cried Paul (2 Cor 9:15, RSV). But there is something unnerving about this epithet, for it suggests as well the ghastly formlessness of Lovecraft's "unnameable." Only at the end of all things will Jesus be fully known for who he is, as John's Apocalypse suggests when in its description of the eschatologically victorious Lord it notes that upon his many crowns "he has a name inscribed which no one knows but himself" (Rev 19:12, RSV). The process of naming keeps going on, Jesus keeps assuming new forms, some comforting, some monstrous. But his true name remains unspeakable until the end. The community of

23 Moretti, "Dialectic," 84 (emphasis in original).

his cult struggles to recognize Jesus as it grows with him in the world, but it is haunted by the realization that it cannot yet name him, cannot yet definitively identify him (which is not to say that he is unknown to it). It can only hold on to the hope that its unending communal construction of his full identity is an asymptotic convergence, and that it is indeed (painfully slowly) "catching up" to who he always was.

Faith can only endure this labor, with its attendant failures. For what does it have that it can directly grasp? What does it possess that could be detached from this uncertain venture of self-commitment? Yes, it has the Jesus of the Gospels, but these after all are no biography but a palimpsest: a farrago of borrowed Syrian cultic legends and dubiously applied Jewish messianic oracles layered over the barely visible lineaments of an obscure enthusiast. It has, too, the heroic early community that preserved his memory, and to which it traces its lineage. But the historian sees only an apocalyptic mystery cult whose ecstatic gibberish ("possession" by the divine spirit of prophecy) supposedly bespoke the controlling presence of "Jesus," an itinerant Jewish exorcist whose grisly death years ago in a shameful public execution was supposedly the setup for his imminent return as God's agent to rule a remade cosmos. What legitimacy is to be found in such an ancestor? It has, finally, the God inherited from Judaism, but does it also have a ready reply to MS's sardonic literalism?

> Nobody, so far as I know, believes in the existence of Yahweh as the OT describes him—a North Arabian mountain god who travelled in thunderstorms and liked the smell of burning fat.[24]

Just so! Nobody could "believe" in such a deity (or such Gospels, or such a church) if this were all there is to be said. But the point of this essay is that there is very much more to be said. Only not, it must be insisted, *instead of* these descriptions (they are true as far as they go), but *about* them. It has been the presumption of this essay that there is no way to expel these disturbing possibilities in purely historical terms, but the Christological proposal has been that faithful witness to the incarnate God might honorably concede them. The Jesus of the past, along with the rest of Christian history simply as past, will never stop speaking hard

24 Morton Smith, "The Present State of Old Testament Studies" [1969], in Morton Smith, *Studies in the Cult of Yahweh*, ed. Shaye J. D. Cohen, vol. 1 (Leiden: Brill, 1996), 39.

words to belief. His ancient warning holds good (John 16:12): we still cannot, even today, bear his words. But faith, if it does not try to stop its ears or shout them down, can turn these dry bones into the living truth of faith. The only comfort to be found, as Jesus promised, is in the *parakletos*, the Spirit. With the Spirit, in the community, belief in this alienating history, contra MS, really is possible. The Christians in their millions, with all their undeniable record of smugness, ignorance, and viciousness, are those whom the divine irony has gifted with the ability to see that whole collection of sordid historical facts for what it is: the saving disclosure of God to all humanity.

As for Jesus' reality now and to come, the incarnational scheme developed in this essay might be imagined this way. The resurrected one has taken the body of the new aeon, ascending the cosmic temple steps to the throne. But there has been no epiphanic moment. Instead, he has trailed his glory behind him in history, like a king's heavy velvet train dragging in the mud. The church is that train, it is Jesus Christ's semiotic or sign-body, the cultural process of never-ending recognition always having to catch up with his surpassing identity (which itself is not complete till the end of human history). Epiphany stretches out in the form of a social process, its sporadic glimmer leaking out through the negotiations of culture. That is why, even today, as Schweitzer said, "He comes to us as one unknown, without a name, as of old."[25]

Out of the scores of ancient Hellenistic mystery cults, one of them, though its stammer can scarcely denominate the one it worships, is still a going concern. To continue, this cult of the unspeakable must keep learning to handle rightly the offense of history, the element of fear that Jesus must bring with him out of the past, even as he delivers his ineffable comfort. This is not that anxiety familiar to the historians of Jesus, the risk (in George Tyrrell's endlessly quoted image) of looking down the well of the centuries only to mistake for Jesus a reflection in the water of the investigator's face. From the standpoint of faith this is, after all, a marginal worry, for history seeks Jesus as a dead fact, fixed in a bygone distance. Only the faith that knows his total claim, the uncontrollable surplus of his humanity, also knows the dread that comes when you look down that same well, only to see the unutterable living thing climbing up toward you.

25 Albert Schweitzer, *The Quest of the Historical Jesus: First Complete Edition*, ed. John Bowden (Minneapolis: Fortress, 2001), 487.

Appendix

Nempe quodlibet epitheton item flecti potest ad usum pium. Invenitur inter inscriptiones antiquas quae in aedibus illustrissimi comites Arundelii visuntur una lingua Chaldaica, effigies fulgenti arulae infaustae Pompeio Magno ex Heliopoli Syrae asportatae, consecratae גלמא בעל *Baal Gulma*, quod interpretatur Domino sine forma sive Deus informis, vocato perperam creator omnipotens et Rex omniae. Quamquam ignotus ut mihi videtur Hebraeis, certe dicit de eodem deo Statius Thebaidos lib. IV *triplicis mundi summum, quem scire nefastum.* Necnon antiquissimo illicitoque cultu veteres certe Arabes hunc deum distortum in medio mundo, numinem caecum et amentem sub nomine *Azatoth* adoraverant, secundum quendam codicem rarissimum flagitiosumque, iam dudum e lingua Arabica conversum, Librum Jures Mortuorum, qui ad me ex bibliothecam V[iri] C[larissimi] Joannis Dee venit. Atque adeo hoc genus daemonorum sidereorum insane venerabantur ut semper praesentes verum tamen figura et splendor carens divinus, ut habet iste liber, *Uti foetor eos noscites; urgent faucibus attamen non videtis.* Sed forsitan numina non modo profana informia aliquando nominent. Ipse eques Kenelmus Digbaeus mihi narravit visionem mirabilem. Anno mortis uxoris eius [i.e., 1633], solus est intempesta nocte intra maceriam hortuli silvae Bragdonii, in vigilia festi natalis beati Johannis Baptistae. Subito adest Dominus noster, sed dissimulanter, quasi vultu deforme. Et tamquam procul vox tristisse mulieris sonat. *Quid*, inquit, *ingens sacramentum, Domine, monstres?* Responditque Christus, *Talis adventus meus longe extractus; regnum signorum valet donec plenitudo gentium intraret: nunc Filius Dei sum et nondum apparuit quid ero.* Quae non intellexit Digbaeus; at verba in postis horti visibiles etiam nunc incidit DEO INFORMI.

John Selden, *De diis syris*

A Note on the Extract

The enormously learned legal historian John Selden, friend of Ben Jonson and Lancelot Andrewes and a pioneering Orientalist, made his European reputation with *On the Syrian Gods* (1st ed. 1617), a study of the pagan deities referenced in the Bible that continually digresses into strange fields of ancient erudition. (See G. J. Toomer, *John Selden: A Life in Scholarship* [Oxford: Oxford University Press, 2009], 211–56 and 841–44.) Among the notes that he prepared for the never-completed third edition of this work (Bodleian MS Selden supra 106 [SC 32266]), but that did not make their way into the *Opera* edited by Wilkins in 1726, was the above (f. 42v). It was intended to be inserted into the treatment of Baal (the first chapter of Syntagma II), evidently following Selden's comments concerning the semantic twist at Acts 17:23, where St. Paul polemically wrests a Christian meaning from the pagan dedication "*deo ignoto*." Incidentally, Selden did not include in his famous *Marmora Arundelliana* (1628) the Aramaic inscription from the Earl of Arundel's supposed copy of "Pompey's altar" (which has not survived, and the authenticity of which is in doubt).

Bibliography

Arendt, Hannah. Introduction to *Illuminations: Essays and Reflections*, by Walter Benjamin. New York: Schocken Books, 1968.

Auerbach, Erich. "Figura." In *Scenes from the Drama of European Literature*. 1944. Gloucester, Mass.: Peter Smith, 1973.

Augustine. "Sermon 52." In *Sermons III (51–94): The Old Testament*. Translated by Edmund Hill O.P. Edited by John Rotelle O.S.A. *The Works of Saint Augustine: A New Translation for the 21st Century*. Hyde Park, N.Y.: New City Press, 2009.

Barth, Karl. *Der Römerbrief, 1922*. Zurich: Theologischer Verlag, 1940. Translated by Edwyn C. Hoskyns as *The Epistle to the Romans*. Oxford: Oxford University Press, 1933.

———. "Unerledigte Anfragen an die heutige Theologie." In *Die Theologie und die Kirche*, 1–25. Zollikon-Zurich: Evangelischer Verlag, 1928. Translated by Louise Pettibone Smith as "Unsettled Questions for Theology Today." In *Theology and Church*, 55–73. New York: Harper & Row, 1962.

Bauer, Walter. *Orthodoxy and Heresy in Earliest Christianity*. Edited by Robert A. Kraft and Gerhard Krodel. Philadelphia: Fortress, 1971.

Benjamin, Walter. "Über den Begriff der Geschichte." In vol. 1, part 2, of *Gesammelte Schriften*, edited by Rolf Tiedemann and Hermann Schweppenhäuser. 1940. Frankfurt am Main: Suhrkamp Verlag, 1974.

Betz, Hans Dieter, ed. *The Greek Magical Papyri in Translation*. Vol. 1, *Texts*. Chicago: University of Chicago Press, 1986.

Bonhoeffer, Dietrich. *Christ the Center: A New Translation*. Translated by Edwin H. Robertson. New York: Harper & Row, 1978. German original available in *Berlin 1932–1933*, edited by Carsten Nicolaisen and Ernst-Albert Scharfennorth, vol. 12 of *Dietrich Bonhoeffer Werke*, edited by Eberhard Bethge et al. Gütersloh: Christian Kaiser Verlag, 1997.

———. *Ethik*. Edited by Ilse Tödt et al. Vol. 6, *Dietrich Bonhoeffer Werke*, edited by Eberhard Bethge et al. Gütersloh: Christian Kaiser Verlag, 1998. Translated by Clifford J. Green as *Ethics*. Vol. 6 of *Dietrich Bonhoeffer Works*, edited by Wayne Whitson Floyd Jr. Minneapolis: Fortress, 2005.

———. *Letters and Papers from Prison*. Translated by John W. DeGruchy. Vol. 8 of *Dietrich Bonhoeffer Works*, edited by Victoria J. Barnett and Barbara Wojhoski. Minneapolis: Fortress, 2010. German original available in *Widerstand und Ergebung*, edited by Christian Gremmels et al. Vol. 8 of *Dietrich Bonhoeffer Werke*, edited by Eberhard Bethge et al. Gütersloh: Christian Kaiser Verlag, 1998.

Braun, Willi, and Russell T. McCutcheon, eds. *Introducing Religion: Essays in Honor of Jonathan Z. Smith*. Sheffield: Equinox Publishing, 2008.

Breton, André. *Manifestoes of Surrealism*. Translated by Richard Seaver and Helen R. Lane. Ann Arbor: University of Michigan Press, 1969.

Brown, Scott G. "Factualizing the Folklore: Stephen Carlson's Case against Morton Smith." *Harvard Theological Review* 99 (2006): 291–327.

———. "The Letter to Theodore: Stephen Carlson's Case against Clement's Authorship." *Journal of Early Christian Studies* 16 (2008): 535–72.

———. *Mark's Other Gospel: Rethinking Morton Smith's Controversial Discovery*. Studies in Christianity and Judaism. Waterloo, Ontario: Wilfrid Laurier University Press, 2005.

———. "The Question of Motive in the Case against Morton Smith." *Journal of Biblical Literature* 125 (2006): 351–83.

———. "Reply to Stephen Carlson." *Expository Times* 117 (2006): 144–49.

Bultmann, Rudolf. "Die Liberale Theologie und die jüngste theologische Bewegung." In *Glauben und Verstehen: Gesammelte Aufsätze I*, 9th ed., 1–25. Tübingen: J. C. B. Mohr, 1993. Translated by Louise Pettibone Smith as "Liberal Theology and the Latest Theological Movement." In *Faith and Understanding*, edited by Robert W. Funk, 28–52. London: SCM Press, 1969.

———. *Theology of the New Testament*. Translated by Kendrick Grobel. Vol. 1. London: SCM Press, 1952.

———. *Das Verhältnis der urchristlichen Christusbotschaft zum historischen Jesus*. Heidelberg: Carl Winter Universitätsverlag, 1960.

———. "Zur Frage der Christologie." In *Glauben und Verstehen: Gesammelte Aufsätze I*, 9th ed. Tübingen: J. C. B. Mohr, 1993. Translated by Louise

Pettibone Smith as "On the Question of Christology." In *Faith and Understanding*, edited by Robert W. Funk. London: SCM Press, 1969.

Burkert, Walter. *Structure and History in Greek Mythology and Ritual*. Berkeley: University of California Press, 1979.

Calder, William M. "Morton Smith." *Gnomon* 64 (1992): 382–84.

Cameron, Ron, and Merrill P. Miller, eds. *Redescribing Christian Origins*. Leiden: Brill, 2004.

———. *Redescribing Paul and the Corinthians*. Leiden: Brill, 2011.

Carlson, Stephen C. *The Gospel Hoax: Morton Smith's Invention of Secret Mark*. Waco, Tex.: Baylor University Press, 2005.

Certeau, Michel de. *La Fable Mystique: XVIe—XVIIe Siècle*. Paris: Gallimard, 1982. Translated by Michael B. Smith as *The Mystic Fable*. Vol. 1, *The Sixteenth and Seventeenth Centuries*. Chicago: University of Chicago Press, 1992.

———. "La rupture instauratrice." In *La Faiblesse de Croire*, edited by Luce Giard. 1971. Paris: Éditions du Seuil, 1997. Translated as "The Inaugurating Rupture, or: How Is Christianity Thinkable Today?" *Theology Digest* 19 (1971): 334–45.

Chesterton, G. K. *The Man Who Was Thursday and Related Pieces*. Edited by Stephen Medcalf. Oxford: Oxford University Press, 1996.

Davies, Philip R. "Method and Madness: Some Remarks on Doing History with the Bible." *Journal of Biblical Literature* 114 (1995): 699–705.

DeHart, Paul J. *Creation and Transcendence: Theological Essays on the Divine Sublime*. Edinburgh: T&T Clark, 2021.

———. "'Ter Mundus Accipit Infinitum: The Dogmatic Coordinates of Schleiermacher's Trinitarian Treatise." *Neue Zeitschrift für Systematische Theologie und Religionsphilosophie* 52 (2010): 17–39.

———. *The Trial of the Witnesses: The Rise and Decline of Postliberal Theology*. Oxford: Blackwell, 2006.

De la Taille, Maurice, S.J. *The Mystery of Faith and Human Opinion*. London: Sheed & Ward, 1930.

Derrida, Jacques. *Of Grammatology*. 40th anniversary ed. Translated by Gayatri Chakravorty Spivak. Baltimore: Johns Hopkins University Press, 2016.

Doyle, Arthur Conan. "The Adventure of the Golden Pince-Nez." In vol. 2 of *The Complete Sherlock Holmes*. New York: Barnes & Noble Classics, 2003.

Ernst, Cornelius. "Theological Methodology." In *Multiple Echo*, edited by Fergus Kerr O.P. and Timothy Radcliffe O.P. 1970. London: Darton, Longman & Todd, 1979.

Frank, Manfred. *What Is Neostructuralism?* Translated by Sabine Wilke and Richard Gray. Theory and History of Literature 45. Minneapolis: University of Minnesota Press, 1989.

Frei, Hans W. "David Friedrich Strauss." In vol. 1 of *Nineteenth Century Religious Thought in the West*, edited by Ninian Smart et al. Cambridge: Cambridge University Press, 1985.

———. *The Identity of Jesus Christ: The Hermeneutical Bases of Dogmatic Theology*. Philadelphia: Fortress, 1975.

Gilby, Thomas. "Appendix 10: The Dialectic of Love in the *Summa*." In Saint Thomas Aquinas, *Summa Theologiae*, vol. 1, *Christian Theology (Ia. 1)*, edited by Thomas Gilby O.P. Cambridge: Cambridge University Press, 1964.

Grafton, Anthony. "Gospel Secrets: The Biblical Controversies of Morton Smith." *Nation* 288 (2009): 25–30.

Groppe, Elizabeth Teresa. *Yves Congar's Theology of the Holy Spirit*. Oxford: Oxford University Press, 2004.

Gruner, Paul. *Menschenwege und Gotteswege im Studentenleben: Persönliche Erinnerungen aus der christlichen Studentenbewegung*. Bern: BEG-Verlag, 1942.

Harris, Horton. *David Friedrich Strauss and His Theology*. Cambridge: Cambridge University Press, 1973.

Harvey, Van A. *The Historian and the Believer: The Morality of Historical Knowledge and Christian Belief*. New York: Macmillan, 1966.

Hegel, G. W. F. *Hegels theologische Jugendschriften*. Edited by Herman Nohl. 1907. Reprint, Frankfurt/Main: Minerva, 1966.

———. *Vorlesungen über die Philosophie der Religion*. In vols. 11–12 of *Werke*, 2nd ed., edited by Philipp Marheineke and Bruno Bauer. Berlin: Duncker & Humblot, 1840. Edited and translated by Peter C. Hodgson as *Lectures on the Philosophy of Religion*. 3 vols. Berkeley: University of California Press, 1984.

Jaspert, Bernd, ed. *Karl Barth-Rudolf Bultmann Letters, 1922–1966*. Translated by Geoffrey W. Bromiley. Grand Rapids: Eerdmans, 1981.

Jüngel, Eberhard. "Die Wirksamkeit des Entzogenen: Zum Vorgang geschichtlichen Verstehens als Einführung in die Christologie." In *Gnosis: Festschrift für Hans Jonas*, edited by Barbara Aland. Göttingen: Vandenhoeck und Ruprecht, 1978. Translated by John B. Webster as "The Effectiveness of Christ Withdrawn." In *Theological Essays*. Edinburgh: T&T Clark, 1989.

———. *God's Being Is in Becoming: The Trinitarian Being of God in the Theology of Karl Barth*. Translated by John Webster. Edinburgh: T&T Clark, 2001.

Kant, Immanuel. "Prolegomena to Any Future Metaphysics That Will Be Able to Come Forward as Science." Translated by Gary Hatfield. In *Theoretical Philosophy after 1781*. Cambridge Edition of the Works of Immanuel Kant. Cambridge: Cambridge University Press, 2002.

Kierkegaard, Søren. *Concluding Unscientific Postscript to "Philosophical Fragments."* Edited by Howard V. Hong and Edna H. Hong. Princeton: Princeton University Press, 1992.

———. *Philosophical Fragments / Johannes Climacus.* Translated and edited by Howard V. Hong and Edna H. Hong. Princeton: Princeton University Press, 1985.

———. *Practice in Christianity.* Translated and edited by Howard V. Hong and Edna H. Hong. Princeton: Princeton University Press, 1991.

Kümmel, Werner Georg. *The New Testament: The History of the Investigation of Its Problems.* Translated by S. McLean Gilmour and Howard C. Kee. Nashville: Abingdon, 1972.

Lacan, Jacques. *The Four Fundamental Concepts of Psycho-Analysis.* Edited by Jacques-Alain Miller. Translated by Alan Sheridan. New York: W. W. Norton, 1978.

Lash, Nicholas. "Ideology, Metaphor and Analogy." In *Theology on the Way to Emmaus.* London: SCM Press, 1986.

Lessing, Gotthold Ephraim. "On the Proof of the Spirit and of Power." In *Philosophical and Theological Writings.* Edited and translated by H. B. Nisbet. Cambridge Texts in the History of Philosophy. Cambridge: Cambridge University Press, 2005.

Lewis, C. S. "Modern Theology and Biblical Criticism." In *Christian Reflections*, edited by Walter Hooper. 1959. Grand Rapids: Eerdmans, 1967.

Loisy, Alfred. *The Gospel and the Church.* Translated by Christopher Home. 1904. New York: Charles Scribner's Sons, 1912.

Lonergan, Bernard. *Grace and Freedom: Operative Grace in the Thought of St. Thomas Aquinas.* Vol. 1 of *Collected Works of Bernard Lonergan.* Edited by Frederick E. Crowe and Robert M. Doran. Toronto: University of Toronto Press, 1988.

Mack, Burton. *A Myth of Innocence: Mark and Christian Origins.* Philadelphia: Fortress, 1988.

Massey, Marilyn Chapin. "David Friedrich Strauss and His Hegelian Critics." *Journal of Religion* 57 (1977): 341–62.

McFarland, Ian. *The Word Made Flesh: A Theology of the Incarnation.* Louisville: Westminster John Knox, 2019.

McGuckin, John A. "The Changing Forms of Jesus." In *Origeniana Quarta: Die Referate des 4 Internationalen Origeneskongresses, Innsbruck, 2–6 September, 1985.* Edited by Lothar Lies. Innsbruck: Tyrolia Verlag, 1987.

Moloney, Raymond, S.J. *The Knowledge of Christ.* London: Continuum, 1999.

———. "The Mind of Christ in Transcendental Theology: Rahner, Lonergan and Crowe." *Heythrop Journal* 25 (1984): 288–300.

Moltmann, Jürgen, ed. *Anfänge der dialektischen Theologie, Teil I*. Munich: Christian Kaiser Verlag, 1962. Edited by James M. Robinson as *The Beginnings of Dialectic Theology*, vol. 1. Richmond: John Knox, 1968.

Moretti, Franco. "Dialectic of Fear." In *Signs Taken for Wonders: Essays in the Sociology of Literary Forms*, rev. ed., translated by Susan Fischer et al. 1974. London: Verso, 1988.

Neill, Stephen, and Tom Wright. *The Interpretation of the New Testament, 1861–1986*. 2nd ed. Oxford: Oxford University Press, 1988.

Neusner, Jacob, ed. *Christianity, Judaism and Other Greco-Roman Cults: Studies for Morton Smith at Sixty*. Leiden: Brill, 1975.

Nichtweiss, Barbara. *Erik Peterson: Neue Sicht auf Leben und Werk*. Freiburg: Herder, 1992.

O'Brien, T. C. "Appendix 1: Names Proper to the Divine Persons" and "Appendix 2: The Holy Spirit: Love." In Saint Thomas Aquinas, *Summa Theologiae*, vol. 7, *Father, Son and Holy Ghost (Ia. 33–43)*, edited by T. C. O'Brien. Cambridge: Cambridge University Press, 1976.

———. "Appendix 2: Faith and the Truth Who Is God." In Saint Thomas Aquinas, *Summa Theologiae*, vol. 31, *Faith (2a2ae. 1–7)*, edited by T. C. O'Brien. Cambridge: Cambridge University Press, 1974.

O'Reilly, Leo. *Word and Sign in the Acts of the Apostles: A Study in Lucan Theology*. Rome: Editrice Pontificia Università Gregoriana, 1987.

Penner, Hans H. "Bedeutung und Probleme der religiösen Symbolik bei Tillich und Eliade." *Antaios* 9 (1967): 123–43.

Provan, Iain W. "Ideologies, Literary and Critical: Reflections on Recent Writing on the History of Israel." *Journal of Biblical Literature* 114 (1995): 585–606.

Quispel, Gilles. "The Study of Encratism: A Historical Survey." In *Gnostica, Judaica, Catholica: Collected Essays of Gilles Quispel*, edited by Johannes van Oort. Leiden: Brill, 2008.

Rahner, Karl. "Some Implications of the Scholastic Concept of Uncreated Grace." In *Theological Investigations*, vol. 1, *God, Christ, Mary and Grace*. 2nd ed. Translated by Cornelius Ernst. London: Darton, Longman & Todd, 1965.

Schleiermacher, Friedrich. *Der christliche Glaube*. 2nd ed. Edited by Martin Redeker. Berlin: Walter de Gruyter, 1960. Translated by H. R. Macintosh and J. S. Stewart as *The Christian Faith*. Edinburgh: T&T Clark, 1928.

———. "Über die Glaubenslehre. Zwei Sendschreiben an Lücke." In *Kritische Gesamtausgabe, Erste Abteilung*, vol. 10, *Theologisch-dogmatische Abhandlungen und Gelegenheitsschriften*, edited by Hans-Friedrich Traulsen. Berlin: Walter de Gruyter, 1990. Translated by James Duke and Francis

Fiorenza as *On the Glaubenslehre: Two Letters to Dr. Lücke*. Atlanta: Scholars Press, 1981.

Schulz, Heiko. "A Modest Head Start: The German Reception of Kierkegaard." In *Kierkegaard's International Reception*, tome 1, *Northern and Western Europe*, edited by Jon Stewart. Farnham: Ashgate, 2009.

———. "Rosenkranz: Traces of Hegelian Psychology and Theology in Kierkegaard." In *Kierkegaard and His German Contemporaries*, tome 2, *Theology*, edited by Jon Stewart. Aldershot: Ashgate, 2007.

Schweitzer, Albert. *The Quest of the Historical Jesus: First Complete Edition*. Edited by John Bowden. Minneapolis: Fortress, 2001.

Smith, Jonathan Z. "The Bare Facts of Ritual." In *Imagining Religion: From Babylon to Jonestown*. Chicago: University of Chicago Press, 1982.

———. "The Domestication of Sacrifice" [1983]. In *Violent Origins: Walter Burkert, René Girard, and Jonathan Z. Smith on Ritual Killing and Cultural Formation*, edited by Robert G. Hamerton-Kelly. Stanford: Stanford University Press, 1987.

———. *Drudgery Divine: On the Comparison of Early Christianities and the Religions of Late Antiquity*. Chicago: University of Chicago Press, 1990.

———. *Map Is Not Territory: Studies in the History of Religions*. Leiden: Brill, 1978.

———. *Relating Religion: Essays in the Study of Religion*. Chicago: University of Chicago Press, 2004.

———. "'Religion' and 'Religious Studies': No Difference at All" [1988]. In *On Teaching Religion*, edited by Christopher I. Lehrich. Oxford: Oxford University Press, 2013.

———. "'Tillich['s] Remains . . .'" *Journal of the American Academy of Religion* 78 (2010): 1139–70.

Smith, Morton. *Clement of Alexandria and a Secret Gospel of Mark*. Cambridge, Mass.: Harvard University Press, 1973.

———. *Jesus the Magician*. San Francisco: Hampton Roads, 2014.

———. *The Secret Gospel*. Middletown, Calif.: Dawn Horse Press, 2005.

———. *Studies in the Cult of Yahweh*. 2 vols. Edited by Shaye J. D. Cohen. Leiden: Brill, 1996.

Solomon, Jon. "Boccaccio and the Ineffable, Aniconic God Demogorgon." *International Journal of the Classical Tradition* 19 (2012): 31–62.

Strauss, David Friedrich. *Die christliche Glaubenslehre in ihrer geschichtlichen Entwicklung und im Kampfe mit der modernen Wissenschaft dargestellt*. Vol. 2. Tübingen: C. F. Osiander, 1841.

———. *Der Christus des Glaubens und der Jesus der Geschichte. Eine Kritik des Schleiermacherschen Lebens Jesu*. 1865. Reprint, Waltrop: Hartmut Spenner Verlag, 2000. Translated by Leander E. Keck as *The Christ of Faith and the Jesus of History: A Critique of Schleiermacher's "The Life of Jesus."* Philadelpha: Fortress, 1977.

———. *Das Leben Jesu, kritisch bearbeitet.* 2 vols. Tübingen: C. F. Osiander, 1835–1836. Translated from the 4th German ed. by anon. [George Eliot] as *The Life of Jesus Critically Examined.* 3 vols. London: Chapman Bros., 1846. Edited by Peter Hodgson. Philadelphia: Fortress, 1972.

———. *Streitschriften zur Verteidigung meiner Schrift über das Leben Jesu und zur Charakteristik der gegenwärtigen Theologie.* Vol. 3. Tübingen: C. F. Osiander, 1837. Edited and translated by Marilyn Chapin Massey as *In Defense of My Life of Jesus against the Hegelians.* Hamden, Conn.: Archon Books, 1983.

Stroumsa, Guy G., ed. *Morton Smith and Gershom Scholem, Correspondence 1945–1982.* Leiden: Brill, 2008.

Tanner, Kathryn. *Jesus, Humanity and the Trinity: A Brief Systematic Theology.* Minneapolis: Fortress, 2001.

Thompson, Thomas L. "A Neo-Albrightian School in History and Biblical Scholarship?" *Journal of Biblical Literature* 114 (1995): 683–98.

Tillich, Paul. *Systematic Theology.* Vol. 2, *Existence and the Christ.* Chicago: University of Chicago Press, 1957.

Toomer, G. J. *John Selden: A Life in Scholarship.* Oxford: Oxford University Press, 2009.

Troeltsch, Ernst. *Aufsätze zur Geistesgeschichte und Religionssoziologie; Gesammelte Schriften, Vierter Band.* Edited by Hans Baron. Tübingen: J. C. B. Mohr, 1925.

———. "Die Bedeutung der Geschichtlichkeit Jesu für den Glauben." In *Kritische Gesamtausgabe*, vol. 6, *Schriften zur Religionswissenschaft und Ethik (1903–1912)*, edited by Trutz Rendtorff. Berlin: Walter de Gruyter, 2014. Translated by Robert Morgan and Michael Pye as "The Significance of the Historical Existence of Jesus for Faith." In *Writings on Theology and Religion*, translated and edited by Robert Morgan and Michael Pye. Louisville: Westminster John Knox, 1977.

———. *Die Bedeutung des Protestantismus für die Entstehung der modernen Welt.* In *Kritische Gesamtausgabe*, vol. 8, *Schriften zur Bedeutung des Protestantismus für die moderne Welt (1906–1913)*, edited by Trutz Rendtorff. Berlin: Walter de Gruyter, 2001. Translated by William Montgomery as *Protestantism and Progress.* Philadelphia: Fortress, 1986.

———. *Der Historismus und seine Probleme: Gesammelte Schriften, Dritter Band.* Tübingen: J. C. B. Mohr, 1922.

———. "Rückblick auf ein halbes Jahrhundert der theologischen Wissenschaft." In *Gesammelte Schriften, Zweiter Band: Zur religiösen Lage, Religionsphilosophie und Ethik*, vol. 2, 193–226. Tübingen: J. C. B. Mohr, 1913.

Translated and edited by Robert Morgan and Michael Pye as "Half a Century of Theology: A Review." In Ernst Troeltsch, *Writings on Theology and Religion*, 53–81. Louisville: Westminster John Knox, 1977.

———. *Die Soziallehren der christlichen Kirchen und Gruppen*. Tübingen: J. C. B. Mohr, 1912. Translated by Olive Wyon as *The Social Teachings of the Christian Churches*. 2 vols. London: Macmillan, 1931.

———. "Was heisst 'Wesen des Christentums'?" In *Gesammelte Schriften, Zweiter Band: Zur religiösen Lage, Religionsphilosophie und Ethik*, vol. 2, 386–451. Tübingen: J. C. B. Mohr, 1913. Translated and edited by Robert Morgan and Michael Pye as "What Does 'Essence of Christianity' Mean?" In Ernst Troeltsch, *Writings on Theology and Religion*, 124–81. Louisville: Westminster John Knox, 1977.

Verheyden, Jack C. Introduction to *The Life of Jesus*, by Friedrich Schleiermacher. Philadelphia: Fortress, 1975.

Veyne, Paul. *Did the Greeks Believe in Their Myths? An Essay on the Constitutive Imagination*. Translated by Paula Wissing. Chicago: University of Chicago Press, 1988.

West, M. L. *Indo-European Poetry and Myth*. Oxford: Oxford University Press, 2007.

Wiles, Maurice. "Some Reflections on the Origins of the Doctrine of the Trinity" [1957]. In *Working Papers in Doctrine*. London: SCM Press, 1976.

Williams, Rowan. *Christ the Heart of Creation*. London: Bloomsbury Continuum, 2018.

———. "Does It Make Sense to Speak of Pre-Nicene Orthodoxy?" In *The Making of Orthodoxy: Essays in Honor of Henry Chadwick*, edited by Rowan Williams. Cambridge: Cambridge University Press, 1989.

———. "The Finality of Christ." In *On Christian Theology*. Oxford: Blackwell, 2000.

———. "Trinity and Pluralism." In *On Christian Theology*. Oxford: Blackwell, 2000.

Wittgenstein, Ludwig. *Tractatus Logico-Philosophicus*. London: Routledge & Kegan Paul, 1961.

Žižek, Slavoj. *How to Read Lacan*. New York: W. W. Norton, 2006.

———. *The Puppet and the Dwarf: The Perverse Core of Christianity*. Cambridge, Mass.: MIT Press, 2003.

Žižek, Slavoj, and John Milbank. *The Monstrosity of Christ: Paradox or Dialectic?* Edited by Creston Davis. Cambridge, Mass.: MIT Press, 2009.

Index